UNQUIET SPIRITS

ESSAYS BY ASIAN WOMEN IN HORROR
EDITED BY BRAM STOKER AWARD®-WINNING AUTHORS
LEE MURRAY & ANGELA YURIKO SMITH
WITH A FOREWORD BY LISA KRÖGER

Whispered Words

"*Unquiet Spirits* is a collection of intimate, insightful essays that will become essential reading for those looking to understand the voice of women of the Asian diaspora in horror. I can't overstate how important this book is."
—Priya Sharma, British Fantasy award-winning author of *Ormeshadow*.

"As an expert in the paranormal I've researched ghosts around the globe, but there's a vast gulf between studying hungry ghosts and fox spirits in scholarly journals, and reading first-hand experience of these extraordinary stories. The pieces in *Unquiet Spirits* are beautiful, enlightening, poignant, and yes, haunting. This is a must-have book for anyone who is interested in the folklore of Asia and how it has impacted the lives of the women actually living it."
—Lisa Morton, Bram Stoker Award-winning author of *Ghosts: A Haunted History*

"A haunting and phenomenally intriguing undertaking. With the variety of perspectives, *Unquiet Spirits* is powerful, poignant, and very, very moving. An emotionally draining experience in the best way possible!"
—Steve Stred, Splatterpunk-nominated author of *Sacrament* and *Mastodon* and reviewer at Kendall Reviews

"It's a manuscript on parapsychology from multiple Asian cultures…a hard critical look into the metaphors inside each ghost and their cultural implications."
— Reed Alexander's Horror Review

"To be heard is a very powerful thing indeed, but first we have to speak. The unique voices in these essays take us into the ways each author's culture honors troubled spirits who enter their homes and souls. There are no simple ghostly shadows here, but a captivating collection of hungry, neglected, abused ancestral beings, with each piece ending in a treasure trove of reference material to inspire and teach. I freely embrace being an unquiet human."
—Linda D. Addison, award-winning author, HWA Lifetime Achievement Award recipient and SFPA Grand Master.

"Fierce and fervid, *Unquiet Spirits* is a grand achievement in its honesty and emotional depth. The pieces within range from academic to conversational and in between—but all shed light on identities and struggles which our world has often tried to quiet. But more than a grand achievement, this collection deserves ascent to the literary canon for both the Asian diaspora and feminism. I'll be shelving my copy alongside the essays of Joanna Russ. Murray and Smith have assembled what could very well be the defining next generation of voices for these intersectional topics. For those interested in horror, women in literature, the Asian diaspora, equality and identity -- this volume is a *must*."
—Austin Gragg, Editor-in-Chief at *Space & Time Magazine*

"The spirits don't whisper in this collection; they roar across the pages—every word carefully selected and earning its place in the essays. These personal stories traverse time and space to be everyone's stories."
—Renata Pavrey, author and poet, reviewer for HorrorAddicts

"Raw, emotional, honest, and empowering."
—Amanda Headlee for The Horror Tree

ISBN Trade Paperback: 978-1-64548-129-4
ISBN Trade Hardcover: 978-1-64548-130-0
ISBN eBook: 978-1-64548-131-7

Cover Design and Interior Formatting
by Qamber Designs and Media

Published by Black Spot Books Non-Fiction,
an imprint of Black Spot Books, a division of Vesuvian Media Group.

EDITORS' NOTE

To retain the diversity of our Asian diaspora, essays in this book retain the English of preference of individual authors.

DEDICATION

For our maternal grandmothers,
Yee Wai Fong and Yuriko Kayoda,
and our mothers, their daughters,
Pauline Thomas and Elaine Marie Grant,
and all our unquiet sisters.

ACKNOWLEDGEMENTS

"We are haunted. We are also the ghosts. Not transparent unsubstantial spirits, who are stuck and unable to move on. Instead, we are grown from the women before us and our own experiences. We have been watered with the tears of hard work and hope, fed hot peppers and sorrow. A force which has learned to consume what haunts us and make it part of us."
—K.P. Kulski in *Tortured Willows*

This book, *Unquiet Spirits*, is a culmination of ghostly voices, the stories of Asian mothers and grandmothers, of aunts and sisters, and nieces and daughters, the unspoken secrets of a diaspora which extends across countries, over cultures, and through generations, and which steps into the shadowy realm of the dead. It is the product of the unquiet spirits who came before us, written to empower those who will surely follow. But this book of personal reflections and essays also owes its existence to people in the here and now, some of whom we feel we must acknowledge. A special thank you to our sister, Geneve Flynn, whose encounter with Lee gave rise to *Black Cranes: Tales of Unquiet Women* and later to *Tortured Willows: Bent Bowed and Unbroken*, and which spawned an incredible community of Asian women writers, many of whom grace these pages. Thank you to our unquiet sisters for trusting us with your powerful testimonies, and to Lisa Kröger for bearing witness and holding space for us. Thank you to Amanda Nelson, blogger at Book Riot, who coined the term 'messay' and freed us with this fresh approach to storytelling. Thank you to author Alma Katsu for her unfailing support and inspiration, and to our incredible publishers Kate Jonez (Omnium Gatherum), Jennifer Barnes (Raw Dog Screaming Press), and Lindy Ryan (Black Spot Books) for sharing our vision to unleash these stories on the world. To influencers and reviewers at sites such as Pseudopod, Nightmare Feed, Space & Time, Tomes and Tales, The Horror Tree, and HorrorAddicts, whose signal-boosting helped us to create a groundswell, and our horror colleagues (simply too many to list here) for their generous endorsements. We're grateful to our readers whose visceral and heartfelt responses galvanised us to do more. Finally, we'd like to thank our families—our partners, David Murray and Ryan Aussie Smith, and our children—for their kind support and encouragement as we stole hours and hours of family time to work on this book, as we walked with ghosts and listened to their stories.

—Lee Murray & Angela Yuriko Smith

TABLE OF CONTENTS

FOREWORD

BY LISA KRÖGER

Ghosts have always fascinated me. They've long been a staple of horror, of course. They've haunted houses, driving innocent families away. They've waited at graveyards, a silent reminder of what once was and what we all will one day face. But it's what makes a ghost that I've always been entranced by.

The ghost stories I grew up with were typical urban legend fare. In Tennessee, where I spent my childhood, the stories that we whispered around campfires or at sleepovers, faces half-hidden in our hands, were usually ghost stories—of the Bloody Mary or White Lady ilk. The stories were ultimately the same. The ghost was often some unfortunate woman who met an untimely death. Usually, at least in my experience, she was wronged by a man—jilted at the altar or unmarried, pregnant, and abandoned. Her death was often by suicide or at the hands of her violent lover. These tales were the literary version of the murder ballad—always about a crime, always about a woman. One I remember the best was a woman who haunted a local bridge. As the story goes, she was young and beautiful, with a long and promising life ahead of her. She was pure, too. That was an important part of the story. Her virtue and innocence were highlighted as if to suggest the "other" kind of woman, the one who was "loose" with her morals, might deserve what was to come. This young lady fell in love with the wrong man. He promised to marry her, and her only crime was that she believed him. Soon, she found herself pregnant. And he ran away, leaving her alone. In some versions of the story, she is so devastated that she jumps off the bridge. In a more terrible version of the tale, she has the baby only to be shunned by her family. It is the rejection of her community that pushes her over the edge, and she jumps off the bridge, infant in arms. Sometimes, of course, the story changes again, and she is pushed—in an attempt for the man to keep secrets buried deep. He gets away in every one of the stories, never implicated in any responsibility for her death. And she becomes a ghost, a constant reminder of what happened to her—and perhaps a warning, too.

It's a sad ghost story, as many of them are. Still, even as a young girl, I learned the lesson of the ghost: there's one path for women, and that is marriage and motherhood. Anything else is death. In these stories, women were presented with one path forward. Outside of being a "legitimate" wife and mother, they had little to themselves. Any life beyond that was cobbled together, piece by piece, from stolen moments. "Good" girls got married. They had children. They lived long lives. They didn't turn into vengeful ghosts. Still, it's funny, isn't it? The ghost woman seems to possess a lot more power and agency than any of those good girls in the stories.

As far as I remember, the woman who turned ghost was never named in any of the stories I heard. Looking back, I guess that was by design. She could be any of us. *She is all of us.*

That's the power of the ghost—and the ghost story.

When Angela Yuriko Smith and Lee Murray first approached me to write the foreword for this book, I was honored—but I was also terrified. I worried I wasn't the person to write these words because who am I, as a non-Asian woman, to introduce these essays by Asian women in horror. After all, these deeply personal thoughts didn't belong to me.

Then I realized that I was here to listen, and only to listen, to the diverse female experiences of the Asian diaspora. With that, I am honored to present these essays to you, the reader.

These are deeply personal thoughts. Within these pages, there are essays about women uncovering their lineage, digging deep for a thread that they can follow, a path that will connect them to those who came before and finally back to themselves. In her essay, Lee Murray explains this connection: "Raised on tales of Red Riding Hood and of the Māori goddess of death, Hine-nui-te-pō, I am defined by my mixed heritage, my experience, and my love for the land which birthed me. Mine is not my grandmother's experience, nor is it my mother's, yet I carry them with me; their decisions, their sacrifices, made in my name, give me strength."

As I was researching *Monster, She Wrote*, I uncovered a long literary lineage of women who had written horror, women who had come before me, who had experienced the birth pains of creation, allowing for the space for me to enter. It was a humbling experience, this connection with my literary foremothers.

It is this connection to foremothers that connects each and every essay in this anthology. By interacting with the folklore, the stories, the legends, and the ghosts of their pasts, each of these women have reckoned with not only parts of their identity that were previously hidden from them, but they also found inspiration for their own writing. In this book, there's a connection to spirits here, to ghosts—because of the power that exists in that role. A ghost is a powerful thing to try and control.

When women have no voice, no choice, they will seek that control wherever they can find it, even if that means shedding their mortal lives for a taste of power in the spiritual form of the ghost. It's almost as if losing a body somehow helps a quiet woman to move into a space that she can fully inhabit, where she can turn her whisper into a roar and finally fully satiate the hunger that has always lived within her.

As women, we live with the weight of expectation—the expectation of what it means to be a woman, as told to us by the world around us. It's a game we had no choice in; we were in the middle of it before we agreed to play. And in that arena, we often lose sight of ourselves. Angela Yuriko Smith illustrates the subject at the heart of this anthology when she writes: "These are stories of women who have given themselves away in pieces."

Now, through the eyes of these writers, the women are being pieced together again—through the power of the ghost story.

The writers of this anthology tell of many different ghosts of the Asian diaspora: the hungry ghosts, the fox spirits, the *kwee kia* (a rather angry ghost baby), and the *tisigui* (a substitute-seeking ghost). These spirits are important, as they are the connective tissue between the writers and a past that they often feel disconnected from (or, in some cases, a past that has been hidden from them, a side effect of immigration and miles of distance). The act of writing, then, becomes a kind of séance, a summoning of spirits to see what we can learn from them. That act is almost always transformative. In one of the essays that follows, called "Fox Daughter," Celine Murray describes what it means to probe into the ghost lore of her own past. "In her eyes, I see a fox, a spirit that now lives in me. And we're angry. Feral. We want retribution."

The other essays in this anthology also evoke this connection to the spirit world. In "Thai Spirits and Longing to Belong," J.A.W. McCarthy describes what it was like to grow up a half-Thai and half-white woman, feeling like a hungry ghost, always searching for that part of herself that she didn't have access to. In "Lucky Number, Or Why 28>58," Eliza Chan examines numerology and luck, especially how it can be a controlling factor in Chinese women's lives. She writes that numbers have a language that can seem "easy." But it isn't always so simple: "There are burdens from generations passed, hopes and fears that cannot always be entirely articulated." Like many other essays in this collection, this one is about trying to understand the past and how that past has unwittingly defined a personality.

I found many of these essays touching, as these writers excavate their lineage for a greater personal understanding, but these essays also challenge the very idea of femininity. In "Becoming Ungovernable: Latah, Amok, and Disorder in Indonesia," the extraordinary Nadia Bulkin grapples with the woman "who is meant to grow from the sweetness of girlhood to the grace of motherhood without ever becoming crass or coarse" and the woman who doesn't fit that definition, and as a result, is labeled chaotic or even monstrous. Tori Eldridge has written a wonderful piece on training female ninjas, going against the Chinese idea of the subservient woman. And Rena Mason examines the "female duality" as seen in the Thai lore of the fox spirit.

These are just a few, of course, of the powerful essays that are contained within this anthology. Each and every essay in this book is important—no word is wasted.

Ai Jiang, in her essay "The Unvoiced, The Unheard, The Unknown, The Unquiet," eloquently summarizes the theme of *Unquiet Spirits*: "I am choosing to be unquiet." Each of the writers in this anthology excavated their past. And in doing so, they perform the difficult task of listening to the silenced voices of the past.

With that connection, they make the choice to be unquiet.

DISPLACED SPIRITS:
GHOSTS OF THE DIASPORA

LEE MURRAY

I am six. It's Saturday morning, and my dad is outside mowing the lawns while, in the kitchen, my Kiwi-born Chinese mum gathers three slender joss sticks into both hands and touches the bundle to the element on the stove. As always, I hope the bamboo sticks will crackle with little stars like sparklers, but instead, their tips glow red, and a curl of smoke drifts upwards on the air. Still holding the burning incense with two hands, Mum bows respectfully towards the open window then places the sticks in a stand on the sill. She repeats the process twice more, fanning out the nine sticks neatly on the holder. For the next half hour, the smoke wisps and swirls its way through the house, permeating everything with its scent of sandalwood and cinnamon. I breathe deeply, savouring the solemnity of this familiar ritual, quiet amid the general busyness of my childhood.

Sometime later, when the sticks have burned out and there is no chance of my hair catching on the smouldering embers, I run my finger along the sill, tracing the letters of my name in the chalky pink ash. Sketching the double ee's is especially satisfying.

It's not until years later, when I'm in my teens, that I realise my mum—like her mother and her mother before her—is a kind of ghost whisperer. She's been sending daily communications to the spirits of our ancestors, messages of calm and courtesy delivered to the celestial realm on those captivating curls of silvery smoke. Because, just as it's respectful to phone your parents now and again to let them know how you're doing, for Chinese families, it's important to maintain regular contact with the dead, to ensure they are nourished and entertained—*to placate them*. You see, if attracting the wrath of your parents is daunting, the misfortune brought on

1

by disgruntled dead ancestors is something else altogether. Those disaffected souls risk becoming hungry ghosts.

Among the best known of Asian spirits, hungry ghosts are typically depicted as bony-limbed creatures with scrawny necks and distended stomachs. Pitiful and emaciated, these disenfranchised souls scrabble on their hands and knees in the dirt, consumed by an unrelenting, unrequited hunger.

> The hunger grows in my belly and in my womb, gnawing at me piece by piece, stretching me dry and insubstantial once more.
>
> —Aliette de Bodard, excerpt from
> "Golden Lilies" in *Asian Monsters*

> …I saw little more than dried skin and exposed bone, the eyes like shrivelled fruits in deep sockets… His voice was thin and weak, as though there were not enough air to pump through that collapsed ribcage.
>
> —Yangsze Choo, excerpt from her novel, *Ghost Bride*

In Chinese culture, people become hungry ghosts because of evil deeds carried out in the course of their lifetime. What constitutes an evil deed, however, is a matter of perception, with generations of patriarchy ensuring that women haven't fared well on that ledger.

> "You must have angered the ancestors."
>
> My heart lurched. "Ghosts! How?"
>
> "I don't know. They usually turn up after a woman has been greedy, don't they? The selfish wife who eats before her husband's guests, the woman who steals away the best portion of the meal for herself—that sort of thing."
>
> —Lee Murray, excerpt from "Phoenix Claws" in *Black Cranes*

The realm of ghosts is full of greedy women who want more than their due. Women who hunger for acknowledgement, acceptance, and fulfilment.

*Was that when you first
began to swell? Your stomach
bulging and burgeoning,
swallowing the bitter,
the burden, the second-hands,
the not-for-yous?
Did your mouth begin to draw
closed like a miserly purse
when you were left behind,
your splendid mind with
only hunger and no choice
but to turn upon itself?*

—Geneve Flynn, excerpt from her poem
"Inheritance" in *Tortured Willows*

Another cause of eternal ghostly torment is displacement. In this case, departed spirits are "without a home nor the sustenance and companionship provided by their descendants" (Liang, 2020). When you die far from your ancestral roots, you risk becoming a hungry ghost. Alarming if we consider the extent of the Asian diaspora in recent centuries—people fleeing poverty and war—helped along by better transportation and Western demand for cheap labour. Imagine the explosion of hungry spirits that vast migration must have caused in the otherworld.

To be fair, even in life, people of the diaspora are disaffected. Those Chinese who left their homes and families for foreign lands did so reluctantly, says New Zealand historian Manying Ip. She asserts "their only purpose was to earn enough in order to leave the hostile country" (Ip, 1990, p. 15). American scholar Paul Sui called them 'sojourners', immigrants who "cling to the culture of their ethnicity" (Sui, 1952). Rose Hum Lee went further, saying a sojourner's "mental orientation is towards the home country" (Lee, 1960). Yet it was precisely their sojourner attitude that prompted the Dunedin Chamber of Commerce to recruit the first Chinese miners to Aotearoa-New Zealand in the 1860s. The chamber considered the Chinese to be "hardworking, inoffensive, and willing to rework

3

abandoned claims [of the Otago goldfields], and they preferred to return eventually to their homeland" (Edwards & Jamieson, 2014, pp. 4-5). Less than five years later, more than 2000 Chinese miners had arrived to take up this backbreaking work. However, the chamber's hope that they would all clear off afterwards didn't quite pan out. Many Chinese never made it back to their families—even in death.

"New Zealand becomes a purgatory where living must take place," says Tan Tuck Ming writing in *A Clear Dawn: New Asian Voices from Aotearoa* (Morris & Wong, 2021). "Once dead, their bodies can be buried in China, in the familiar soil where they were born. Here, they grow old, denied a pension by the government, shuffled along to deserted gold claims they mine in solitude and ultimately die in. Many of them are mired in unending grief." (p. 255)

> *They say it still rains in the ruins of our youth. So, they say at times rain splatters onto our distant corpses, our toes. And rumor has it that we are still alive. This spring God plants birds in heaven again, and the wild plants bloom at once and disperse their scents, but now, you all refuse to go back to being dust and mud. You spirits, roam your old beloved towns with your invisible ankles, you glare at our live sleeping bodies. Will we be able to resist you all? Will we be able to return you safely to death?*
>
> —Ch'oe Sung-ja, from her poem
> "Prayers to Ancestor Spirits" in *Anxiety of Words*

The resourceful miners came up with a solution, forming subscription-based cooperative societies, Cheong Shing Tong, to look after poor and elderly Chinese immigrants and to help them return home. Moreover, if members died, the societies would ensure their remains were repatriated. The first 'coffin' ship, carrying the exhumed remains of several hundred deceased miners from New Zealand, arrived in Guangdong in 1883, prompting the charter of a second ship, the *S.S. Ventnor*, by respected Dunedin businessman Choie Sew Hoy. Carrying 499 southern Chinese—including Choie Sew Hoy himself, who died not long before the departure date—and nine elderly Chinese granted free passage to attend to the dead, the ship set sail for Hong Kong on 26 October 1902. But disaster struck, and the ship was wrecked off the coast of Northland:

"... she struck a submerged rock off Cape Egmont and was holed forward. The engines were reversed, and the ship managed to get free. As there were no suitable dock facilities at Wellington, the master decided to proceed to Auckland via North Cape for repairs. In the meantime, the pumps were brought into use, but these could not cope with the water. By 9 p.m. on 28 October, when *Ventnor* was about 10 miles off Omapere, Hokianga Harbour, the ship became unmanageable, and it was apparent that she would soon founder. Although all boats were launched, 13 lives were lost when the captain's boat was sucked under with the ship" (Edwards & Jamieson, 2014, p5).

The Chinese chartered another ship hoping to salvage the remains, but the zinc-lined coffins were too deep to be retrieved. All those poor souls lost—508 if you include the unfortunate attendants who were sucked under the ship and slurped up by the ocean.

But that number is only half the story. It says nothing of the wives of the dead men; women left behind in the old country to raise children and look after elderly relatives. It says nothing of the miners' mothers and their unwed daughters. Women who, as a result of the tragedy, and long-held patriarchal constructs, were doomed to join their menfolk in the realm of hungry ghosts. No one ever mentions them.

the old ones are all gone now
though their ghosts still roam this isle
where the willows whispered warnings
all the while

—Lee Murray, excerpt from her poem
"Willows" in *Tortured Willows*

My grandparents weren't among those who came in those first brave cohorts. My grandfather, Yee Paleon, a former general in Chiang Kei Shek's nationalist army, joined his brother in New Zealand in 1940. We're not sure which route he took or if he came directly from China. My grandmother, Wai Fong, the youngest of Paleon's wives, escaped the Second Sino-Japanese War to join him here a year later with their newborn daughter. By this time, New Zealand had undergone half a century of anti-Chinese sentiment, reinforced by legislation, exorbitant poll taxes, language tests, fingerprinting, and exclusion of Chinese from naturalisation and pensions. In 1905, a crippled and elderly Chinese man named Joe Kum Yung was shot dead in broad daylight in Wellington's Haining Street by protestor Lionel Terry, who resented the influx of Chinese to New Zealand. Hatred towards the 'Yellow Peril', as the Chinese were called, was widespread, the murder splitting public opinion (Fensome, 2014).

In 1943, my mother is born. Her parents name her Pauline, an anglicisation of her Chinese name. In 1947, she and her parents become permanent residents. It takes almost twenty years from the date of their arrival for my grandparents to gain citizenship. When Paleon and Wai Fong die, in 1968 and 1989, respectively, they are buried in the sprawling old cemetery on a hillside in Karori, Wellington. So far from their native villages, are my grandparents hungry ghosts? Perhaps they would be if my mother and her siblings did not take care to nourish their spirits.

> Your mother might be a ghost herself; you didn't know. No one had thought to tell you, although they said other things—mean, sunken, tortured things. Things with thin bony limbs and slender necks. Swollen bloated-bellied things which wormed their way beneath your ribs, pushing aside your lungs, where they took up residence: pulsing, and pulsing, and pulsing ...
>
> —Lee Murray, excerpt from
> "Frangipani Wishes" in *Black Cranes*

I know my mother remembers and honours her parents— knowing her deep affection for them, that is a given—but this summer, over a cup of tea, I ask her if there are others she honours when she lights her joss sticks. Mum looks off into the distance and shrugs before speaking of great-great-grandfathers, of great-aunts, and uncles. She offers no names for the people who went before, the people back in China.

"Did you know any of them?" I ask.

My mother pulls a face. The kind you make when there is something disagreeable on your plate. There's just her paternal grandmother, who she'd met for the first time on a visit to China in 1947 when she was just four.

"What was her name?"

"I don't know," Mum says, "but it'll be recorded somewhere."

How strange it is that my mother cannot name her own grandmother. I think about my Māori friends, many of whom can recite the names and deeds of their ancestors, going back to the time before demi-god Māui fished up the land from the sea.

After the 1947 trip to China, my nameless great-grandmother came to live with the family in Wellington. Strict and humourless, she wasn't a favourite of my mother and her siblings, not the least because of her cruel treatment of Por Por (my maternal grandmother, Wai Fong). Although, I imagine a Chinese mother-in-law can't help but be disdainful when a son's wife has seven daughters. Girls are of no value, merely chattels in their father's lineage. I wonder, though, since my great-grandmother was far from home and never likely to return, if her attitude arose because she knew her own soul was at risk. A destiny like that is enough to make anyone mean-spirited.

"What about on Por Por's side of the family?" I ask my mother.

She shakes her head. "There's no one. From the time she left China, Por Por never saw anyone in her family again."

Por Por did go back to China, though. More than once. The first time, during that 1947 trip, she scoured the country for news of her family, a sorrowful hunt for survivors of the war. Her village was unrecognisable. Of those who remained, none could say what had happened to the family. There was rumour of a cousin, but no trace was found. Not even the gravesites.

My family is full of displaced ghosts.

In the sixties, my mother married a Kiwi of European descent—a *gweilo*-devil. For this courageous act of love and defiance, my mother risked a lifetime ostracised from her family and an afterlife of hunger for her greediness, for the sin of wanting more. Barely five feet tall on her tiptoes, she is a source of wonder and strength to me. Yet, for all the hardships my mother has endured, at peril of her afterlife, she holds no regrets.

As for me, child of a devil, I am a contradiction. Despite being born in New Zealand, I am not truly Kiwi, nor am I properly Chinese. I am fluent in two languages, neither of which is Cantonese, my rightful maternal language. I would not have been able to speak to my ancestors in real life, so how can I imagine holding a conversation with them in death? What do I know of words spoken in swirls of smoke? I've never lit a joss stick in my life.

An old Facebook meme popped into my head, the one about tradition being peer pressure from dead people, usually accompanied by a picture of a skeleton, or Lisa Simpson holding a lecture pointer.

Well, I didn't have to let family tradition define me.

—Lee Murray, excerpt from "Phoenix Claws" in *Black Cranes*

It's true, I can ignore all that social conditioning. This is a new country, I tell myself. The rules are different here. Things have moved on.

I was a third-generation true-blue Kiwi; I knew more words in Māori than in Chinese, owned a pair of gumboots, loved Marmite, and understood the off-side rule.

—Lee Murray, excerpt from "Phoenix Claws" in *Black Cranes*

Only what will happen to my grandmother's ghost when my mother has gone? What of my precious mother? Who will entertain her and nurture her if not me? And what of those others, women who sacrificed so much that I might be born and raised in relative safety in this golden land? Those women are without names: great-grandmothers and great-great-grandmothers, all lost to the realm of ghosts. I am failing in my filial duty, and the burden feels too much to bear.

She's lost and I worry she will fade away into smoke and I will forget that she even existed at all. Funny how we build our own hells. The prisons we erect from grooves of our passing to and fro, until the road no longer exists, but only a hall framed with impossible walls.

We build these things because we love.

—K.P. Kulski, excerpt from her novella, *House of Pungsu*

The story of the Chinese miners has a happier ending. Over time, the ocean did its work, and the coffins broke apart, releasing the miners' bones; they washed up on windswept Northland beaches and were discovered by the Māori people of the region, of the Te Roroa and Te Rarawa *iwi* (tribes). Auspicious because Māori and Chinese cultures have a lot in common, particularly when it comes to honouring our dead. The Māori tribespeople gathered up the bones and buried them, hiding them in caves and hollows near the beach. Special, sacred places. For a century, the Māori people nurtured these gravesites, passing on the whereabouts through oral histories in case the descendants of those nameless dead should come to look for them.

> The instinctual respect with which these bleached bones were treated speaks to the similarities between the way both [Māori and Chinese] cultures perceive death, and a shared belief that the ancestors are always present and must therefore be treated with the respect they deserve.

—Jayden Boyle in *Health Central: The Death Series*

In 2007, New Zealand filmmaker Wong Lui Shueng learned of this guardianship by the local Māori. She set about raising awareness among the Chinese community, prompting numerous delegations of Chinese to Northland to thank the Māori for their stewardship. In the years that followed, an extraordinary connection has formed between the peoples of both cultures. As well as this vital fellowship, memorials and plaques were erected, services held, welcoming the souls of the lost miners, and laying them to rest with respect and honour.

Of course, in the time since the wreck, those ancestors lost to the sea hadn't been forgotten by the Chinese, but the trauma was so great and the loss so shameful that people didn't speak of it.

Over time, sons and daughters died, new generations were born, and memories grew murky until only the anguish remained.

> Some things you knew already. Some things you knew before you were born; they were revealed to you in the rhythm of your mother's heartbeat and in the echoes of her sighs. Later, you heard it in the closing of doors, in the scuff of a suitcase, and the low hum of a ceiling fan.

—Lee Murray, excerpt from "Frangipani Wishes" in *Black Cranes*

Now that they'd been recovered, the ghosts of the dead miners clamoured to tell their stories, further research eventually leading to the discovery of their names in some old archives. "They were anglicised names, phonetically recorded, and with no further details of home village, nor age," explains commentator Renee Liang (2020), herself a second-generation Chinese New Zealander. "Still, they are the names."

The ghost women, though, remain nameless.

"It's not so unusual," my mother says. "Addressing a person by their true name was considered disrespectful, as it can attract the attention of angry spirits." To avoid this, Chinese people tend to use nicknames or relational names. Women, especially, are given relational names—Auntie. Daughter. Grandmother—in part because a woman's identity is connected firstly to her father's lineage and later to her husband's family. Unwed women have no family, no children; they are the 'leftover women' doomed to an afterlife of hunger. These strongly misogynist attitudes are slowly changing in China. Still, for people of the diaspora, cultural traditions remain strangely static, embedded in the moment that the family quit their country of origin.

> … for so long I have only known myself as daughter. A name of relationship, dependent on another, never singular or solitary in identity. Are we not defined by our relationships? I ponder these questions with heaviness. How does a woman know herself devoid of human connection? Like the wife in grandmother's story. What was *her* name. What did she think of herself? What do *I* think of myself?

—K.P. Kulski, excerpt from her novella, *House of Pungsu*

In 2021, a researcher working on a project about Chinese women refugees to New Zealand saw an article I'd written about my family and contacted me to clarify some details. These were sparse, sanitised, and inaccurate. My grandmother's name had been listed incorrectly, so she was one of the last women investigated, the last refugee included in the book, which was about to go to press. For that reason, her children—including my seventy-eight-year-old mother, who was shocked to learn she is considered a refugee despite being born here—were excluded from the fellowship offered to other women in the project.

"I think the stiff permanence of official archives with their incomplete, and sometimes inaccurate, information ... accounts for some of the alienation and erasure suffered by New Zealand Chinese women and their children over the past century," I told the researcher. "Even the legal term 'refugee' is problematic, implying, in my view, a certain 'otherness' which doesn't reflect the way many Chinese women fully embraced this country and our community as the home of their hearts." (Murray, 2022, pp. 477-479)

Isn't it enough that Aotearoa-New Zealand was the home of their hearts? Would that spare our grandmothers an eternity of hunger and pain? Is New Zealand far enough away from China that the new diaspora might evade haunting by hordes of unnourished ancestors—or were those early miners prophetic when they named the country the Land of Ghosts.

The publishers of the eventual book, *Farewell Guangdong*, send their file to China for printing, where it is held up for many months, purportedly the result of COVID-related shipping delays. Yet, I can't help but wonder if my grandmother, Wai Fong, and all those other pioneer women whose names are recorded in the book had some hand in its delay, their hungry spirits conjuring the misfortunes that would allow their desperate souls to linger on familiar soil.

Why does this happen? Why must we fight even in the afterlife to know our womanhood? To be free?

—K.P. Kulski, excerpt from her novella, *House of Pungsu*

"I am descended from hungry ghosts," writes Rosabel Tan (2021), an Australian-born Korean who moved to New Zealand when she was eight. "They are those I cannot name. The grief I hold for them is difficult to navigate because the past isn't lost. It just feels hard to claim. Remembering them is another journey. But in the meantime, I have another lineage. It's the one that has shaped me, the people whose paths have pulled me forward. Imagine a future, it says, and imagine you in it."

I, too, am descended from generations of hungry ghosts. A child of the diaspora, I may not know my ancestors' names, nor can I picture their faces, but I feel sure they know me. Didn't I introduce myself to them when I wrote my name in the joss stick ash on my mother's windowsill? But I cannot meet them halfway. There is too much distance between us, too much time elapsed. Aotearoa-New Zealand is my home. Raised on tales of Red Riding Hood and of the Māori goddess of death, Hine-nui-te-pō, I am defined by my mixed heritage, my experience, and my love for the land which birthed me. Mine is not my grandmother's experience, nor is it my mother's, yet I carry them with me; their decisions, their sacrifices, made in my name, give me strength.

> I am power. The power that I didn't know I had, wasn't allowed to develop. That which I knit into my soul, the vessel grown for the benefits of others. A name obscured and forgotten against yours. No more will I be a mere identity created from the rib of man. The secondary to the primary.
>
> I am fire and whole and full and forged from my own fires.
>
> I know all this now.
>
> I will imprint the knowledge on my soul and as I am more again and with it, I will break the world.
>
> As grandmother pushes me, I feel us all fall into each other simultaneously. We are one. I am whole.
>
> I think of walls.

I think of being contained.

Then I think of tearing it all down.

—K.P. Kulski, excerpt from her novella, *House of Pungsu*

So, to the women who travelled before me, you beautiful voracious unquiet ghosts, let me nourish you with my stories, which are built on your stories and your suffering. I will raise our unquiet voices, not, as you have done, on ephemeral curls of smoke, but on the written page. Though I walk in another realm, let me write to you of a new world without walls, in which no woman hungers.

inside
a man-crafted
box of woman-should
a starving ghost
I let her go

—Lee Murray, "Fury" in *Tortured Willows*

REFERENCES

De Bodard, A. (2016). Golden Lilies. In Helgadóttir M. (Ed.) *Asian monsters: Fox spirit book of monsters #3*, (pp. 55-62). UK: Fox Spirit Books.

Boyle, J. (2018, June 12). Hungry ghosts no more: nourishing the souls of early Chinese miners in New Zealand. *Health Central: The Death Series*. Retrieved from https://healthcentral.nz/hungry-ghosts-no-more/

Ch'oe, S. (2006). Prayers to Ancestor Spirits. In *Anxiety of Words: Contemporary Poetry by Korean Women* by Ch'oe, S. Kim H, & Yi Y., translated by Choi D.M. (p. 45). Massachusetts, USA: Zephyr Press.

Choo, Y. (2013). *The Ghost Bride*. London: Hot Key Books. Retrieved from https://www.amazon.com/Ghost-Bride-Yangsze-Choo-ebook/dp/B00JTJEVIA/

Edwards B., & Jamieson B. (2014, April). *Archaeological Assessment of the SS Ventnor Shipwreck, Hokianga Harbour mouth, NZAA Site No: O05/350*. 4-5. Retrieved from https://www.nrc.govt.nz/media/uulctuhe/ss-ventnor-assessment-sheet.pdf

Fensome, A. (2014, Dec 28). Murder aimed to spread 'yellow peril' message. *Stuff*. Retrieved from https://www.stuff.co.nz/national/crime/64512110/murder-aimed-to-spread-yellow-peril-message

Flynn, G. (2021). Inheritance. In A. Y. Smith & L. Murray (Eds.). *Tortured willows: bent, bowed, unbroken*. (p. 50). Independence MO: Yuriko Publishing.

Ip, M. (1990) *Home Away from Home: Life Stories of Chinese Women in New Zealand*. (p. 15). Auckland, New Zealand: New Women's Press.

Kulski, K.P. (2022). *The House of Pungsu*. Bizarro Pulp Press. (pp. 65, 80).

Lee, R.H. (1960). *The Chinese in the United States*. (pp. 69-85, 326-27). Hong Kong: University of Hong Kong Press.

Liang, R. (2020, October 9). Naming our ancestors lost in the Hokianga. *Newsroom*. Retrieved from https://www.newsroom.co.nz/naming-our-ancestors-lost-in-the-hokianga

Murray, L. (2020). Phoenix Claws. In L. Murray & G. Flynn (Eds.). *Black cranes: Tales of unquiet women*. (pp. 61-77). Los Angeles, CA: Omnium Gatherum.

—Frangipani Wishes. In L. Murray & G. Flynn (Eds.). *Black cranes: Tales of unquiet women*. (pp. 188-201). Los Angeles, CA: Omnium Gatherum.

Murray, L. (2021). Willows. In A. Y. Smith & L. Murray (Eds.). *Tortured willows: bent, bowed, unbroken*. (pp. 2-3). Independence MO: Yuriko Publishing.

—Fury. In A. Y. Smith & L. Murray (Eds.). *Tortured willows: bent, bowed, unbroken*. (p. 32). Independence MO: Yuriko Publishing.

Murray, L. (2022). In Lee, L. (Ed.) *Farewell Guangdong: Refugee Wives and Children Arrive in Aotearoa New Zealand, 1939-194*. (pp. 477-479). New Zealand: The Chinese Poll Tax Heritage Trust.

Siu, P.S. (1952). The Sojourner, *American Journal of Sociology. 82*, 34-44.

Tan, R. (2021). How to feed a hungry ghost. *Verb Wellington*, Retrieved from https://www.verbwellington.nz/essays/how-to-feed-a-hungry-ghost.

Tan, T. M. (2021). Seven mournings of the Chinese Gooseberry. In Morris, P. & Wong, A. (Eds.), *A Clear Dawn: New Asian Voices from Aotearoa* (p. 255). New Zealand: Auckland University Press.

FOX DAUGHTER

CELINE MURRAY

A few years ago, my partner and I visited Dunedin's Lan Yuan Chinese gardens, the only authentic Chinese garden in New Zealand and one of very few outside of China. The design of the garden is perfectly cultivated to reflect the harmony of nature, its winding paths offering glimpses of the landscape, each angle giving a new view of the trees, pagodas, river, and lake, an arranged beauty made of many facets that cannot be perceived all at once. Along the outer wall of Lan Yuan is a corridor with information about the history of the Chinese community in New Zealand. Near the end of the corridor, a panel describes the ships sent to return the remains of dead miners to China, the loss of the *S.S. Ventnor,* and the souls she was meant to transport home. Their families left grieving an irreparable loss—predecessors of people just like me, a Chinese New Zealander on my mother's side. When I read about the *S.S. Ventnor,* a creature inside me snarled in pain.

Then this summer, when I visited my paternal grandmother, I asked her to tell me about our Māori lineage. She brought out a cardboard box filled with Scottish history—family trees, crests, tartan. Among the memorabilia were two photos and a slip of paper. The paper included the name of my *iwi* (tribe) and a list of daughters and the Scotsmen they married. The first of the photos was a copy of the Charles Frederik Goldie painting of my ancestor, Atama Paparangi, a famous Māori chieftain. The second was a minuscule photograph of the first mixed Māori-Pākeha woman in our family. A new face of a woman who caused a metamorphosis in our history. She was the first step towards newness. I thought about her values, the knowledge she brought from her ancestors, and the cultural texture that never made it to me. In her eyes, I see a fox, a spirit that now lives in me. And we're angry. Feral. We want retribution.

Help!
It's trapped in my ribcage
Jagged little teeth, needling claws
Frenzied scrabbling and biting
It hurts me all the time
I want you to love it

The *huli jing* is a Chinese nine-tailed fox demon, a shapeshifter capable of appearing human, but often at a cost. In some forms, the fox must kill and consume human flesh. Others must search for human skulls to fit over their head before they can transform.

> The fox spirit straightened the skullcap, moist with blood, atop her head then stepped over the decapitated corpse from which she'd taken it. Her hind paws transformed into petite, human lotus feet adorned in pointy shoes embroidered with golden silk. This visit her name would be Júhua, like the chrysanthemums woven into the fabric near her toes. The eight tails behind the fox spirit became long braids, winding themselves into intricate loops and circles, concealing the bone that aided her in keeping a human guise.
>
> Tottering on useless feet, Jú couldn't roll the headless woman down the hillside. She kicked the body, wincing as pain ravaged the deformed foot and shot up her leg and into her torso. (Mason, 2020, p. 127).

Fox demons are contradictory creatures, often malevolent and dangerous. However, they also contain the capacity to be good. Though she is a demon, the huli jing is also a spirit who, through perseverance, might become a celestial being. This endeavour may take one hundred, or even one thousand years to achieve, and may leave a trail of viscera and bone behind her.

Thus, the essence of the fox demon is a painful yearning to be more than what they are. As a queer woman from Aotearoa with both Chinese and Māori heritage, and an invisible disability, this absence of a complete identity claws at my heart. I am perpetually a minority, consistently faced with the threat of not-enough-ness. Filled with an ever-present hunger for more of myself.

Am I afraid of being a ghost?
Or jealous
That they can disappear
And I cannot.

As a spirit, this Asian monster shares many traits with the dead. Both ghosts and fox spirits represent a transformation into a new form. Both are hungry to find their missing celestial culture. But huli jing are not just spirits. They are also demons tied to a physical form. Unlike ghosts, they cannot be separated from their body, nor can they flee any physical threats. They can bleed; they can be hunted and killed. Unlike the dead, a fox demon is a creature with her back against the wall. Her existence depends on her ability to toe the line between worlds, to appear benign, and without malice.

Foxes are closely connected to the dead, often living in the same caves my Chinese ancestors were buried in. I hunger after my own dead ancestors, for the bones of Chinese miners lost at sea. I want to measure their skulls to see which might fit on my head. One day, I also hope to feel complete.

> She lifted to the moon and howled: it was a howl made by steam passing through brass piping and yet it reminded me of that wild howl long ago, when I first heard the call of a hulijing.
>
> Then she crouched on the floor. Gears grinding, pistons pumping, curved metal plates sliding over each other—the noises grew louder as she began to transform.
>
> She had drawn the first glimmers of her idea with ink on paper. Then she had refined it, through hundreds of iterations until she was satisfied. I could see traces of her mother in it, but also something harder, something new. (Liu, 2016, pp. 33-34)

The fox demon at her most threatening is always a beautiful young woman. Those around her see her as a temptress, a seductress, who will twist a man's mind, take his power, and perhaps his life. Her feminine cunning is evil and untrustworthy. In the Tang dynasty, stories were told of two historical Chinese queens associated with the fox spirit: Da Ji of the Shang dynasty and Bao Si of the western Zhou dynasty. Both women are remembered as being malevolent and hard to please. To win their favour, the kings they married began to mistreat their people for the queen's entertainment, leaving them vulnerable to attack from their enemies. Thus, each fox spirit queen is presumably at fault for the downfall of their kingdom.

As a child of mixed heritage, I see the faces of the fox spirit in the women of my family, those who married outside their culture, an act expected to ruin the integrity and respectability of their husbands' family. Society is afraid of the fox spirit's deception, and what she may be hiding beneath, so she is forced to use these same skills to survive. Changing her form, she moulds herself into a good wife, hiding her pointed ears and sharp teeth. In passing, I learn about a kitsune, a Japanese great-great-great-grandmother who married into our family and who lived during the Japanese-Sino war. In the enemy territory of her new home, she gracefully swept away her old culture with a flick of her tails, never to be discussed again. Her identity becomes a secret passed on only in the whispers of her fox children. I try on her skull.

A fox's tail is not easily hidden. –Chinese Proverb

Queen Da Ji is believed to have invented foot binding as a way of hiding her own little fox feet. Though the fox demons of myth are cunning and skilled deceivers, her disguise is never complete. If you look closely, you might notice an ear, a tail, a patch of fur, a slanted eye. No matter how skilled an actress, she will always be betrayed by how she looks.

My dad has fair skin. He sunburns badly and has freckles all over. Growing up, I assumed I was the same, checked 'New Zealand European' as my ethnicity on forms, believed I was part of a safe majority. I studied linguistics at the University of Otago, in a city with strong Scottish roots—another culture of mine, passed down from my dad. There, I was disillusioned by a woman whose first words to me were to ask after the colour of my skin. As she did, the skull I had worn over my own began to tighten, squeezing at my brain until I was forced to remove it. Even now, I struggle to wear this disguise. I am always afraid someone will see the Chinese fox that lies beneath.

Conversely, other fox-forms I possess feel too subtle to wear comfortably. To claim my Māori heritage, I have to defend the validity of my cultural connection without the support of the language, the personal relationships with my iwi, or the connections to my landscape that should have grown alongside me. Disabled for more than five years, I find others respect my limitations most when I have a walking stick in my hand and often forget when I leave the cane at home.

"The concept of a Chinese New Zealander," wrote scholar Manyip Ng in *Dragons on the Long White Cloud*, "is not so readily accepted by those who feel that only Europeans and Māori can be true New Zealanders ... such covert racism undermines their birthright, subverts their identity and poses serious challenges to their self-esteem and sense of belonging. Chinese New Zealanders, like descendants of all migrants whose physical traits mark them apart from the dominant culture are 'hyphenated' personalities destined to move between distant worlds, the boundaries of which are shifting all the time." (Ip, 1996, p. 34)

Perhaps the tragedy of the fox demon lies in her inability to land on one form. She is unable to fully show herself amongst the hostile eyes of the community, yet she must always carry some aspect of the fox that distinguishes her as an outsider. Is this why my great-grandmother bit back at her own Māori culture, though it was as much a part of her as Chinese culture is part of me? Was she defending her hidden identity or lashing out in revenge for never being seen as herself? I am angry at her for biting me, but as I try on her skull, I am also angry on her behalf.

Without fox demons, no village is complete. –Chinese Proverb

Though the fox demon has typically been feared, there is a seed of hope for her. As a shapeshifter, her reputation has faced many changes throughout history. In the Tang dynasty, many Chinese people treated fox spirits with respect, believing them to be dangerous only if mistreated. With compassion and kindness, perhaps there could be a space for the fox spirit amongst us, a chance for her to show her face and to form connections within the community without needing to blunt her claws.

> "However old one might be, stories never die. Folktales, legends, family mysteries, the childhood of our parents, the youth of our grandparents, the soil that birthed our ancestors, and the land they walked upon call out to us. The past wants to speak to us. Where can we go if we know not where we came from? And where could we go if we knew? Immigrant literature enriches the lives of both, writer and reader. While the former painstakingly cultivates a treatise of their heritage, the latter devours books filled with culture and traditions from around the world. In learning about each other, we learn about ourselves. And what we learn about ourselves, we teach to future generations, so that stories linger through time and space, and 'ours' and 'theirs' become one." (Pavrey, 2022, p.175)

My mother is also a writer, and in her writing, I see her fox spirit in how she honours our ancestors, shifting from joss sticks to words to guard their spirits. "...to the women who travelled before me," she writes in her essay in this volume, "you beautiful voracious unquiet ghosts, let me nourish you with my stories, which are built on your stories and your suffering. I will raise our unquiet voices, not, as you have done, on ephemeral curls of smoke, but on the written page. Though I walk in another realm, let me write to you of a new world, a world without walls, in which no woman hungers." When I read my mother's essay, I learned that the bones of the Chinese people that were lost from the *S.S. Ventnor* washed ashore in Northland and were cared for by the Māori people who lived there. That the people of Te Rarawa, my own Māori ancestors, shouldered the weight of their bones. For a moment, my fox demon is as calm as the Lan Yuan gardens. She is sated. Another skull is added to the pile, one of one thousand steps towards finding the truth of who I am.

I understand
that the mountains of my ancestors are distant,
the details of their faces sometimes obscured by cloud.
I understand
that from here
you cannot know how large they are,
that their shadows are long,
stretching across my mind.
And still
I don't want to be defined by your near-sightedness.
Everything I am
I am, entirely.

REFERENCES

Lui, K. (2016). Good Hunting. In Helgadóttir M. (Ed.) *Asian monsters: Fox spirit book of monsters #3*, (pp.21-34). UK: Fox Spirit Books.

Ip, M. (1996). *Dragons on the Long White Cloud: The Making of Chinese New Zealanders*. North Shore City, NZ: Tandem Press.

Murray, C. Unless otherwise stated, poems in this text are the author's own previously unpublished work.

Mason, R. (2020). The Ninth Tale. In L. Murray & G. Flynn (Eds.). *Black cranes: Tales of unquiet women.* (pp.127-141). Los Angeles, CA: Omnium Gatherum.

Pavrey, R. (2022). Travelling the world in search of home: an exploration of immigrant literature that connects writers to old roots as much as it connects readers to new lands. In Sharma S. & Kanger K. (Eds.) *English literature: Themes, perspectives and appropriations,* (pp. 169-176). New Delhi, India: Rudra Publishers and Distributors.

SOME THINGS ARE DANGEROUS, BUT CAN BE LIVED WITH: THE GHOST BABY OF MALAYSIAN MYTHOLOGY

GENEVE FLYNN

I've never met my Aunt Rosemary; she died when my mother was only four or five years old, but her spirit has laid its delicate, restless touch on my life. Her story, her *kwee kia*'s voice, will continue to echo through the generations that follow.

According to Southeast Asian lore (Khairunnisa & Wardhaningsih, 2020; Laranjo et al., 2013), a kwee kia is a creature made from the spirit of a deceased human fetus, often aborted or stillborn. The ghost baby has many names and transcends several cultures. It is called a *toyol* in Malay, *tuyul* in Indonesian, *komantong* in Thai, and a kwee kia (ghost child) in Hokkien.

Brought to life by a *bomoh* (Malaysian shaman) through black magic, a kwee kia is usually the size of a toddler, with a large head, red or black, clouded eyes, pointed ears, fanged teeth, long nails, and green or grey skin. The creature is kept in a jar and must be fed with blood, either through breastfeeding or from the fingers or toes of its keeper. Despite its ghastly origin and description, the kwee kia is relatively harmless and is only used by its owner to steal or cause mischief.

However, under the direction of a malevolent or neglectful master, a kwee kia can become monstrous, and any riches gained will be at great personal cost. The ghost child is often passed from generation to generation and may grow stronger over time. Once created, it can be difficult to destroy.

Several Asian transnational female authors have reimagined traditional myths to tell stories of otherness and liminality from their perspectives of diaspora (Satkunananthan, 2020).

Yangsze Choo (2013), a Chinese Malay author, adapted the concept of the hungry ghost to explore themes of filial duty, gender, and sovereignty. In *The Ghost Bride*, Choo repurposes the mythology to allow her protagonist to unpack traditional cultural norms and to reclaim the power to steer her own life.

Cassandra Khaw, another transnational Chinese Malaysian, reinvents the legend of the hungry ghost in her short story "Some Breakable Things" (2016) to depict the pain of loss, difficult relationships, and things left unsaid.

The hauntings in both works hold up for consideration the tension between the cultures of the authors' countries of origin and the countries they now call home. They dissect the differences in gender expectations, societal norms, what is real and unreal, and the echoes of the past.

In my short story "Little Worm," (Flynn, 2020), which is the final entry in the award-winning anthology *Black Cranes: Tales of Unquiet Women*, I adapted the myth of the kwee kia to represent the suppressed hopes and ambitions of the protagonist's—Theresa's—mother. I amplified the hereditary and vampiric nature of the ghost child to personify the trauma and lessons we learn from generations past. The kwee kia became the embodiment of an unquiet phantom: something that is passed down from generation to generation, beginning with trauma, morphing and shaped by each age, and which can never be discarded.

When Lee and Angela invited me to contribute to this collection, my first thought was to expand on this exploration and delve further into my family history. My mother has told tales of her childhood, her experiences as a daughter, wife, and mother, and of the death of her older sister. However, these retellings seemed to be fragments of a whole. I wanted to trace the entire narrative, follow the tendrils that lead back to the formation of my family's kwee kia, and examine how this urban ghost story could be adapted to interrogate generational trauma.

ROSEMARY

My maternal ancestors are of Chinese descent and have lived in Malaysia for several generations.

Aunt Rosemary was twenty years older than my mother and the eldest of four children. Rosemary was absent for much of my mother's early childhood as she went to boarding school and then earned a scholarship to study medicine in Australia. My mother only ever remembers seeing her once, on Rosemary's wedding day, when, as a young child, my mother helped her get dressed for the occasion. In most ways, the sisters were strangers.

Rosemary returned to Malaysia and married a young doctor, Too Joon Swan, and they moved away from her hometown for his training. He was afforded a small bedsit as part of his internship and, being only one of around sixty doctors in the whole of Malaya at the time, he was on-call most nights. Believing that the tiny room was no place for his new bride, my uncle sent Rosemary to live with his father and his father's wives.

The months after marriage can be some of the hardest for a new bride in traditional Chinese society. Sons have an unbroken sense of belonging in the family. They will continue the family name, remain in the family home, and inherit the family assets. They will also have the weight of preserving the family honour and status. Daughters, on the other hand, are viewed as extra mouths to feed until they are married off. When a wife enters her new family, she is often deemed a threat to the bond between mother-in-law and son. The wife only gains a true sense of belonging when she creates her uterine family—her children. Her status rises if and when she is able to produce sons (Eastman, 1988).

Rosemary never felt part of the family. She was sometimes mistreated, and her husband's family spoke a different dialect to her own. She and Too Joon Swan clashed many times about her placement. Desperately isolated and homesick, she asked her parents to visit. They declined but bought her a car so she could drive back and forth to see her husband.

One night after a party, only a few months after they were married, Rosemary and Too Joon Swan argued terribly. Distraught, she drove off into the night. She needed glasses for driving but, for some reason, was not wearing them. The road forked around a large tree; on one side was the Catholic cemetery, on the other, the Christian graveyard. Rosemary crashed headlong into the trunk, crushing the bonnet four feet and severing both her legs. Witnesses say tears were on her face when she died. In a cruel turn of fate, her husband, the only doctor in the area, was called to attend.

Like the death necessary for the creation of a kwee kia, my Aunt Rosemary's story was a life cut short.

CHRISTINE

My grandmother, Christine, wept and refused to leave her bed for a week. She began to smoke and gamble heavily, often playing mahjong with friends for several days and nights at a time. She would hurriedly cook for the morning, then return after dark, leaving my mother to prepare the evening meal. The happy family atmosphere was fractured, and nobody was allowed to speak ill of Rosemary, nor even utter her name. All the photos of her were removed, and there was no commemorative shrine. My grandmother did not attend Rosemary's funeral.

The eldest surviving child, Ronald, was at boarding school. The remaining children—David, the second son, and my mother, the youngest—were still living at home and required care. My grandparents doted upon David and nursed him for his health issues. But my grandmother, who was already somewhat distant, became cold and neglectful towards my mother.

My mother bears an uncanny resemblance to Rosemary: she has been told that she looks, speaks, and walks like my aunt did, and her name is Rosalind. As a young woman, she was often mistaken for her sister. After my aunt's death, friends and family would accidentally call my mother by her sister's name, sending my grandmother into a fury. My grandmother fought with my grandfather to move away from their hometown to escape; the family would move several times before finally settling.

After my grandfather passed away in 2003, my mother found a small tin box while sorting through his belongings. She had never seen it before; it was something my grandmother had hidden away. Inside, were the missing photos of Rosemary. Although my grandmother never brought out the box of photos, and would say she had three children—never four and one who had died—the box had survived every relocation. My grandmother had created a form for the kwee kia.

My mother also found the police report of her sister's death in my grandfather's safe. Although nowhere on the report is suicide recorded, my grandmother suffered terribly from the guilt of not visiting Rosemary when she had been so unhappy.

Controlling behaviour is a common response to trauma. After investing so heavily in their first daughter, my grandparents refused to make the same mistake with their second. The sudden loss of Rosemary and my mother's likeness to her sister created a powerful anxiety in my grandparents. The fear of losing so much again was coupled with their traditional patriarchal values, and the road before my mother narrowed to a single, airless path.

However, anxiety is a liar and a thief. While it seems that expending energy to avoid the source of worry affords us control, this effort only feeds the fear. It allows its shadow to grow (Centre for Clinical Investigations). Soon, it eclipses everything, spreading into every waking moment. We spend more and more energy trying to run from or placate this devious monster, only to find that it is insatiable.

The kwee kia is much the same. A sacrifice of blood seems to bend it to its master's will, but over time, it only grows stronger and becomes increasingly entrenched. In their effort to assuage the apprehension they must have felt for my mother, my grandparents instead nourished the creature haunting them. It grew bloated and noxious in the dark corners of their home.

There is a Chinese nursery rhyme that has been passed down from my great grandmother to my grandfather, to my mother, to me, and now to my children. It was the inspiration for the title of my story "Little Worm" and has an eerie, prescient parallel with the kwee kia in this essay. The following is a translation:

Point little fingers
Point to the little worm
Little worm, hatch!
Fly to the lychee orchard
The lychees are ripe
The house is full

In light of the kwee kia in my family, this might be a fitting interpretation:

Take notice
See the daughter
Daughter, blossom!
Fly to the new home
The new family grows
The family prospers

In this case, the daughter's chance to blossom in her new home is cut short. The house, the family, is never full again.

ROSALIND

This kwee kia, this trauma, irrevocably altered my mother's childhood, and the value and understanding she developed of herself.

With parents who had withdrawn from guilt and grief, my mother became cook, cleaner, and later, carer for my great-grandmother after she had a stroke. She was to be prepared for a life as a filial daughter, wife, and mother. Her brother, David, showed little academic aptitude; however, my grandparents pulled strings in order to secure his place in the local boarding school, then sent him to Australia to study. In contrast, although my mother easily passed the examination for entry to the boarding school, my grandfather was reluctant to send her. She argued her case and was allowed to attend, but when she graduated from high school, her education would go no further.

My mother learned that her identity was embedded in service to others, that the authority over her life belonged to someone else, and that girls and women, regardless of their intelligence or ability, did not have the same opportunities as boys and men.

My family (mother, father, older brother, and I) emigrated to Australia in 1983. The Women's Liberation Movement emerged during the 1960s and into the 1980s, compounding the cultural shock for my mother of relocating to a western society. My mother was caught between traditional Chinese beliefs of patriarchy and filial duty and the western ideals of equality and individuality. This constant tension meant a difficult path. Once, her friend told her to lie on the floor. Confused, my mother asked why. Her friend said she spent all her time being a door mat for everyone; now, it was the friend's turn to walk all over her. It was a blunt and shocking wake-up call.

The next few years were characterised by seismic shifts in our family dynamic. My mother battled to emerge from the shadow cast by the kwee kia and traditional Chinese values; often, her most tenacious antagonist was herself. She would vacillate between staunch feminism—sometimes tarring all men with the same brush—and subverting her own feelings and wants for the sake of others. She would also struggle to find the balance between being my friend and my parent. Her own mother had been aloof and uninvolved; my mother endeavoured to be a close part of my life, but it was sometimes difficult to navigate between and understand the boundaries when my mother herself was unsure of them. Without effective modelling, how was she to know how to be different? The kwee kia had grown pernicious and pervasive.

Eventually, she divorced my father, ending a desperately unhappy marriage, and went on to earn a master's in Asian Studies. She became a successful businesswoman and ensured that all three of her children had the opportunity to attend university. She was determined that I, her only daughter, would never be in a position of economic and social disadvantage in any relationship.

Although it seems that my mother had managed to silence the demon baby, I still hear its cries ringing in my ears.

GENEVE

My own navigation through daughterhood, wifedom, motherhood, and career person has not been without its own confusion. Although my mother spoke of feminist beliefs, her behaviour often still reflected her upbringing and the long reach of the kwee kia. She continues to run around after others, still performing the role of the sudden adult, cook, cleaner, and carer that was thrust upon her when her sister died. She will still ring me up to remind me that the council rates are due, and she still cooks and cleans for my two brothers, who are now fifty and thirty-seven.

Having this modelled since I was born, I, too, find it difficult not to constantly 'do' for others and to put my own aspirations or needs aside. For a long time, in my own relationships, I did whatever I could to present the face of what I believed was the perfect woman.

And that definition is difficult to pin down. My mother has expressed disappointment that although I earned two psychology degrees, I did not go on to have a career after graduation. Instead, I got married and became a stay-at-home mother. I entered a traditional relationship and poured my time and energy into my family. I can only imagine the anxiety this choice stirred in my mother. She must have felt that I was taking the path she had worked so hard to escape. This was the voice of the kwee kia, only it was speaking through my mother's rejection of its original form.

The conflicting parenting styles that characterised my upbringing means that I swing between independence and service, often with extremes. I clearly remember the tumultuous years of seismic shifts before, during, and after my parents' divorce to be as perilous and unpredictable as trying to cross a half-frozen lake. One minute discarded dirty socks were ignored, the next, my mother would lash out in frustration, then return to tidying after everyone. Try as I might, I haven't managed to avoid inconsistency in my own parenting. I often hear echoes of my mother when I scold my sons for leaving their dishes on the counter or dirty towels on the bathroom floor. And then I go around and pick up after them.

Although I grew up in Australia, I still feel the weight of expectations of what a 'good' daughter, wife, mother, and woman should be in terms of Chinese culture. Even in the previous sentence, I'm aware that I've listed all the ways in which I am connected to others before how I may simply be myself. Intellectually, I know that the right and fair thing is for work and responsibility to be shared. Still, on the occasions that I don't follow my mother's example of taking on the lion's share, I feel tremendous guilt.

I have become so entangled with the kwee kia that it seems impossible to separate from it. In my poem "Inheritance" (Flynn, 2021) from *Tortured Willows: Bent, Bowed, Unbroken*, I spoke of this experience. As Yangsze Choo and Cassandra Khaw did, I took the hungry ghost and used it for my own purpose.

Inheritance
What was it like
being the brightest spark
with the dimmest road
that narrowed and ended
with a sudden cliff
and walls all around?
Was that when you first
began to swell? Your stomach
bulging and burgeoning,
swallowing the bitter,
the burden, the second-hands,
the not-for-yous?
Did your mouth begin to draw
closed like a miserly purse
when you were left behind,
your splendid mind with
only hunger and no choice

but to turn upon itself?
Was that when you learned
to forever chase the proof
that you were good,
you were smart,
you were worthwhile?
When did I take up
the chase and the very
same hunger and how
did I learn so easily
to begin devouring
myself, never sated,
never full, one hungry ghost
just like the other?

THE NEXT GENERATION

Are my children and the generations that follow then doomed to forever be twisted and tortured by a spectre that was formed long before they were even born? How do I break the pattern of wrestling with, pushing against, and ultimately still being caught by such an insistent apparition?

The answer, I think, lies in the act of telling stories, specifically *ghost stories*.

What is a haunting but an echo from the past? Something formed from a traumatic event that hasn't finished all it has to say. Something that we may have tried to live with, live around, live past, but that continues to shape and mould us. Some hauntology theorists believe that these spectres have secrets, and once the secret is uncovered, understood, and categorised, and the haunting returned to the order of knowledge, we will be cured of the harm that ghosts cause in our lives. Still, others view ghosts as an opportunity to accept that we don't and can never truly know all, or at least that we don't yet have the language to comprehend everything a haunting has to teach us (Davis, 2005).

Ghost stories provide us with that parlance. When Lee Murray wrote "Frangipani Wishes" (Murray, 2020), it gave voice to an ancestor, someone who was silenced and buffeted by hungry ghosts:

> Since the moment you were born, generations of hungry ghosts swirled around you, teasing the air, your breath, your hair. Not your fault, although First Wife and Little Wife and the entanglements who dwelled in your father's villa, those living repositories of secrets, they blamed you still. They whispered behind their hands, hiding smiling teeth, muttering, uttering, chattering. Your mother had unleashed them, they said, spawned them as she spawned you, let the starving ghosts escape into the night. A hundred dragon's teeth could not drive out such demons. Nor a thousand dragon teeth ground to powdered dust. It was as well she was gone. (pp. 188-189)

This lyrical, dream-like journey unveils the wounds that formed the haunting and ultimately, provides a way to comprehend an incomprehensible act.

My grandparents never told my mother why she wasn't allowed to attend university. They did not explain why life altered so terribly for her after the death of someone she barely knew. Perhaps this essay is a way to unpick what haunted them, and to come to some form of peace.

Writing stories and creating myths can help us to process trauma. It's often easier when there is something tangible to push against, something with a goal or meaning, and therefore something with a weakness that we can use to overcome the horror it represents.

Matt O'Connell (2020) has a pungent way of putting things in his article on generational trauma and horror: "We need a face that we can punch. We need a heart that we can stake. We need to give ourselves a fighting chance in the story we're going to tell … it's not exactly surprising that each great wave of popular horror can be read as a way to narrativize—and thereby process—real, generational traumas."

The kwee kia represents an effort to write a generational trauma as an entity—something that has rules, limitations, governance, an outline—and allows objective distance. It makes the wounds of the past easier to examine and also provides a moment of clarity for me to see my parents for what they are: human. They, too, hear spectres crying out from generations past. This essay was difficult for my mother to read, but I think and hope that it has helped her to reframe some of the cruel moments in her upbringing.

Narrative forms are spectral: an opportunity to investigate and receive our history and to contemplate what could have been. We cannot tell a story without resurrecting the past; it is sometimes perilous and often painful but altogether necessary. The ghost story allows a way to conceptualise the ghost's origins, its influence, and finally, its relative containment.

In my story "Little Worm" (Flynn, 2020), Theresa comes to accept that her mother's kwee kia was born from necessity: a way to cope with traumas and pressures present at the time. It cannot be separated from her mother, nor can its cries be ignored. Instead, she honours its existence and accepts that there are things in this world that are dark and not fully knowable, but she has been given a chance to learn.

A line in the final paragraphs captures the nature of the kwee kia and its parallel to generational trauma:

"… some things were dangerous, but could be lived with." (p. 220)

REFERENCES

Centre for Clinical Interventions. (n.d.). *The vicious cycle of anxiety.* Retrieved from https://www.cci.health.wa.gov.au/~/media/CCI/ Mental-Health-Professionals/Panic/Panic---Information-Sheets/ Panic-Information-Sheet---03---The-Vicious-Cycle-of-Anxiety.pdf

Choo, Y. (2013). *The Ghost Bride.* London: Hot Key Books.

Davis, C. (2005). Hauntology, spectres and phantoms. *French Studies, 59*(3), 373-379. Retrieved from https://doi.org/10.1093/fs/kni143

Flynn, G. (2020). Little Worm. In L. Murray & G. Flynn (Eds.). *Black cranes: Tales of unquiet women.* (pp.202-220). Los Angeles, CA: Omnium Gatherum.

Flynn, G. (2021). Inheritance. In A. Y. Smith & L. Murray (Eds.). *Tortured willows: bent, bowed, unbroken.* (pp. 48-49). Independence MO: Yuriko Publishing.

Eastman, L. E. (1988). *Family, field, and ancestors: Constancy and change in China's social and economic history,* 1550-1949. Oxford: Oxford University Press.

Khairunnisa, A., & Wardhaningsih, M. (2020). *A book of Indonesian ghosts: A field guide of ghosts in Indonesian myths.* Indonesia: PT Cerita Nusantara Asia.

Khaw, C. (2016, September). Some breakable things. *The Dark.* Retrieved from https://www.thedarkmagazine.com/some-breakable-things/

Laranjo, R., Martinez-Erbite, K., & Santos, Z. J. (2013). Intersection of Asian supernatural beings in Asian folk literature: A pan-Asian identity. *Proceedings of the Asian Conference on Asian Studies* 2013, 15-24. Retrieved from https://papers.iafor.org/wp-content/uploads/ papers/acas2013/ACAS2013_0102.pdf.

Murray, L. (2020). "Frangipani Wishes" in L. Murray & G. Flynn (eds.). *Black cranes: tales of unquiet women.* (pp. 188-201). Los Angeles, CA: Omnium Gatherum.

O'Connell, M. (2020, June 4). Living through horror: How generational trauma shapes our monsters. *The Luciferian Dominion*. Retrieved from https://luciferiandominion.org/how-generational-trauma-shaped-our-apocalyptic-storytelling/

Satkunananthan, A. H. (2020). Transnational hauntings, hungry ghosts: Malaysian Chinese Domestic Gothic fiction. *SARE, 57*(1), 37-54.

THE SUBSTITUTE

YI IZZY YU

To feel so wronged that one hangs oneself is indeed bitter! Before she was a person and was unaware, afterwards she was a ghost and was still not enlightened, but the hardest to bear was the moment when she finished putting on her makeup and tightened her sash. Therefore, after she was dead she had forgotten everything else, except for this moment and this place. Still doing over again what she had done is the only thing she could not forget.

—Pu Songling (1640–1715), *Liaozhai zhiyi* (1766/2005)

孵
[Hatchling]

When I was a kid, my friends and I loved roaming the yellow dirt streets of my grandma's dying village and finding deserted houses to explore. Inside, we pawed through debris for treasures: shiny nails and interesting shapes of wood or pottery. Sometimes, we even found clay tiles unflaked from mosaic wall art. Their patterns were explosions of eddying color as if each were imprinted with mysterious galaxies.

I always felt a buzzing joy stepping into these abandoned places—whether they were ancient with packed-mud walls and *kang* stone beds with stoves beneath to keep you warm during winter; or modern concrete husks, doorless and yawning because their ornate wooden doors had been sold for money.

But beneath my joy, I would feel unsettled, would want to snatch the nails and tiles and flee before there was a hatching disturbance in the dim light. Before *she* appeared, dangling, reeking of blood and moldy rope.

Every child remembers a death that stands out above all others. That glows blue and holy with significance. My great-aunt Wang Peiyu's suicide was that for me. Every dark and empty space has been haunted by her hanging ghost's presence since.

鬼

[Ghost]

There are hundreds of ghosts in Chinese thought. Stink-faced ones and ghosts with mouths like blazing torches. Tumor-covered ghosts with long curling tongues that lap at their own pus, venomous ghosts that shapeshift into insects, and lust ghosts that manifest as arid, drought-causing winds. There are hungry ghosts and messenger ghosts, alcoholic ghosts who hang around the smell of liquor, and ghosts who prefer the odors of lavatories. Gentle ghosts hoping wistfully for offerings and ghosts who trick people into the bone-littered dens of tiger masters (Ji, 2021).

But the *tisigui*, the "substitute-seeking ghost," is the one that most terrifies me.

Commonly portrayed as the long-tongued ghost of a young wife who has hung herself, it seeks to trick others into dying in the exact same manner. If it manages this, it will be freed from its earthly limbo to reincarnate, leaving behind its victim to become a substitute ghost in its place.

To achieve its goal, the substitute ghost creates illusions. Put your head through a stranger's car door to give directions and find yourself hanging in his basement. Slip a lover's jade bracelet onto your wrist and find you have slit it.

The substitute ghost doesn't always need illusion, though. The right words whispered at the right time—say after a vicious family argument—can do the trick.

For several centuries in China, a major field of inquiry among male scholars was what substitute ghosts whispered to cause women to kill themselves.

婦
[Wife]

My great-aunt Peiyu liked salmon. Every year, her family in the northeast sent her a few boxes—the red, fatty fish meat crusty with salt. Peiyu would steam the fish, serve it on buns, and eat it with great ceremony beneath her favorite apricot tree. Once, when my mom was eight, she asked Peiyu to share a piece. The answer was no.

Overall, Peiyu's childhood was happy. She was at ease in the world and her life—at peace as only a well-loved child can be. But this all changed when she entered a family-arranged marriage at seventeen.

The man was tall and movie-star handsome, with fair skin, long hands, and a charming manner. He was a great catch. Except for this: he quickly decided that he loathed his new wife, a conclusion his mother arrived at, too.

So after Peiyu delivered two daughters instead of the hoped-for boy, the mother-in-law gave Peiyu's husband permission to take a second wife. Her name was Enli, and she was ten years younger than the by-now twenty-eight-year-old Peiyu.

Everyone adored Enli. Her beauty was ethereal, her laughter quick and pleasing to hear, and she seemed genuinely concerned with everyone's welfare, even Peiyu's. Whenever they met, she would ask gently about Peiyu's health and slip her tiny gifts.

But my great-aunt couldn't stand the sight of Enli. Who could blame her? The husband moved to Enli's village, where he started a new life, leaving Peiyu and their two daughters to his parents. He and Enli turned out to be the great loves of each other's lives, while my aunt was just a background figure in their opera, some little scrawl of drying ink on a misty mountaintop.

溺
[Drowning]

When I hit my early twenties, my parents start to freak out that I'm still single and decide on an arranged marriage for me. Why not? Theirs had been arranged, as had the marriages of those before them. I tell them I don't want to get married yet.

It's time to grow up, they say.

The men my family brings for me to meet are not bad at all. I'm just not ready.

There is Feng, an ICU doctor who writes poetry about his patients and has two pet angelfish whose daily lives he records in a research log. He is pure and lovely.

There is Hong, a promising battalion commander in the navy who lives in the beautiful seaside city of Qingdao.

Eventually, I can't hold out any longer against my parents' wishes and accept an offer. The man is the blandest of the bunch—with a flat emotional affect that I tell myself is a sign of emotional maturity. He feels like an easy and undangerous choice, at first anyway. Besides, he works at the university like me, and his well-off family has long ties with mine.

I stick with him for a year. My friends and cousins envy me. All my furniture is fine antiques. I feel like I'm drowning.

示
[Apocalypse]

One of the earliest depictions of a substitute ghost, or something very much like one, is found in the fifth-century apocalyptic Taoist text, *The Scripture of Divine Incarnation*. Composed to graphically depict the consequences of not following the doctrines of a particular school of Taoism, it details how in the final days, eighty million three-foot-tall ghost soldiers, under the guidance of the great ghost king, will rise from their graves to punish those who have ignored the Three Caverns revelations and have scorned the way of the Tao.

From one side of the land to the other, the ghosts will sweep in massive herds—delivering death in hundreds of flavors. Some deaths will involve drowning, via illusion and force, at the hands of drowning victims turned ghosts.

During this dark time, no body of water will be safe, and any seemingly solid piece of sunlit field is possibly a body of water. Plague traps will be disguised as grass, tree, rock, and even fruit. Picking an apricot might trigger the escape of the Ninety-six Varieties of Sudden Death.

Everything will be suspect.

理

[Principles]

The substitute ghost is a controversial ghost in Chinese history. While other revenge ghosts make sense in terms of *bao*, the karmic repayment of debt, the tisigui illogically seeks victims that have done it no wrong and damns them to the same fate. Therefore, many classical scholars found the concept ridiculous and an insult to reason and cosmic justice.

I sympathize with these ancient sentiments but think bao and release from suffering are the wrong places to look for the substitute ghost's motivation. The right place is in everyday human behavior.

Don't the living also punish those who have done us no wrong because of past experiences? Don't we engage in repetition-compulsion and restage early traumas, morph from victims to victimizers?

How can we expect better than from a deranged ghost?

We insist others speak our languages, cite our authorities, adopt our family customs and doctrines, and take up our belief in gods or lack thereof. We seek to infect them with the memes with which we have been infected.

Richard Dawkins, the staunchly anti-supernatural, evolutionary biologist who coined the term "meme" saw them in fact as "living structures, not just metaphorically but technically," literal mental viruses that like biological genes seek to reproduce themselves in hosts and turn their brains into vehicles for propagation (Dawkins, 2006, p. 207). In this behavior, memes bear some similarity to the strategic larvae of the aquatic horsehair worm, which allow themselves to be consumed by mayfly larvae because they know these insects will eventually metamorphose into prey for crickets on shore.

Once inside the crickets, the worms grow into writhing, foot-long black threads which infiltrate the cricket's entire body, stuffing it like a toy and seeping neurochemicals that take control of its brain. As a result, the cricket develops an overwhelming attraction to certain qualities of light. This makes moonlit water shimmer irresistibly and brings the normally water-averse cricket to water's edge (Ponton et al., 2011). Here, the worms issue their final command: *jump*. As the cricket drowns, impossibly long worms—one after the other—flit into the water to lay eggs and start the cycle anew.

Far from the substitute ghost's behavior being out of step with the deep principles of the cosmos, it unsettlingly aligns.

縛
[Bondage]

Peiyu couldn't fight her husband's second marriage. She could not ask her domineering mother-in-law, "How could you remarry your son when I'm here and healthy?" Tradition gave the mother-in-law such a right, especially if the first wife hadn't given birth to a son. The worst part was that no matter what happened, the first wife remained duty-bound to serve her parents-in-law. She was their property. This was her fate. Thus, the saying:

> *Cry out to the sky if you like, but there will be no response.*
> *Cry out to the earth, but it will remain still.*

紅
[Red]

In the old days, women sometimes tried to become substitute ghosts on purpose. It was their only shot at power, and so they prepared carefully.

First, they acquired a red robe. Red is the color of *yang* energy, a kind of spirit camouflage, a color that fools household gods into believing that ghosts are nothing more than the astral-projecting souls of dreamers which flutter thick as moths at night.

Next, the women picked an auspicious night.

Not much after this except the knotting of a rope. Except courage and determination. Except rage and despair.

The women climbed on what they needed to climb—say a stairwell, a chair, a roof. Then just like that, they jumped into power. Jumped to emerge something different and terrible. Something unstoppable. Something no one owned.

傷
[Wound]

When I told my mom I wanted to know more about Peiyu, she said, "Why? She died so long ago. No one liked her much even then."

But as Mom talked, her attitude softened. Soon, we were both almost crying.

"How could I have not appreciated the pain of my own aunt's life until this moment?" she said. "How could I have forgotten so much? They made Peiyu prepare the outfits for her husband's second marriage. Did you know that? That husband and mother-in-law of hers.

"Your grandma said to me once that if she were in Peiyu's place, she would have scratched the husband's face open—all the way to the bone—so that the guests could see her pain. But Peiyu was one of those women who dare to love but don't dare to hate."

行

[Capable]

In "Ghosts Seeking Substitutes: Female Suicide and Repetition," Rania Huntington observes:

> One can imagine how the narrative of the ghost seeking a substitute would be useful not only to the family trying to explain a suicide, but to a woman rescued from her failed suicide attempt. Rather than claiming her own feelings of rage or despair facing the people who had elicited these emotions, she could offer a narrative in which she was more victim than perpetrator. Claiming such a narrative might not be entirely false: a woman contemplating suicide might well think of models, of other people, remembered or imagined, who had committed suicide. (Huntington, 2005, p. 20)

When I read this passage in graduate school, I recall how sometimes after a fight with my dad, my mom would shout:

"Wang Peiyu did it. So I'm capable, too. Don't think I'm not."

In the darkest days of my first marriage, when the only way I could breathe was to go on long drives with all the car windows down, I would think of my mom's words and how I must be capable as well. I would think about how nice it would be to die and reincarnate into a different life, would think about my ashes buried on a sunny hill. My death seemed better than a divorce, which would devastate and disappoint his family and mine. They all felt so happy about our union. The only one not happy was me.

世

[Incarnation]

During the first part of her life, my daughter Frankie keeps resetting, forgetting much of what happened in the years previous, as if pages were being ripped out of the book of her mind—at least until around the age of five when memories become stickier, providing a foundation for the building of self. The age of five is coincidentally the same age that child psychiatrist Ian Stevenson says most children start to forget past life memories (Bering, 2013).

Reincarnation strikes some of my friends as a hard-to-swallow proposition. I don't know why. After all, incredibly we began our present existence as a microscopic tadpole and a holy glowing orb—before being reborn to water-breathing fetus, to color-shocked infant, to shell-shocked adult.

Every few years we forget; we reinvent ourselves. The child us, the adult us. The us before and after coming out. Before and after our parent's death, or relocation to a new city.

Same but not the same. An old self forgotten until an old friend remarks, "Remember when?" And we feel deep vertigo as a piece of forgotten self or forgotten event rises like a body before sinking again.

Immigrants understand the deep truth of reincarnation better than anyone, understand the sheer number of lives we can live within the span of a single one.

Russian doctors who become custodial workers in Canadian country clubs.

African engineers who work at Lube-n-Go.

Thai nurses who open pizza shops.

Those who enter or leave romantic relationships understand this, too. The "you" you were with them, the "you" who disappears.

It is said in China:

When a woman marries, it is as if she is being reincarnated into a second life within her existing incarnation. If you find a good family, it is like being born into a good life. But if you are delivered to poor family circumstances, you are done.

門
[Door]

I'm twelve when CeCe, a strikingly beautiful girl who everyone falls in love with, joins my junior-high class. One evening, I'm gushing to my mom about how every day students peek into our homeroom to see CeCe's otherworldly face when she stuns me by revealing that CeCe is the descendent of Enli, Peiyu's replacement, and her spitting image to boot. She also reveals more details about Peiyu's hanging.

My mom was a teen when it happened, and she and my grandma helped lower the body and prepare it for burial. "Peiyu's face was purple except where blood vessels burst and made pink stars," my mom tells me. "And that tongue. It was just like they say it is after a hanging. Very long and inhuman."

"How hard it is to hang yourself?" I ask my mom.

"For Peiyu," she replies, "it was incredibly hard. She was older when she did it and needed help to even walk because of a stroke. So she hung herself from a doorknob. Rolled and flopped her way from her bed like a fish, tied the rope to the knob, and then slowly used the weight of her body to hang herself by straining forward. It must have taken every last bit of her strength."

骨
[Bone]

The substitute ghost's targets are never happy-go-lucky. They are bullied by in-laws, the victims of adultery and abandonment, or lonely and depressed for other reasons. Traditional Chinese theory holds that ghosts and demons can only hurt those low in yang energy, those weak in mind or body; or those crippled by fear, guilt, and other negative emotions.

It is the interplay of spectral influence and mental or physical illness that makes a victim vulnerable. In this way, supernatural pathogens are like natural ones such as cold and flu viruses. Resistance to both requires the shoring up of yang energy via diet, herbs, and meditation.

There are, however, also ways to prevent or defeat a substitute ghost that are unique to it. Take murder bones, which spark into existence the moment a suicide's neck snaps. If destroyed, they cause a substitute ghost to disappear or—if action is taken soon enough—prevent one from forming.

To find this bone, stomp the ground, stab the earth with a sharp object, and then dig beneath the hanging body. You'll find it a few feet down in the dirt—a neck bone cleaner and whiter than you've ever seen a bone (Zhang, 1985).

引

[Entrainment]

One of the most mysterious suicide bridges in the world is the Overtoun Bridge in Scotland. Since the 1950s, over six hundred dogs have inexplicably jumped from this bridge into the deep gorge below, many to their deaths.

Several explanations have been offered for this behavior, ranging from optical illusions to the beguiling scent of mink, and sound frequencies emitted from a distant submarine base. These have all been disproven. Moreover, none fit the fact that the dogs jumped from the exact same spot on the bridge and appeared, according to some owners, to be in a trance when they leapt. Some of the dogs that miraculously survived even made a second attempt later.

Dogs are not the only species capable of such peculiar behavior. In 2009, over the course of three days, twenty-eight cows threw themselves off a Swiss cliff hundreds of meters high.

Just like dogs and cows, people have their suicide bridges and cliffs. In China, there is the Nanjing Yangtze Bridge from which 2000 people have leapt since it was built in 1968. Going further back, the eighteenth-century writer Ji Yun records how after a traveler's deadly fall from a Chengde Mountain peak, people in the village below began to go insane and throw themselves off the peak, too (Ji, 1995).

"Resonance," a therapist friend says. He tells me that certain places, dense with electromagnetic or geomagnetic energy, are imprinted with traumatic events, patterns that seize control of sensitive people and cause them to play out ghost loops—as if they are moving to the same piece of music or are pendulum clocks tocking into sync.

I like his theory. It fits with the Chinese idea that both places and people are patterns of energy that interact with your own being and with one another. Nevertheless, I forget it until a few months later when, while doing story research on anomalous copycat murders and suicides, I come across a 2007 Paloma, California case where a man started acting radically out of character after he and his partner moved into a new house—a change accompanied by strange noises, phantom lights, and his eventual suicide by gun. Later, his suicide was discovered to repeat, in exact detail, one which occurred in the same house years before (Mishlove, 2020).

棄

[Forsaken]

Peiyu's older daughter visited her constantly—except during the autumn wheat harvest in her husband's village. This was when Peiyu hung herself, at the sweltering moment her daughter was threshing golden braids of wheat.

When she heard the news, the daughter cried her heart out.

She had not suspected the degree of her mother's suffering. To everyone, Peiyu's fate was no more remarkable than a worm drowning in a puddle. A miserable-looking woman with a miserable life? What was unusual about that?

Not one of us, not me, not you, understands the pain of others, and so we take their misery too lightly—at least up to the point they take their life.

The substitute ghost refuses to forget its misery or its pain, however, refuses to let you forget. It replays its bloody execution again and again until finally you demand the show be shut down once and for all, the bone dug up, the bridge closed, the cycle broken.

The tisigui is a voice for all we don't see. The date rapes and debt, the bouts of opioid addiction, anxiety, and depression. The Uyghur camps and prison systems. The dark deeds of science and history.

After China's one-child policy went into effect in 1980, limiting families to one child, around sixty million Chinese women went "missing." While twenty-five million were later found to have been left off census registration lists, the brunt of the rest were victims of sex-selective abortions, the withholding of health care, brutal neglect, and infanticide.

Millions upon millions of women.

In my village you saw these tiny victims occasionally—abandoned on the stoops of shops and temples, while others were left in the woods and the fields, or guiltily carried to the water.

Villagers would patrol to look for baby girls before wild dogs or the cold could get them. Still, no one could prevent the occasional glimpse of a blob of white in the currents, a tiny water-logged body floating away after being drowned. I was told that if I ever heard a baby crying from the river at night to ignore it. Those who answered such a call ended up drowning.

Such horrors are not exclusive to the one-child policy. Since the old days, female infanticide has been common in China because sons could take care of their parents financially, while daughters were bound to their husband's families.

In the third century BCE *Han Fei Zi*, it's disclosed:

"Parents' attitude toward children is such that when they bear a son they congratulate each other, but when they bear a daughter, they kill her" (as cited in Lee, 1981, p. 164).

女

[Daughter]

Growing up, I was keenly aware that my parents were disappointed I was not a son because they would communicate this in a thousand tiny ways.

Every so often, my father would hand me a piece of paper with a handwritten logic puzzle that my paternal cousins, who were all boys, had solved. His face would always be bright in anticipation of my success. "Let's see if you're as smart as your cousins, Yi."

I wanted to make my father happy. But the truth was that while I was smart, one of the top students in my class, I was never smart in the logic puzzle way.

The puzzles wanted me to calculate how many kilometers it would take to get to so and so after such and such; or to figure the number of trips to get a wolf, a sheep, a man, and some cabbages safely across a river. But I'd get lost in wondering about the backstories of the cabbages.

So while my father's face tightened, and the long minutes slowly ticked by, I stayed silent, face burning, until my father at last gave up on me.

Eventually, my father grew to love my peculiar mind. Still, to this day, there are moments where I can tell my parents regret my being a girl—usually connected to my mom making a comment during a family gathering.

"You should have heard your aunts carry on. My son this. My son that. As if pointing out I failed your father."

Having overheard everything while cooking with relatives, I knew my aunts meant to imply no such thing, that my mom is voicing her own feelings through my aunts, her feelings that she failed my father through my not being a boy, her feelings that I failed her by extension.

Nevertheless, as a filial daughter I always try to comfort her about her lack.

索

[Rope]

In some old stories about the substitute ghost, a search of a house after a ghost appears reveals a hidden rope that stinks of blood—wasted away over the years so that it looks more like a scribble in the air than a rope. If planted in an enemy's house, it will summon a substitute ghost.

While a search of a Chinese home today would likely turn up no such rope, one does regularly find other talismans, simulacra, material metaphors, and magical substitutes.

For example, when my mom visits America to help with my

daughter Frankie's first year, she wraps her first cut of hair in red paper and tucks it into a high place so that Frankie will grow tall.

When I later find this charm, I recall similarly discovering a gleaming steel axe and a heavy bronze lock, wrapped in red cloth and hidden in a stack of old clothes, when I was a teenager.

After hemming and hawing, my mom confessed to visiting a shaman when I was a baby because I was sickly and wouldn't stop crying. They warned her that I had one foot in this world and one foot in another. Consequently, it would be hard to keep me safe and close without magical intervention. One to cut my ties to the other world. One to lock me to home.

At the time my mom told me this, I found it silly. Mostly, I still do. But here it is, years later. I, my parents' only child, have left China, leaving them to grow old alone with no child to care for them.

Sometimes I wonder what would have happened if I hadn't unwrapped the axe and lock and broken the spell.

結

[Knots]

During Frankie's first year, my mom, Frankie, and I all sleep snuggled together, and late at night she shares things that she has never shared before.

In this way, I learn about a man she was once in love with and would have married if her family hadn't rejected him as a match. She tells me that although she grew to love my father after their marriage, she sometimes dreams of this man. "He played basketball very well," she whispers in the blackness of the room.

She tells me other things during these night-time episodes as well, the two of us just voices in the dark, our bodies invisible, while Frankie softly gurgles between us and touches our faces with her tiny fingers.

"It was hard to be a woman in the old days," my mom says. "Not just in your grandma's time but in mine, too. You girls today have no idea. We were considered so low. We were expected to put our family's feelings ahead of our own."

When she tells me this, I think of how she practically disowned me during my divorce, the sharpness of her words, the disgust in her eyes. But I realize her decision to discuss this issue now is an apology, as close as she can come. That she may be even admitting that she admires me for striking out on my own.

One night the conversation turns to Peiyu.

"It's awful to say," she confesses, "but sometimes I think about how relieved Peiyu felt to be released from this life. She must have felt so at peace to not be disliked anymore, to be no one's bother. How wonderful is that?"

幣

[Coin]

People who drive taxis in Yantai have learned over time that some roads are not roads. They are instead illusions constructed to cause you to drive over cliffs or into walls. So they carry extra coins.

When approaching an area where such roads have been reported (always at the sites of deadly accidents), the taxi drivers roll down their windows and toss out these coins, cold little pieces of metal flashing the moon. Imbued with energy and intention, the coins prevent illusory roads from forming—or if such a road has already appeared, cause it to disperse like fog.

I'm not sure why substitute ghosts of such immense power can be defeated by a spatter of coins. Maybe they take them as an offering, and it's just enough acknowledgement of their existence that they are satisfied without having to resort to murder.

And maybe, too, the same question could be asked of human beings and fiat currency. Why do symbolic pieces of colored paper drive self-value and murder?

Then again, maybe it's never about coins or flowers or paper replicas for ancestors' graves or sweetheart cards or ropes. Maybe all these things are simply focal points for energy, emotion-flavored "information hypostasized into objects" (Dick, 2001, p. 259), and thus we the living and they the dead are equally vulnerable to symbols.

美

[America]

When I fled the arranged marriage that was not what I hoped, leaving my parents broken-hearted that I was not the daughter they thought, to step into a country that turned out to be quite different from what I imagined, my funds were low.

So at two a.m., I took a subway from the JFK airport to my cheap hotel room in Queens instead of the more expensive taxi option, despite never having ridden in a subway before. This was a mistake, and I ended up getting off at the wrong stop on the wrong line in the dead of night.

The subway platform was dark: all flickering light, people stink, and haunted absence.

Suddenly, I noticed two strange men watching me, eyeing the ungainly suitcase I was lugging, my whole old life whittled down to fifty pounds, a fifty pounds that had battered and bruised my legs so much in the last twenty-four hours that my legs would look dyed green the next day.

They're not watching you, I told myself. *And if they are, they're just curious.*

But when I tried to put distance between us, the men followed. And when I turned a corner, so did they—even increasing their pace.

With each quick footstep and squeak of suitcase wheels, my panic rose. I imagined becoming just another statistic on my first night in America, proving my whole family right about my foolishness.

Then suddenly I saw someone else ahead—blurred faces and figures resolved into a couple leaning against each other as they waited for a late-night train.

"Hey," I said loudly, smiling and waving and hurrying toward the couple as if they were my best friends in the world, which is what they felt like in that moment. "Hey! So sorry I kept you waiting!"

Finding me more complicated prey than they thought, the men abruptly changed direction and bolted up an exit. When I finally reached the thoroughly confused couple, I said: "Sorry, I thought you were someone else."

路
[Road]

Sometimes, I wonder how my life would have turned out if I hadn't agreed to marry my ex-husband in the first place. If I didn't make an escape that caused so much pain for my parents, who to this day can't quite understand why I wanted a divorce from such a good family, why I left our country to become a citizen of a new one, why I left them to fend for themselves in their old age.

I have no easy answers. It's entirely feasible I would have immigrated anyway—or, if I knew that my parents would later refuse to move abroad, I would have stayed to the end.

But I do know I have a beautiful daughter. She is eight, and her middle name is Lu, which means "road" or "way." It is not a Chinese tradition to have a middle name, but I gave Frankie this one because I want her to see clearly what roads lie ahead and choose for herself where she wants to go.

臉
[Face]

Not far from where Wang Peiyu hung herself is my grandma's place. Her neighbors tell us that the people who moved into Peiyu's house after her death have reported strange occurrences, including seeing the ghost of a woman at night.

Above this ghost's neck is nothing but a writhe of hair, and below it nothing but a white shirt and pants floating in midair. Faceless, this ghost is impossible to identify. She could be any one of us.

REFERENCES

Bering, J. (2013, November 3). *Ian Stevenson's case for the afterlife: Are we 'skeptics' really just cynics?* Scientific American Blog Network. https://blogs.scientificamerican.com/bering-in-mind/ian-stevensone28099s-case-for-the-afterlife-are-we-e28098skepticse28099-really-just-cynics/

Dawkins, R. (2006). *The Selfish Gene.* Oxford University Press.

Dick, P. K. (2001). *Valis.* Gollancz.

Huntington, R. (2005). Ghosts seeking substitutes: Female suicide and repetition. *Late Imperial China, 26*(1), 1-40. https://doi.org/10.1353/late.2005.0007

Ji, Y. (1995). *Yuewei caotang biji* (H. Shao, Trans.). Shanghai guji chubanshe.

Ji, Y. (2021). *The Shadow Book of Ji Yun: The Chinese Classic of Weird True Tales, Horror Stories, and Occult Knowledge* (Y. I. Yu & J. Y. Branscum, Trans.). Empress Wu Books.

Lee, B. J. (1981). Female infanticide in China. *Historical Reflections / Réflexions Historiques, 8*(3), 163–177. http://www.jstor.org/stable/41298766

Mishlove, J. (2020, January 15). *Poltergeist agents with Barry Taff* [Video]. YouTube. https://www.youtube.com/watch?v=V6F_h3dIh1M

Ponton, F., Otálora-Luna, F., Lefèvre, T., Guerin, P. M., Lebarbenchon, C., Duneau, D., Biron, D. G., & Thomas, F. (2011). Water-seeking behavior in worm-infected crickets and reversibility of parasitic manipulation. *Behavioral Ecology, 22*(2), 392-400.

Zhang, C. (Ed.). (1985). *Yuchu xinzhi.* Hebei renmin chubanshe.

THE UNVOICED, THE UNHEARD,
THE UNKNOWN, THE UNQUIET

AI JIANG

I often feel as though I'm a wandering spirit, both in the land I was birthed, China, and the land I've immigrated to, Canada. Settling in body does not always mean settling in mind and spirit. There are ghosts called *di fu ling*, bound to places of attachment or burial, and I often wonder if I were such a ghost, where would I be bound? China or Canada? Who's to say I'm not a ghost already? As ghosts represent a strange in-betweenness, foreigners or outsiders to the world (Lee, 2004), a feeling I'm no stranger to.

A hairdresser once told me I looked like a person with unvoiced, complex thoughts. There was no previous context for this statement, nothing I said that had triggered this thought—at least not that I'm aware of. He said it out of the blue as he snipped away at my dead ends, without meeting my eye. And I wondered how could someone who saw me perhaps once every few months make such an observation that friends of mine only realized a decade into our friendship, that my husband realized only after receiving reflective letters I sent from abroad, that my family still don't realize? They say those who are nearest and dearest to us know us best, but perhaps sometimes those are the people from whom we hide ourselves most, and perhaps those are the people who are sometimes most blinded to the pain we hold inside.

For the first time, I am choosing to be unquiet.

ON MOTHERHOOD

In late 2021, after an argument with my husband, my sister clutched at my arms in the washroom as I sat in a heaping mess on the floor. She was hugging me; I was hugging myself. Hugs were too awkward—at least for me, at least for me with my family. This was an embrace, of sorts. It felt comforting, but it also felt alien. My sister was born in Canada, five years after I was born in China. She did most of the hugging in the family. Outside of her spontaneous and cringey—though I appreciate it much more now—embrace, I don't remember what it feels like to hug anyone in my family. In this moment, both cradled and caged within my younger sister's arms, I sat on the floor in a crumpled heap yelling, "Why me?"

My sister's voice blurred with my wails. "I'll do it. I'll have the children."

To which I'd responded, "It would be too late."

Not having children was not an option, though I'd like to think I'm making headway in changing this mindset, yet there is still a long way to go. But why must it be like this?

My aunt called me later that night, asking me if it were true that I said I didn't want children and insisting that I must, that it's my duty, that it's what *life* is all about. I'd told her that many of my friends have similar thoughts to me: many women now choose not to have children—not all of us are meant for children after all, and we shouldn't *have* to have them just because we're women. It felt like a slap in the face when my aunt questioned the nature of my friends, the ones who didn't—don't—want kids, calling them "monsters" and "unnatural" and "unhinged." It was then when I realized nothing would make my relatives happy—unless I became more or less exactly like them. In my poem, "Tongue Work" (Jiang, 2021), I touch on the way women are often silenced and treated like modelling clay—not only by men but also by other women in their lives:

> *They watch your cave bleed,*
> *giving you no choice but to leave.*
> *But to leave is more dangerous*
> *than staying, working, twisting*
> *the soft flesh like moulding clay*
> *into a shape that only they want to see.*

My aunt then asked what I was planning to do with my life, and I told her I was considering a PhD. She tsked and said, "Take it easy. There's no need for such high education for women. Let the men handle the work."

That was the last thing I wanted, and what I loathed to hear most. It was impossible for me to be the niece she imagined, the daughters who followed these words within our family.

"Do some part time. An easier job that doesn't require too high of an education."

Part of this desire to set higher goals, to rebel against my aunt's thinking that women must be below men, manifests in my story, "Missing Dolls Around the World" (Jiang, 2021):

> The husband didn't want Second Doll to work full time and certainly didn't allow her to wear the makeup she had on now to work.
>
> "There's no need ... especially for a job like *that*," he had said.
>
> Second Doll stayed. And she smiled. And she blinked back liquid pain that burnt the lower lids of her eyes, lined them red.

But I'm ambitious; I hunger for knowledge. Yet, for much of my family, their traditions, their culture, there is a rigid path to life for women: childhood, then education—but not *too* much education, then work—but not *too* rigorous, then motherhood. I say "their" because I'm uncertain what *my* culture is. It has become a strange mixture of my upbringing in Canada, and the tradition and values ingrained by my grandmother who couldn't—can't—let go of her past, even as the world is moving forward. In "The Year of the Niu" (Jiang, 2021), I explore the duality of my identity, which I elaborate on in this essay: "The water: a fragile balance of cultures pushed against each side of her body."

Further on rebellion, particularly the resistance of women against their traditional roles, Pu Songling's work supports the reclamation of control by women and their freedom of choice. His work emphasizes "[t]he identity of ghost ... as a metaphor for all the oppression of women" (Zheng, 2020, p.757) through the story of "Nie Xiaoqia", highlighting how traditions can be changed, challenged, and women can find success and should be allowed individualism both with and without men and tradition.

Half my family come from the countryside, rural Shanghu, with little formal education, while the other half attended colleges of some form, living mainly in the city of Changle. My life, compared to the lives of much of my family in the past, is a luxury and is privileged. But it is also bound by traditions I cannot seem to escape. In "Tea Party for the Living" (Jiang, 2021), I explore a past that took place in the country and its contrast to Canadian city-life, and how no matter how much one changes, returning to one's homeland unleashes all the tradition and culture buried within: "Unlike when I'm out with friends on the weekends [in Canada], here [in Shanghu] I'm quiet, docile. I don't laugh or speak over anyone; I only listen and speak when spoken to." In the story, the narrator encounters the ghosts of her ancestors, and in Chinese culture, ancestral ghosts often appear as a guide, when the living feel lost, aimless. They serve as a reminder of our roots. In the story, the spirits of the narrator's grandparents appear, offering guidance on how to reconcile with divided and fractured identity. Sometimes, I too wish to have such an experience. But one thing I learned while writing this story is that I will never truly forget my past, no matter how long I've been away from it.

In high school, I found my mother in her bedroom, crying. (There really is something about women crying in domestic spaces). For the first time in my life, she lashed out at me—with words— with such viciousness I didn't realize was possible coming from her fragile, bird-like frame, replacing her usual kindness and patience.

She yelled, "Why do I have to go through this?"

"I want to move out."

"Could you just be … better?"

"Why does no one understand me?"

"How could she [grandmother on my father's side, who lives with us], also a mother, not understand me?"

"Why is everyone against me?"

And in unspoken silence, "But why can I not leave?"

Because she is a mother.

I haven't seen another instance of this explosion of emotions, but recently, in a quiet whisper, my mother told me, "I am a little hotel." I wrote a poem in the middle of that very night with those words as the title, highlighting the violence, the enduring nature of motherhood. And as selfish as it may sound, I realized I do not want to be a mother. But my mother, to me, is a hero. To show such love, such care, even when it seems she receives barely half in return. I cannot imagine anyone stronger than a mother.

> *But sometimes, even I forget*
> *that beneath withered, wrinkled, time—*
> *stamped hands, there once was a woman,*
> *who loved her guests, those who entered*
> *and left, those who stood guard*
> *at the door, until my floors became empty,*
> *and the only reminder of my guests*
> *are their footprints, first muddy,*
> *then dried dirt, sown across my carpets,*
> *and greasy handprints along the walls—*
> *and no matter how hard I scrub,*
> *they don't leave unless I rip*
> *out the wallpapers, but even then*
> *I cannot escape because I am a little hotel.*
>
> (Jiang, 2022, "I Am A Little Hotel")

ON GENDER AND POWER

My grandmother has five children, four of whom are daughters, four of whom have sons. And she has one son, my father, who, of all his siblings, only has two daughters. The irony. The irony of all the praying, the wishing, the working, and the migration, for something that my grandmother couldn't control, only to be met with disappointment. This wouldn't matter if not for the fact that it's tradition for men to pass down the family name to their children, meaning my sister and I can't—or can we?

The passing down of the family name is something—that seems to me, at least—that has lost its meaning over time. I often question what is the significance of a family name, what meaning does it have now, and what is it we have accomplished that makes us worthy, special, that makes the act of passing on a family name a necessity? What is it we must be remembered for? Our history? Our achievements? And regarding last names, why must we, as women, follow the last name of our husbands? Be referred to as So-and-So's wife like we no longer belong to ourselves? Why are we Mrs. Husband's-First-or-Last-Name? When I married my husband, a friend called me Mrs. My-Husband's-First-Name. I corrected him immediately.

My grandmother always had, still has, a preference for boys, sons. She had placed immense pressure on my mother when she produced only daughters. My sister and I were meant to have another sibling, but they were lost before they barely began forming within my mother.

"If they're a girl, remove her. Keep the child if it's a boy." It was the most cruel and heartbreaking thing my grandmother could have said to my mother as she experienced her miscarriage, and yet, she did. But, regardless of these words, my grandmother is not innately a cruel woman. Her tradition forces her to speak these words, to want a son, to feel like a failure if her daughter-in-law failed to produce a child who could carry the last name of the family.

But what does it mean to build a legacy?

On the role of men in Fujianese culture, they're regarded as the head of the family, placed on a pedestal, but also heavily relied upon to pave the way for the family's success and future. My grandmother was a single mother after her husband passed, when my father had barely began walking, and her low wage as a farmer placed even more pressure on my father to become successful. He has become successful—to me, he has. But there is a certain power, entitlement, that I believe is ingrained in my father because of his gender and the expectations that culture and tradition bestowed upon him. And perhaps this is what inspired a part of the Third Doll's background in "Missing Dolls Around the World" (Jiang, 2021):

Third Doll bowed his head, hands tightened into fists at the sides of his body. He was only fourteen, had only begun high school this year. Why must he carry the weight of his family, his mother's pain, responsibility for his sister's future in his barely calloused hands?

As a father and man, my father never fails to demonstrate the power he has in the family. "I am your father" is not so much a funny phrase outside of *Star Wars*, when I'm upstairs and my father is downstairs in the living room, demanding that my sister and I hand him the remote within his arm's reach. No, this is not ableist. He's perfectly fine, healthy, mobile. This is the demonstration of a power he's been handed because of his gender—a birthright that daughters, mothers, grandmothers cannot enjoy just because we are female. It is an engrained sense of unconscious entitlement for the "bread winner".

I've found that in much of my writing, there is an absence or lacking fore fronting of the father figure. The male figure is often a shadow, much like my own father—who is an amazing and hardworking man, but, at times, far too stoic and incomprehensible in his manner and actions—that haunt the background of my stories. But my father too is struggling with the role that has been chosen for him, fitted to him. He knows nothing else but the set identity he was born into. Much like us—my sister, my mother, my grandmother, and me—he too had little choice, even if it seemed as though he had the most options. In "The Catcher in the Eye" (Jiang, 2021), the father figure I present is a workaholic, who is obsessive over his success and demands acknowledgment from his family:

> I suspect he was only trying to get attention, acknowledgement, not that our attention would've been enough for him; not that any of us would have noticed or cared... Before I left the kitchen, I looked back for a moment and saw panic in my father's eyes as he, in haste, launched into speaking about another recent achievement of his.

Though my father does not demand us to acknowledge his success, I often wonder if he silently seeks it.

ON MARRIAGE

Marriage is the coming together of two individuals, the combination of families, but why does it feel like the absorption of the wife into the body, the identity, the voice of the husband, where we drown and keep drowning and will continue to flounder as though no one can hear our wails muffled by the endless and dense sea that is our husbands' voices? My husband does not dictate the voice in our relationship or speak for us or instead of me as "we", but I often find myself asking him to speak on behalf of us, or requiring his validation before I speak, and I wonder if it's a sign of respect or groomed cultural docility. I'm fortunate to have a husband who views me as an equal, but not every relationship has such equal balance, where some might diminish the presence of their spouses or significant others so the dominant individual's voice is the only one that can be heard.

> *They force the seal and drop ropes*
> *lined with thorns and their own roses*
> *dipped in colours only they accept*
> *and replace your echoes with theirs.*
> *They laugh at your silence*
> *while sitting on thorns like nothing.*

(Jiang, "Tongue Work," 2021)

In Fujianese culture, we have the tradition of bride wealth, where the groom's family must offer the bride's family a certain amount of money for the marriage to occur. While the bride's family must also offer money (for the bride to keep), it often feels as though we're being sold to our husbands. My parents tell me not to see it as such, but I can't help the thought from wandering into my mind: marriage as a transaction.

It is both a spoken and unspoken rule that you must dedicate your life to both the old and the young, and for wives, to your husbands. But then what time do you have to yourself? There's only the discovery of the world through childhood that you barely make use of before having children of your own, and the freedom of old age that you can't enjoy because it's too cold, or too hot, or too early, or too late, or you're too exhausted to enjoy what years you have left. I don't mean to be morbid, but how unfair is it to always have to sacrifice, to stunt, to stall our own growth for the sake of others, where some of us may become bitter, loathing, wretched beings? We are allowed to be selfish, and that should be acceptable. They say humans tend towards chaos, but really, I think humans often cause other humans, those nearest and dearest to them, towards chaos even when they're well-meaning in their intentions.

ON IDENTITY

I am a first-generation immigrant but feel as though I'm second-generation, yet compared to my Canadian-born sister who is fully second generation, I feel removed from that identity as well. As a part of a strange wave of 1.5-generation children, who were born not of this land called Canada, and experienced, briefly, their land of birth, but raised predominantly on foreign soil that has become like a mother, I find myself often questioning my cultural identity. Yet the things that I've been introduced to and taught during childhood, no matter how brief, are internalized within me forever.

To my culture, I may seem the least filial, least loyal, rebelling against traditions, my elders, and my family. We don't need to stand out, or so they say, we just need to do "our job", "our duty", perform our "roles", live life as "we should", in the rigid and "appropriate" structure laid out for us with each milestone an immobile mound awaiting us at each checkpoint. I am shunned for being too Canadian, for being not Canadian enough, for being too Chinese, for not being Chinese enough. Though I was born in China, and can speak Chinese, I cannot read and write it. And though I can understand Fuzhou hua, I cannot respond in it. "What is the difference / between screaming and singing, / when the words of our mother tongue / become inseparable from the words of English?" (Jiang, "Singing and Screaming and Silence," 2021) But there is often the expectation that I should know the language, read it, write it, speak it, when my mother tongue is not so much a mother tongue anymore. And this makes me feel as though I am ill-fitting wherever I go.

> Third Doll's mother was not unlike the relatives and strangers I've encountered, who always asked, "How can you not know Chinese if you're Chinese?" And all I could answer with was "I'm sorry," in English, before leaving them standing, open-mouthed, speechless. What else could I have said? (Jiang, "Missing Dolls Around the World," 2021)

I wonder if I will ever feel truly at home anywhere. Even after making a home in Canada, there is still a lingering sense of loss, a detachment, from something I've feared and despised, the tradition I rebelled against, because it's something so deeply rooted in my identity that I will miss even if it has only fractured me while it is present, while it remains, eating away at my identity. Sometimes I wish I were white, but other times I am grateful I'm not. This contradictory debate within my mind took the form of "Don't Scratch" (Jiang, 2022), where a creature, who never felt as though they fit in, learns to embrace their otherness:

> My limbs tingled as though a thousand fine hairs were plucked from their roots. But the green of my skin would not leave, only darkened by the rays of light now gone. How I wished I were not the colour of unripe leaves before the peak of spring.
>
> I clawed at my neck, wanting nothing more than to rip off the moss to reveal what was within: blood and organs—something human.

CLOSING THOUGHTS

But don't misunderstand me: as much as I might antagonize some of my family in these flurries of passionate words, they are people who inspire me, touch me, motivate me, in ways no others can because of the hardships they've faced, ones I've seen, some I've also experienced, the pasts they come from, the futures they've created with their bare hands for themselves and for me. It's just, sometimes, having all these people living together in the present makes things a little more challenging. I don't regret my family, and I won't apologize for being different, but I won't remain silent any longer.

Unquiet women are many and plentiful, but in my life, I've encountered several unquiet men, waiting to break from the chains of tradition as well—some realizing with greater clarity than others. But some may continue to wander, much like the women, unable to escape the realms of past customs and ways. A map may be something many of us need, but it's not one we can create for each other.

"I look up and notice the threads above me, tangled and threatening" (Jiang, 2020, "Dancing With Etta"). For the first time, I notice my own threads—society and family controlling my actions and decisions like a puppet. But unlike puppets, we can release ourselves and cut our own strings. And I encourage you to raise scissors and blades over these threads over your own head and allow yourself both your fears and desires. And perhaps through stories of spirits and ghosts, we can further explore our place in this world; within, without, and between cultures; and in confronting our cultural and existential fears, anxieties, and angst, we might become more human, and less of an unsettled spirit.

REFERENCES

Jiang, A. (2020, October). *Dancing With Etta.* Maudlin House. Retrieved from https://maudlinhouse.net/dancing-with-etta/

Jiang, A. (2021, December). *Missing Dolls Around the World.* The Dark Magazine. https://www.thedarkmagazine.com/missing-dolls-around-the-world/

Jiang, A. (2021, January). *Singing and Screaming and Silence.* Rejection Letters. Retrieved from https://rejection-letters.com/2021/01/07/singing-and-screaming-and-silence/

Jiang, A. (2021, November). Tea Party for the Living. *Prairie Fire Press, 42*(3). Retrieved from https://www.prairiefire.ca/shop/fall-2021-volume-42-no-3/

Jiang, A. (2021, November). *The Catcher in the Eye.* The Dark Magazine. Retrieved from https://www.thedarkmagazine.com/the-catcher-in-the-eye/

Jiang, A. (2021, October). *The Year of the Niu.* Flash Fiction Magazine. Retrieved from https://flashfictionmagazine.com/blog/2021/10/19/the-year-of-the-niu/

Jiang, A. (2021, September). *Tongue Work.* Claw & Blossom. Retrieved from https://clawandblossom.com/issues/issue10/tongue-work-jiang/

Jiang, A. (2022, February). *Don't Scratch.* Tales From Between. Retrieved from https://talesfrombetween.wordpress.com/dont-scratch-by-ai-jiang/

Jiang, A. (2022, December). I am a Little Hotel. *Uncanny Magazine.* vol 49.

Lee, K. F. (2004). Cultural translation and the exorcist: A reading of Kingston's and Tan's ghost stories. *MELUS: Multi-Ethnic Literature of the United States, 29*(2), 105–127.

Zheng, Y. (2020). Writing about women in ghost stories: subversive representations of ideal femininity in "Nie Xiaoqian" and "Luella Miller". *Neohelicon, 47*(2), 751–766.

THAI SPIRITS & LONGING TO BELONG

J.A.W. MCCARTHY

I could tell you about the spirit *krasue*, the floating head and entrails of a cursed young woman who roams the countryside looking for flesh and blood to consume.

I could tell you about the *pret*, ghosts of greedy people cursed with tiny mouths so they can never satiate their endless hunger.

Or I could tell you about *phi pop*, the restless spirit who possesses living bodies and devours their hosts' intestines from the inside.

But I won't, because I don't know any more about these spirits than what a few online articles tell me.

What I can tell you is that these Thai spirits all have something in common: they are often women, and they are always searching, always hungry.

As a half-Thai and half-white woman, I have been searching and hungry my entire life. I exist in this intersection, no matter how much—or how little—I know about my heritage.

The truth is, I know very little about my Thai heritage. It was my mother's culture, only tangentially mine, like when a friend asked about the curry on the dinner table, or when people scrutinized my face and asked, "What *are* you?" Because I looked more like my white father, I could choose which half I wanted to present to the world. I could be white; my eye shape and thick, dark hair subject to nothing more than passing curiosity. I could be white when the bigots we encountered in every new town yelled at my Thai mother in parking lots and grocery stores, "Go back to where you came from!"

Still, I was often subject to inspection. Though I didn't receive the threats my mother did, there were always reminders that I was different, that I didn't fit in to outside eyes, even within my own family. My mother had to assuage my confusion when an employee at my elementary school believed her to be my nanny at pickup. She had to assure me that she was indeed my birth mother when I came home in tears after a third-grade teacher used me as an example of adopted students in class. It soon became apparent that my life would be easier if I let people believe I was entirely white.

Perhaps this is why I know so little about my Thai heritage. My parents gave me the most popular girl's name in the US at the time, so I could fit in. Even my middle name is very common—not Thai. We went to Catholic church while my mother reserved her Buddhism for the privacy of our home. I was often the only biracial kid in my classes, but that was something I could keep to myself. My lunchbox held cheese sandwiches and chips, same as my white classmates.

It's not that my mother didn't try to teach me. As a child, I learned some basic words, practiced writing those beautiful curving characters, even learned a traditional Thai dance with my curious white friends. My father encouraged me to explore my Thai heritage, to proudly proclaim my ethnicity on school forms and in classroom discussions. My mother encouraged me to check the "white" box on those same forms and to keep my Thai half to myself if I wasn't sure about the company I was in.

Eventually, I became a selfish teen and lost interest. I looked white enough by high school that I rarely got more than passing curiosity when I offhandedly revealed my Thai heritage. Friends who came over might've been mildly surprised to see my mother, but it wore off quickly and we were on to the next cool band, the latest episode of *The X Files*, the newest bit of gossip going around school.

This is also the time I began to resent my dominating whiteness. With three to five other Jennifers in every one of my classes, I longed for a Thai first or middle name so I could differentiate myself. I felt plain, uninteresting, common. As my interests turned to making art and velvet chokers and bands like PJ Harvey and The Cure, I desperately wanted to stand out from the jocks and the cheerleaders, all those picture-perfect white kids in my very white town.

Like krasue and the pret and phi pop, I was searching. I was hungry.

I could say telling ghost stories is in my blood—I want to believe it—but I can't be sure. I was born to be a storyteller, though, raised by a storytelling mother who encouraged my creativity from an early age. She told me stories about princesses and castles, and illustrated them as she spoke. As I grew, I fed my hunger with books, writing my own stories, sketching my own illustrations. My mother didn't tell me about the Thai ghosts, but she sensed my hunger and she fed it. She and my father both gave me all the room in the world to search.

What I found was the darkness, and—even better—my love for it. My earliest stories were about sentient sunflowers, teens squatting in abandoned mausoleums, couples who wake up one day suddenly conjoined. My parents never restricted the books and movies I consumed, so my work was likely influenced by seeing films like *Poltergeist* and reading books like *Carrie* at a too-young age. Still, even without these stimuli, I believe I would've found the darkness eventually.

The racism my mother endured in the US was insidious, and, in many ways, it is the darkness that's been chasing me, that I find myself writing about time and time again, even decades later. Guilt is the other half of that darkness—my own guilt. Because I could often pass as white when I needed to, I got very comfortable on that side of the line. I hopped back and forth between wanting to fit in and wanting to stand out. I was white until somebody looked at my face long enough or was bold enough to ask. I was Thai when I got good grades, because that was what was expected of Asian kids. When I was making art, I got to pick who I wanted to be; people were looking at my drawings, not my face. When it was time for college, I could apply for that scholarship for Asian students. When the kids in my class complained about "the Chinese" stealing their fathers' jobs, I could slump down in my seat and be selfishly invisible again. I got to witness firsthand the things some white people say when they think there are no people of color in the room.

Most of my fiction is rooted in the same longing to belong and guilt that's been a part of my life from the first moment I learned that being of mixed race made me different. In recent years, I've written about women who go to extreme lengths in order to achieve their skewed perception of perfection (McCarthy, 2021), women who welcome possession as a way to become someone they deem better (McCarthy, 2019), women who find a way to work with their doppelgängers so they can trade places (McCarthy, 2021a). It's all bodily change (body horror, my favorite sub-genre) while the mind continues to be plagued by delusion. These women I create are blinded by comparing themselves to others whom they perceive as better, never once believing themselves to be anything other than less-than. They don't feel whole and they're searching—willing to do anything—to find their other half.

I guess I've been writing about myself.

I'm a hungry ghost, still roaming all these years later, greedy and angry and only vaguely aware of why. Instead of devouring flesh and blood, my tiny mouth screams on the page. Not too loud, though.

Don't be too loud. Don't draw too much attention to yourself.

My mother had to live this way in order to protect herself, to protect me. Look away, pretend you didn't hear those slurs; *maybe we'll go to the grocery store on the other side of town today.* No one threatened me due to my ethnicity because my mother shielded me, hustled me to the safety of the car, made sure she was the one who got the brunt of the hate so I would know those words and gestures were not directed at me.

So I have a common Western name. My skin grows paler by the day (hello, Pacific Northwest). I get to flit between cultures at will, possessed by self-doubt and that nagging feeling that I'm an interloper who doesn't belong anywhere. I can be invisible in ways that my mother cannot. The thing is, though, she never wanted me to be invisible.

First, as a child, I stayed quiet and leaned into whatever anonymity I could get so that I would fit in among the kids at my predominantly white schools. Then, as a teenager, I found rebellion in the angst of being ordinary, of being *almost*: almost unique, almost interesting, almost Asian. I wanted to be known for something other than being the almost-Asian, almost-white girl. Then, the more I blended in, the more I longed to be seen, coming to a point where I was willing to be known for being almost-Asian, if that was all I could get.

I wrote this whole time. Almost-horror. Almost-honest. The "me" in these stories sought adventure, independence, the bravery to stand up and defend my mother, to be seen. This "me" was special.

I was an almost-author. I was first published at nineteen, when I got to read my piece at the magazine launch party before being quickly escorted out of the bar venue because I was underage. Then I was an almost-artist. I went to art school, dropped out, went back, showed in a gallery, got my degree. Half-author, half-artist. I stood on each side of the line, but never at the same time. Then I stepped away.

Life happened. I partied, travelled, had some fun. I got mired in the endless loop of work and relationships and survival that we all do. Then, five years ago, after not thinking about writing or art for over a decade, a story idea popped into my head, and I had to write it.

I haven't stopped since.

Perhaps I'd been suppressing myself all those years, a pret who learned to take small bites with her tiny mouth, trying to undo the curse of her own greed. The krasue in me was still roaming, even those times she thought she'd sated her hunger. My phi pop possessed a lot of bodies, but they never quite fit. It took some time, but I found a way to express what was haunting me. With a keyboard and a decade of un-sated spirits, the real me burst free.

Five years in and I've found some success with my writing, the validation that maybe I shouldn't have allowed this dream to lie dormant for so long. No one in the horror community seems to care that I'm half-Thai and half-white; if they're looking at me, I can say with confidence it's for my skill, not my face. Here I am in this comfortable spot, but I still feel like there are two sides and I don't belong on either one of them.

If there's a submission call for people of color (POC), I question if I'm Asian enough to fit into that category. Am I a fraud because I'm half-white? Will editors look at my very white name and think of me as an intruder, trying to con my way into a space where I don't belong? Will I be taking up a spot from another author who is more Asian than me?

The truth is, I'm not Thai enough. This has nothing to do with my race—my white half—my insecurities, or even how I perceive myself. I am not Thai enough because I wasted my formative years focused on fitting in to the detriment of my own heritage. My mother tried to teach me to speak, read, and write in Thai in the safety of our home, but I wasn't interested, not when there were slumber parties and school dances and trips to the mall. My friends' parents thought it was so interesting that I was mixed race, that I had a Thai mother, but I didn't want that kind of attention. Whether it was crude jokes or well-meaning but inappropriate fascination, I didn't want any of it.

Now, as an adult, I see how much I missed out on. I see how I contributed to making my mother smaller in this world. I can't imagine what it was like for her, as a young woman in the 1970s, to take the almost unimaginable leap of leaving her friends, her family, her career, her entire life behind to follow the man she loved to another continent. Yes, it was her choice, but she didn't just leave an old life behind for the promise of something new. She left behind the safety of fitting in. Of belonging.

All these years later and I'm still exploring who I am, where I fit in, and if that place—that intersection—is a place of my own making. There doesn't have to be a line down the middle; I don't have to choose between two separate halves. It's as organic and free-flowing as the blood in my body, the ideas in my head. It's hard to say it (*don't be too loud*), but I'm learning to say it as well as believe it: I belong. I'm laden with guilt and regret, but I'm still writing. On the page I release the demons, though they never leave for long. As I dig a little deeper, finally making an effort to learn about my Thai heritage—as I should've done all those years ago—my white half has gotten to know krasue and the pret and phi pop; my Thai half has learned to embrace them. My two halves cannot exist without each other, so I am finally acknowledging that they are one whole. And when those tortured spirits come back, I start all over again with a new story, a new way to satisfy them.

We are hungry women, and we will never stop searching for our next meal.

REFERENCES

McCarthy, J. A. W. (2021). With You As My Anchor. In *Sometimes We're Cruel and Other Stories*. (pp. 35-55). USA: Cemetery Gates Media.

—McCarthy, J. A. W. (2021a). Exactly As We Are Meant to Be. In *Sometimes We're Cruel and Other Stories*. (pp. 119-131). USA: Cemetery Gates Media.

McCarthy, J. A. W. (2019). Luksaw. In Gerrard J.F, Cho A., & Tham, W. (Eds*.) Immersion: An Asian Anthology of Love, Fantasy & Speculative Fiction*. (pp. 143-160). Canada: Dark Helix Press

LUCKY NUMBERS, OR WHY 28 > 58

ELIZA CHAN

Growing up in the UK, being lucky depends very much on chance. Good fortune shines upon you in the most random of ways. There are tricks to wish for it with crossed fingers or shamrock leaf. Avoid bad luck by throwing salt over your shoulder or touching wood. Little things. Covertly done, with a foolish grin to ensure no-one thinks you're taking it too seriously. Superstitions. Irrational fears. It rarely encroaches into business, culture, or even architecture.

What I've learnt over the years is luck is a much more all-encompassing affair within the Chinese community. Invisible spirits pushing and pulling the threads of your life. Luck is finite. One person's fortune is another person's misfortune. Good luck can be courted, cajoled, and persuaded to get on your side. Bad luck must be avoided, head down and avert eye contact so that it passes you by. Grip your house keys, cross the road, and dial your friend as you walk home.

Seven is the most common lucky number in the west. It was my favourite number growing up, and I still like it for the occasional lottery ticket. The seventh son of the seventh son. Seven deadly sins. Seven magpies in the "One For Sorrow" nursery rhyme. But numbers and word play are intertwined in Chinese culture. Word play is huge in the Cantonese my family speaks. A tonal language where "ma" can mean a number of things from horse to mother dependent on inflection. Numerology is a part of that: seemingly innocuous numbers are rendered auspicious or inauspicious dependent on similar pronunciations with other meanings. Especially if you are a woman.

TWO MAKES IT STRAIGHTFORWARD. OR AT LEAST IT SHOULD.

Two is generally a good luck number. A homophone for *easy*. And doubling things can only be good. Double Happiness—literally the character for *joy* written twice—is commonly used in wedding decorations.

Should we? Or shouldn't we? My future husband and I looked solemnly at each other. Hesitating. We were certain about being together: the proposal had happened, the answer a resounding yes. We weren't even arguing about the style of wedding we wanted. What we were stuck on, was whether or not we should look up auspicious dates.

When my eldest sister got married, relatives went to a fortune teller to find a good date. A common practice in Asia, choosing dates is not just about when your venue is available. It's about securing good luck for the couple. But the date they chose, the only date with availability in the next two years that was also auspicious, was bad luck for people born in the year of the sheep. Guess which year my other sister was born? As a result, she spent the morning of the wedding hidden in a hotel bathroom.

I didn't want that. For my guests, for myself, I didn't want anything to do with fortune tellers and auspicious dates. I didn't believe in it. But I also knew that if we didn't check, someone would. Parents, grandparents, random nosy aunties. If the knowledge was out there, it would linger like a cloud around the proceedings. So in the end, we looked. Sighed in relief to find our date was fine.

Then my mother forbade my aunt and cousin from attending. My cousin got married two months before me, you see. A finite pool of good luck meant we would clash. I imagined us brides as tigers circling warily, teeth bared to rip chunks out of one another. The victorious bride raising a sweat and blood-stained bouquet above the beaten hulk of her competitor. Good fortune flocking above the two of us like a murmuration.

I fought it. Shouted and slammed down the phone. Pleaded with my mother, my aunt, my cousin. It was my wedding, wasn't it? But it did not work. Instead, what worked was—dare I use the word—reason. A glamping wedding under the trees bore very little resemblance to a traditional Chinese ceremony. And the official registry office portion was on a different day. Didn't some people say the bad luck risk was only if events were within the same month rather than two months apart? These loopholes reassured my mother that the superstition had not been ignored. Simply adjusted. By the time the wedding day arrived, my mother declared loudly that she had brought about the perfect weather. After all, she'd earned the good fortune.

FOUR IS FOR DEATH. AND HOW TO AVOID IT.

Four. A near homophone for *death*. And fourteen—*definite death*. A major problem extending far beyond the connotations of unlucky number thirteen. Pervasively infecting many aspects of life.

I was a teenager when I first visited Hong Kong. Standing in the elevator watching the numbers tick upwards, I distracted myself from the sticky humidity by looking at the buttons. Hong Kong was my first experience with high-rise apartment blocks. Rows and rows of buttons representing each floor like I had only seen in films. Even at my grandparents' modest apartment block, there were more than thirty floors, and this was nowhere near the height of the shining skyscrapers at the waterfront. It was then that I realised some buttons were missing: 4, 14, 24. I thought the buttons had been removed, floors abandoned due to cursed spirits. I imagined hitting the emergency stop just after the 23rd floor. Prising open the doors to find a secret level haunted by Sadako from *The Ring* (Suzuki, 2003). It didn't occur to me that the floors had been renumbered.

Years later, when looking to buy, I found a home which fitted most of our needs in the UK. But it was number fourteen. The unluckiest number of all. And as much as I tried to rationalise it as a superstition with no basis, once known, it's difficult to ignore. Bad luck would wrap its cold arms around me every time I stepped through the door. Sowing doubts. In the end, we didn't even view it.

I grew up in a house with a name rather than a number, so we didn't have to worry about numerology there. Still, my mother put a special octagonal mirror and scissors over the front door. If evil spirits tried to enter, the mirror deflected them, and the scissors would cut them asunder. The explanation gave me no comfort, nor did my stilted attempts to explain it when I had friends over. Instead, I ducked and ran through the door lest the scissors judged me wanting.

The spirits my mother was afraid of, those that led me to see her as irrational and old fashioned, are not just a provincial thing. Not when buildings all over Hong Kong have no 4th floor, 4th block, or apartment number 4. Telephone numbers and licence plates with 4 are simply not sold. Thirteen, although not traditionally unlucky, has been adopted as well. Just in case. This is the accepted norm by young, educated professionals and the older generation alike. In some Hong Kong hospitals, staff have banned red foods, especially red dates, as the term sounds like *early red*—heralding heavy blood loss. Science and superstition operating together where I had not expected them to.

FIVE IS FOR ABSENCE. THINGS YOU ARE NOT.

The number five in Cantonese sounds like *not*. Parental love was often shown through chastisement. Don't go out too late. Don't forget to dry your hair. Don't eat too many fried foods. Don't write about monsters. Write about happier topics instead. Think about the baby.

My husband looked at me, brows knitted as he held the phone. What baby? The hypothetical baby that we were not even trying for at that point. But relatives are forthright with unasked for advice. Why haven't you had a baby yet? Just a couple—one girl, one boy— make your parents happy. Repeated constantly, nagging like they are merely asking you to treat them to dinner. Filial respect is of course very important, and bearing sons the expected goal of all women...

Take, for example, the pig. I grew up with a western notion of pigs: lazy, dirty creatures who wallow in mud. Yet in Chinese culture, the most extravagant piece of bridal wedding jewellery is an oversized 24-carat gold pig with piglets dangling from its nipples. Heck, you can push the boat out and get three tiers of chubby pigs, each the size of saucers, hanging around your neck. Pigs are happy. Fat because they are well-fed and content which can only be a good thing. And they, as the necklace suggests, have lots and lots of babies. Fertility, wealth, and happiness—massive positives in Chinese culture where pigs are symbols of abundance. And if you do not have a family then you can't possibly be content.

Women are still commodified, even if this is with an awkward laugh and the excuse that it's just tradition. My mother was in primary school when her parents changed her name. Her new name meant *calling boys*. They wanted a son and their daughter's purpose—her very name—was to summon one. And my mother passed this purpose down, like a heavy chain of reproach around my neck. You were meant to be a boy.

Straight A's at school—if only you were a boy.

Helping with all the housework—if only you were a boy

Studying medicine at university—if only you were a boy.

My parents didn't burden me with quite as literal a name as she had. But they called me *truth*, for the reality that I ... was not a boy. In case I forgot, my mother liked to tell the story of my name when friends and relatives visited. Whenever I did not affirm my mother's gendered perception of how a woman should be—demure and ladylike—it was blamed on that same unfortunate fact. At first, I felt guilt for never making them fully happy. Somehow, I chose my gender in the womb, against my parents' wishes, family predictions, and even fortune tellers' projections. But over the years this hardened to resentment. A burden I didn't want to pass on to my own children.

When I finally became pregnant myself, I avoided caffeine, alcohol, and soft cheese. Said goodbye to sushi for nine months and reluctantly swapped out my coffee for herbal tea. But then that extra layer of Chinese rules threatened to suffocate what few freedoms I had left. No cold drinks. No watermelon. No lifting pretty much anything ever. No sewing. No DIY. No moving house. Some of the rules made a certain archaic sense to them; others were simply nonsensical in the modern world. Most parents need to decorate a nursery. Or have a cold drink now and then. I bridled against the watermelon taboo so much that I secretly bought one like it was illegal drugs. Gorged myself on it. Against all rational knowledge, a curl of fear lingered in my stomach alongside the sloshing watermelon juice. What if? What if something did happen to my unborn baby? Would I come back to this moment, to my moment of defiance and regret it? That's what superstition does. Sows the seeds of doubt.

My mother told me that she'd dropped a needle on her pregnant belly when she'd been carrying my sister. Some clothes had needed mending, and she hadn't believed the superstitions either. But her mistake explains why my oldest sister has a pinprick hole near her ear. Other stories are more severe. Miscarriage and disfigurement served as cautionary tales. It's your fault. You were warned. And you—the woman, the mother—are solely to blame when things go wrong. As if there isn't enough self-doubt and fear swirling inside. That nail you hammered into the wall, that parcel you moved from the doorway, that ice cold glass of water on a hot summer's day. That's on you. You ignored the rules and let the bad luck seep in.

EIGHT IS FOR FORTUNE. A CULTURAL OBSESSION

Luck and wealth are often interchangeable in Chinese culture. A good fortune would be to have an absolute fortune. Just as there are bad luck numbers, there are also good. Eight sounds like *wealth* and who doesn't want that? Eighteen—*definite wealth*. Twenty-eight—*easy wealth*. Four or five oranges prepacked in a net are no good. But redistributed as a bag of eight and you have yourself a respectful gift for visiting a relative.

Growing up in the UK, my family didn't celebrate lunar new year to the same extent as families in China. I still had to go to school. There were no fireworks or firecrackers in 1990s Glasgow. We were lucky to get a community centre performance of off-key singing and a lion dance. But we did know the importance of luck. My sisters and I helped clean the house in the days before new year to ensure we started the year right.

Celebratory food in the west is often about treating yourself. A fancy meal out. A roast turkey with all the trimmings. Cheese boards and desserts. Overindulgence. It's not about luck. For Chinese, it's both. At lunar new year, traditional foods are word play for good luck. Fish sounds like *surplus* and symbolises prosperity. The words for new year glutinous rice cake sound like *higher year*, implying doing better in any and all aspects of life. Tangerines sound like *luck*. Each food has their role in shepherding good luck across the house, as well as merely being tasty.

And, of course, there were red envelopes to receive. Alongside litanies of good luck blessings about doing well at school, growing up quickly and following your dreams, red envelopes were good luck gifts of money. Keep the luck, my mother would say as she discreetly took the money from my hands to restuff into different envelopes and pass back to other relatives like a return volley. Even the red envelopes were reused until thin and worn, sealed with a smear of sticky rice.

Perhaps that was why I disliked the colour red: I struggled to see the benefits. The round red lanterns strung across Chinatown. The colour of paper tablecloths at the Chinese restaurant where I would sit as a tennis match of Cantonese chatter went over my head. The colour of traditional Chinese wedding dresses, paired with ostentatious gold embroidery and jewellery. I hated it because it looked like set dressing to me. Dated, and more like TV shows than my everyday life.

I voraciously consumed Chinese period dramas as a child. It gave me access to a world I wanted to understand. A world of honourable martial arts clans and sword-wielding heroes. The women were either young and feisty or old angry spinsters. Nothing in between. And the journey that took them from the former to the latter was often due to misfortune of their own doing. Vanity. Arrogance. Lack of respect for their elders. These were the role models my mother would point to. Be more modest like her. Not the real-life role models of my mother and aunties who worked long hard hours in Chinese takeaways. Who had sun-spotted skin from working in the rice fields. Who spat and swore and most definitely were not quiet. Be like me and you'll have to live a hard life, my mother said. I'd rather you be someone else.

Numbers shaped my mother's life. Three for the cities she lived in: Hong Kong, Glasgow, and Dundee. Three for the daughters she had in a new and foreign country. For me, it's the number one. One for the medical degree I quit when I decided to be myself. One for my own child, whom I raise with love and luck in the hope that will be enough.

The language of numbers seems easy on the surface. Concrete digits with mathematical solutions. But knowing the numbers does not mean knowing the whole equation. There are burdens from generations passed, hopes and fears that cannot always be entirely articulated, especially when my first language is my mother's fourth. It's more than just a language barrier but also a chasm of age and attitudes.

REFERENCES

Suzuki, K. (2003). *The Ring*. Translated by Rohmer R.B. & Walley G. Japan: Kadokawa Shoten

FALLEN LEAVES, NEW SOIL

YVETTE TAN

Behind every haunting is a story of heartbreak.

I am a Filipino woman of Chinese descent. My paternal grandparents and my maternal grandmother all hail from the same tiny island in Fujian, China, and my maternal grandmother is from Bulacan, Philippines. My father's parents raised their children in as Western a way as possible. As far as I can tell, my mother and her siblings were raised with a mix of Filipino and localized Chinese customs.

To this day, I find it hard to fully relate to my Chinese side, since my siblings and I weren't raised in the "traditional" way, unless it involved something unpleasant—mostly customs we didn't understand and weren't given a proper explanation for, or traditional Chinese medicine, which tended to taste awful. I accidentally found a way to connect with my Filipino roots however, and that was through the supernatural.

The thing about growing up in the Philippines under the dictatorial government established by then President Ferdinand Marcos from 1972 to 1986, is that mass media was regulated under pain of, well, death, among other things. Only news that put the administration in a good light could be reported. A side effect of this is that bad news got out anyway, and since it wasn't reported in legitimate news sources—which people tend not to trust because of their bias against the government—bad news tended to take on a life of its own. It became gossip, which morphed into whispered warnings. And sometimes, these warnings turn into urban legends.

I was a quiet kid, which meant I got to eavesdrop on a lot of adult conversations. And in what seems like a specifically 80s phenomena—or my brain homing in on interesting things—there was no line drawn between gossip about real people and stories that involved the supernatural. For example, after a trip to an uncle's chicken farm in Batangas province, my sister's nanny shared some gossip she'd heard from the farmhands: the chickens were dying because they were being eaten by a *tikbalang*, a lower mythological creature made up of a human body and a horse's head.

Scholar Maximo Ramos, locally heralded as the dean of Philippine folklore and whose books provide the majority of the sources modern folk writers take inspiration from, quotes Lucetta K. Ratcliff's essay "Philippine Folklore" published in the *Journal of American Folklore* in 1949:

> "They have bodies like those of men, but their heads are similar to those of horses. Their limbs are said to be so long that when they sit their knees reach above their heads. When they laugh, all you can see is mouth." (Ramos, 1990, p. 28)

In hindsight, the farmhands could have been telling tall tales about natural chicken deaths, but there are more obvious carnivores to choose from than the tikbalang.

This story fascinated me because I never would have linked tikbalangs to chicken theft, as I figured horses would be vegetarians. Of course, there are the Mares of Diomedes from Greek mythology that ate human flesh, so maybe the idea of a meat-eating horse-like cryptid isn't so farfetched. I've only used the tikbalang in my stories twice, once in passing in a street party scene in "Sidhi" (Tan, 2021), a tale about the blurring of drugs and religious ecstasy, and as a protagonist in "The Last Moon" (Tan, 2021), which accompanied artwork that adorned the Philippine booth in the 2021 Frankfurt Book Fair. My fascination with tikbalangs tends to be more about their strength and speed than their diet, which I feel will play a part in a future story.

This blurring of real and supernatural extended to mass media, despite the previously mentioned bias towards the government-sanctioned narrative. There was a hugely popular celebrity show in the 80s where the host would present supernatural happenings around the country as legitimate news stories in between reports of the latest showbiz scandal. The host had stories like "Woman gives birth to fish," complete with an interview with said woman, her fish-child swimming in a basin alongside her.

And there were urban legends. The one I remember the most, and have used in my fiction, is how parents would tell their children not to go out at night because they would be kidnapped and sacrificed to appease elementals in construction sites.

I use this urban legend in my story "The Bridge" (Tan, 2021), which is told from a child's point of view. Not only is it a retelling of the urban legend, but it also touches on one of the weirder parts of the Marcos dictatorship, that of Ronald Joaquin Marcos, the Bionic Boy Wonder, a young man with psychic powers who was rumored to have been adopted by Ferdinand Marcos (Licauco, 2018). My favorite of his many alleged feats is his being able to use a toy telephone to make real phone calls to anywhere in the world, which also appears in the story. (International calls were expensive in the 70s and 80s. This was an important talent to have!).

This sacrificial ritual, where a live creature is killed or walled into a structure to ensure its strength, is common in many cultures. The practice survives in the Philippines in the tradition of killing a chicken and letting its blood drip on a site before construction begins.

The urban legend behind this was that when the dictator built a bridge across a strait, some construction materials fell into the water and killed a water elemental, whose parents cursed the First Lady so that she grew scales. The only way to appease the spirits was to offer children in sacrifice. So children began disappearing, and the First Lady was cured.

This cautionary tale could be a way for parents to keep their children indoors at night. The dangers back then were certainly very real, and were scarier than any ghost story. People did disappear in the night, their bodies usually found dumped in a nearby field. The term for it was "salvage," so when you said, "a man was salvaged," it meant a man had been abducted and killed, and his body dumped in a random spot. The bridge was constructed in 1972, before I was born, and I heard the story in the early 80s in Manila, far from the province it was said to have occurred, which is testament to how long the tale survived and how far it traveled.

Another urban legend which arose under the dictatorship had to do with the Manila Film Center, hurriedly constructed in 1982 in time for the first Manila Film Festival. One night, some scaffolding collapsed, burying 169 construction workers under quick-drying cement (De Guzman, 2019). A media blackout was imposed, so the government could save face, and rescue did not commence until nine hours after the accident.

Because of this media blackout and the callous dismissal of the lives of the construction workers, a story grew around the tragedy that the administration wanted the building constructed immediately, so the workers' limbs were simply hacked off and their bodies left in the cement. The story has been debunked (*i-Witness*, 2005) even by people not sympathetic to that regime, but it persists, and the Film Center remains abandoned to this day, with many ghost stories surrounding it. On a side note, a psychic friend said that the supernatural activity in the area stems from the building being abandoned for so long and not from the tragedy that gave it its bad reputation. A side note to this side note is that the more I immerse myself in folklore, the more psychics I seem to encounter. It could be a case of like attracts like, or it could be that Filipinos tend to be more accepting of the supernatural, even in modern times. But urban legends weren't my only sources of inspiration.

The Philippines had a vibrant film industry in the 80s, and this included horror movies. My mother never took us to horror movies (and I would have been too scared to watch anyway), but I was exposed to them through TV commercials. This is how I learned of the *tiyanak*, a goblin who takes the form of a new-born baby to lure unsuspecting people into its clutches. I use the tiyanak in my story,

"Stella for Star" (Tan, 2021), about a gay couple who adopts a baby that turns out to be a tiyanak.

I'm wary of the supernatural, but at the same time, also deeply fascinated by it. This is why Filipino folklore influences so much of my writing: because it encompasses real life, to an extent. My approach to hearing about supernatural encounters is that whether I believe the storyteller or not isn't important, but that the person telling the story believes it is, and that's the mindset I bring to my writing: you may not believe what my characters have gone through, but they do, and they have the scars to prove it. It's also why I don't write about Chinese ghosts: because I've never experienced them. I don't mean an actual encounter with an entity, but the act of listening to how others have reacted to them in real life.

Here's something I noticed about the Chinoys (Chinese Filipinos) I've come across: they brought a lot of their culture with them when they migrated from China—food, language, traditions, and superstitions—but they don't seem to have brought their ghosts. Even my Chinese immigrant grandparents' personal supernatural encounters were viewed through the lens of Christianity.

As a girl in China, my paternal grandmother had a vision of what she learned (after she converted to Christianity) were angels going up and down between Heaven and Earth in what she would later describe as an escalator, though it also sounds like a celestial tractor beam. They were speaking a strange language. Decades later, as a mother in the Philippines, she was surprised to hear my youngest uncle practicing lessons in that same tongue. She got excited and asked him what language he was speaking. It turned out that he was learning Latin.

I'd never met my maternal grandfather, but the family story is that he was a Taoist who converted to Christianity but kept sliding back into his old ways. He would summon spirits, get tormented by them, and could only banish them by ringing a bell and proclaiming Jesus Christ as his Savior. I was raised Protestant from birth, so this story was told as a cautionary tale about the evils of paganism. It was only as an adult that I realized, after recounting the story to someone who was spiritual but not a Christian, how rude it must have been to the spirits to be summoned and then driven away. Except for my father's death, around which I crafted a fictional supernatural narrative in my story "Daddy" (Tan, 2021), I tend not to use personal anecdotes in my fiction, for no other reason than it isn't the right fit at the moment.

The few Chinese ghosts I did come in contact with were through the Hong Kong movies that were popular in the Philippines in the 80s. (There's a popular 2004 Filipino film about a Chinese ghost, but that creature was invented). This was the height of the popularity of the *jiangshi*, or Chinese jumping vampire. Since my only experience with horror films in the 80s was through TV commercials, what I saw of the jiangshi was their comedic effect. They didn't seem like ghosts that could be taken seriously because they hopped around with their arms outstretched in front of them and could be stopped by putting a spell written on a piece of paper on their foreheads. And because my only exposure to comedy then was basically slapstick, I didn't know that it was possible for a funny movie to be poignant, too.

I recently watched *Mr. Vampire*, the 1985 Hong Kong supernatural comedy that popularized the jiangshi and laid the foundations for its cinematic lore. Not all jiangshi are vampires. Sometimes, they are zombies. But they are zombies for a different reason than that depicted in pop culture and traditional voodoo. Zombie jiangshi were intentionally created by funeral workers, so that the corpses would be easy to transport (Mok, 2020). Travel was difficult in ancient China, so it helped greatly if the bodies could move by themselves. The corpses that became vampires did so not because of a human spell, but because they had, according to the movie, "one last breath"—or an unfulfilled desire.

The Chinese have a saying that translates to "Falling leaves return to their roots." It was very important for the *huaquiao* (migrant Chinese), to return to the land of their birth, even if it meant they only returned to be buried there. Returning dead people to their hometowns was an actual job in ancient China, and it's believed that the way the corpses were carried gave rise to the legend of the jiangshi. When you realize the longing and homesickness that gives rise to these supernatural creatures, your laughter turns to sadness, even if the movie you're watching is a comedy.

I asked the Chinoy cultural group I'm part of why there aren't any stories of Chinese ghosts on Philippine shores, and the answer I got was that there are stories, but they're only reported in Chinese newspapers. I don't read Chinese, so I can't have read about them, but it doesn't explain why I haven't *heard* any stories.

My experience doesn't mean Chinese Filipinos don't believe in ghosts. Many Chinoys observe the Ghost Festival, locally known as Ghost Month, the seventh month of the lunar calendar when the spirits are said to roam the earth. It generally has the same rules as Mercury Retrograde, but with offerings to and ceremonies for the dead. Key traditions include no signing of contracts during this month, no trips (unless planned beforehand), no big purchases, and no celebrations. There is also apparently a small temple in San Fernando street in Binondo, Manila, incidentally the world's oldest Chinatown, dedicated to "ghosts," or souls without families. It was constructed so, as a friend put it, "wandering ghosts have a place to stay." Before the temple was constructed, the creek below the San Fernando bridge used to claim at least one life a year, either through suicide or accidental drowning. In the 50s, someone put up a small epitaph below the bridge to honor the lost souls. It was removed in the 90s when the temple was constructed, and it's reported that the deaths and drownings have lessened considerably since then. The temple is filled with donated statues of Chinese deities, so not only is it a place for lost souls, but also a place for unwanted images of worship. But again, these tend towards superstitions and ancestor-based spiritual practices more than supernatural creatures.

There may be another explanation for the lack of specifically Chinese supernatural creatures on Philippine soil. Chinoys tend to be very superstitious, and a popular superstition is that you don't talk about things you don't want to attract. Could this be why, unlike other cultures who have brought tales of their supernatural creatures to the countries they migrate to, the Chinoys have left theirs behind?

None of these explanations make me feel closer to my Chinese ancestry. I'm too far removed in terms of lifestyle and influence to be an involved participant—part of me will always remain an outside observer. I have no ties to China, except through blood, and possibly vague bragging rights because my three Chinese grandparents come from Gulangyu, an island that's now a UNESCO World Heritage Site because of its architecture.

I've touched on my dissociation with my ancestry only once, in a story called "Fold Up Boy" (Tan, 2012), where a Chinoy girl encounters the ghost of an immigrant boy who was killed in one of the many massacres the Spanish colonial government regularly conducted against the Sangleys (what the Chinese were called during the Spanish era).

Someone from the cultural group explained that since we're Filipinos who happen to be of Chinese descent (*huaren huayi*), for us, "falling leaves return to their roots" has become "fallen leaves take root in new soil," pertaining to the land that may have been a new home to our ancestors, but is the only home we've ever known.

Perhaps this is why Filipino supernatural stories resonate so much with me, and why I feel like an observer, almost a tourist, to Chinese spiritual traditions. Behind every haunting is a story of heartbreak, and though my blood may be mostly Chinese, my heart is wholly Filipino.

REFERENCES

Asia Cultural Travel. Gulangyu Island. Retrieved from https://www.asiaculturaltravel.co.uk/gulangyu-island/

De Guzman, N. (2019, November 7). The Mysterious Curse of the Manila Film Center. *Esquire*. Philippines. Retrieved from https://www.esquiremag.ph/long-reads/features/manila-film-center-haunted-a1729-20191107-lfrm2

GMA7 (2005). "Multo ng Nakaraan Film Center". *i Witness*, GMA 7, 2005.

Licauco, J. (2018, November 1). This bionic boy's life: what happened after malacañang. *ANCX*. Retrieved from https://news.abs-cbn.com/ancx/culture/spotlight/11/01/18/ronald-joaquin-marcos-the-bionic-wonder-boy

Mok, L. (2020, October 29). Halloween special: what are Chinese hopping zombies? Meet jiangshi, the undead horror film villains made famous in cult 80s Hong Kong movie Mr Vampire. *South China Morning Post Style*. Retrieved from https://www.scmp.com/magazines/style/news-trends/article/3107548/halloween-special-what-are-chinese-hopping-zombies-meet

Ramos, M. D. (1990). *The Creatures of Philippine Lower Mythology*. Quezon City, Philippines: Phoenix Publishing House.

Tan, Y. (2021) *Waking the Dead and Other Stories*. Mandaluyong City, Philippines: Anvil Publishing Inc.

Tan, Y. (2012) Fold Up Boy. In Tan C. (Ed.) *Lauriat: A Filipino-Chinese Speculative Fiction Anthology*, (pp. 141-156). Maple Shade NJ: Lethe Press

LADY NAK OF PHRA KHANONG: A LIFE INSPIRED BY THE FEMALE DUALITY ARCHETYPE

RENA MASON

My most cherished childhood memories revolve around cooking in the kitchen with my mom and listening to her tell ghost stories from Thailand. Fortunately for me, this tradition continued well into my adult life. But as I grew, I realized her accounts resembled precautionary tales of innocent women whose lives had gone wrong and then they became bad. For my mom, and most Thais, several of these stories are not fiction but have been re-told as fact for generations, integrating them into Thai history and culture.

As a teen, I wondered why the stories were always about women. Out of matriarchal and cultural respect, I never asked my mom back then. I also feared how she might respond. Every recollection of the lore I'd heard focused on Thai women who'd been good girls, good women, good sisters, wives, and mothers who had done everything right in life. Then a random tragedy would befall them, causing them to become angry, vengeful, frightening—turn evil. Men in these stories played a lesser protagonist role, their parts often short-lived once they discovered the angry ghost and then got rid of it and became the hero, or died and became a martyr.

These archetypes have long been told and written of in Asian stories, most recognizably in Pu Songling's *Strange Tales from a Chinese Studio*, a collection of fantastical and supernatural tales where women in one form or another are to blame for the plights of honest men. Many of his stories were about the *huli jing*, shapeshifting fox demons, depending on their tails, the number of which defines their hierarchy.

At sleepovers, slumber parties, then later just hanging out with my friends, we'd exchange ghost stories to scare one another, but I'd never recount one of my mom's tales. I'd make up new ones because I worried what my mom's stories might insinuate regarding her perceptions of me. Most of my friends were their mothers' *little angels* and *princesses*, so their stories centered around why teen girls, always with boyfriends, shouldn't talk to strangers, sneak out of the house, or go unsupervised to parties. If I'd have retold my mom's stories, maybe they'd have thought my mom considered me promiscuous, unlucky, or more than that, that I lived under some dark cloud and something bad would happen to me. Think of Carrie's mom from the Stephen King novel. No one wants to be friends with *that* girl. Already othered for my Asian appearance, being the "victim girl" archetype by my own mother in scary stories wasn't the least bit appealing, so I kept her stories to myself. Until now.

Mae Nak of Phra Khanong, the Lady of the Phra Khanong region, is the most famous Thai story of all time, right along with the story of Phra Ram, essentially the Thai Buddha. These two accounts can be broken down from a Jungian psychology perspective as the strong male *persona*, able to wear a mask and function in the public eye yet keep their true selves hidden, and the female unconscious *anima*, the irrational soul. It is this "irrational" side of a woman that plays a strong part in Thai and other Asian ghost stories.

This misogynistic mindset is so ingrained in Thai culture that even in modern-day Thai horror films, the duality of the good-turned-evil female archetype continues to be popular. This can be found with the most recent success of *The Medium* (2021), directed by Banjong Pisanthanakun, where a young Thai woman becomes possessed after her mother won't permit her to take on the generational role as the family's medium in a hill country village of Thailand. The punishment for this refusal begins with the young woman exhibiting minor personality changes, such as the use of bad language and lashing out in anger, and then escalates quickly with promiscuity and violence, ending with the young woman wiping out her entire family, village, and all the monks from the local monastery. At least in this case, there is no male archetype hero. Pinsanthankun also co-wrote and co-directed *Shutter* (2004) and Thailand's biggest box-office sensation *Pee Mak* (2013) among other films. The movie *Pee Mak* is a re-telling of Mae Nak's story from her husband Mak's point of view, where the term *pee* denotes respect.

Pee Mak is a more hopeful adaptation compared to the love-turned-horror story most Thais know. There are numerous versions of Mae Nak's tale, but the way I remember it, it happened a long time ago (almost 200 years from what I am able to gather, after the Siamese-Vietnamese War, which lasted from 1831 to 1834.)

Mae Nak was pregnant with her first child when her husband Mak was called to war. While he is away in battle, Mae Nak and her unborn son die in childbirth. Mak eventually returns, and the local villagers he passes on his way home warn him that his wife and child are dead. He does not believe them, goes home, and is relieved to find Mae Nak and their newborn son at home. Mak reaccustoms himself to domestic life and tends to his property and family.

When Mak goes into the village for supplies, the villagers continue their attempts to convince him his wife and son are dead, but Mak refuses to believe them. Then one day, while he's working outside and Mae Nak is in the kitchen preparing a meal, she drops a lime that rolls to the other side of the room. Through a gap in the wall, he sees his wife's arm stretch the length of the house to pick up the lime. At once he knows the villagers were telling the truth, and his wife is a ghost. He takes off through the jungle in horror, and she chases after him.

With his ghost wife fast on his heels, Mak hides behind a *Nat* bush that Thai ghosts fear because it has sticky leaves. Unable to find him, Mae Nak changes course, and Mak makes a run for it to a local monk to exorcise her. Blaming the villagers for her beloved's change of heart, and with the full power of two spirits (hers and that of her unborn son's), Mae Nak goes on a killing spree. When the monk and Mak return, they are able to capture Mae Nak's ghost in a clay pot that they then toss deep into the Phra Khanong waterway.

As a young girl of five, if that, hearing this story scared me because any and all ghosts were frightening at that age. And yet I wanted to hear more of them. As a teen though, this story made me wonder why my mother had retold it so many times. Did she worry I might fall deeply in love, be abandoned by my husband, and then die in childbirth? Strangely enough, she only now confesses that she did fear her daughters might fall in love too young, move far away, and not meet our potential of becoming intelligent, independent— yet close to family, women. She may have had some anxiety because she'd gone through a miscarriage at a young age, which put her in a coma for several days due to blood loss. She may also have had extraordinary foresight because in 1992, her fourth daughter, my little sister, was driving home late one night and passed out behind the wheel because of a ruptured ectopic pregnancy. The car went off the road, hit a tree, then turned over in a creek, killing my sister.

Despite what Thai men might say or think, Thais are matriarchal. The women of the family by blood share very close bonds. My mom has always believed there's a strength, a power, in a group of women, a sisterhood. Now that I'm older, I understand better what she means, particularly when it comes to female siblings in a family. It is only outside the country, with Western influences, that sisterly ties have more of a tendency to break down. In that, my mother was right; I do not stay in touch, as she would wish, with the remaining two sisters in my family. Perhaps what she'd really meant to relay by telling these stories was that in the end, being a Thai woman is being dealt the lower hand in a way that will make us have to work harder for any success. Many mothers, no matter where they're from, instill this same ideal in their daughters, but maybe not at such an early age, and through paranormal horror tragedies.

My mother's haunting stories had stayed with me as I'm sure she'd intended, and it's more apparent now how they influenced my work both as a medical professional and as an author. Growing up I never considered myself a storyteller on her level, even after I began my writing career over a decade ago. Maybe because she told them as nonfiction: *This is a real account, taken from a true event.* That warning on movies and book jackets still affects how I'll react to a story today. Thais use the word *phi* when referring to general ghosts that haunt the night, but for so many of their stories the term phi isn't used in the names, especially when it comes to Mae Nak, which confirms they believe her story to be more of an historical account than folklore.

The scarier the tale my mother told, the more it stuck in my mind like a bootcamp of fear, exercising my brain through horrific tales to build mental strength and endurance compared to physical training. This cerebral fortitude served me well as a registered nurse who'd specialized in the fields of oncology, home health, and the operating room. As an author, I'm able to combine the knowledge of both when writing the physical and mental human limitations of my story characters.

The duality of the Asian female archetype can clearly be seen in my short story "The Ninth Tale" where a *huli jing* on her way to celestial ascension for that ninth fox tail is irritated with the practice of foot binding. She toys with her lover and his new fiancée because she is jealous but also to uncover whether the human couple's love is true. At a point in the story, the fox demon shapeshifts into a man to uncover secrets but maintains their female *anima* to discover the truth as well as to entertain themselves, while also portraying a strong male *persona* in both their female and male forms. They are mostly good, and although they may have killed a couple of people in their quest, they feel justified in doing so, thus lessening their *anima*, irrational, bad behavior. Once ascended, the foxtail demon requests to be sent back down to deal with the practice of foot binding. In the excerpt below, I use the good-to-bad-girl archetype for the fiancée as well as for the fox demon, Jú.

A strong, intelligent farmer has no need for pretty things.

"Not many people can afford the luxury of daydreaming on the river. What is it that you do?" Jú said.

"I help my mother with chores at home."

"A good girl then?"

"I'm to be married soon. I think my family has allowed me more free time to think on my future."

"That's happy news."

"Yes, but ..." (Mason, 2020, p. 131)

For this story, I mainly wanted to use colors and how they are viewed and perceived in Asian cultures in the different scenes—much in the way Zhang Yimou does in his films. Two of my favorite examples are: *Hero* (2002) and *House of Flying Daggers* (2004). But I also wanted to take a beloved character like the playful Monkey King (who is always male) and make the fun trickster character predominantly female. The Monkey King is the main character from the novel *Journey to the West*—so much to unpack with all of the "what" that made this story important to me, but authors oftentimes weave personal hidden meanings and messages into their stories for the astute reader to find.

In the beginning of "Jaded Winds," recently re-released in *Asian Ghost Short Stories* by Flame Tree Press, the antagonist in the story is confronted by the ghost of his wife whom he drowned in the San Francisco Bay. He murdered her because she was unable to bear him sons. "Jaded Winds" is my ethnic version of *A Christmas Carol* (1843); the story goes on with the antagonist being visited by demons warning him impending doom is near, but unlike Dickens's story, the antagonist meets his destruction. His end is camouflaged by the great earthquake of 1906.

> Ming Li woke to the sounds of a skeleton in motion, flat percussions reminding him of primitive bamboo wind chimes. The clacking came from the bed mat behind him. Last week, on their third wedding anniversary, he'd strangled his wife to death as she slept there.
>
> [...] Ming dumped the body in the Oakland side of San Francisco Bay. Now her gu nu bone demon returned for his soul. (Mason, 2015, p. 173)

Feeling called upon by the need to tell the story of the antagonist's wife in "Jaded Winds," I wrote "Fathoms' Embrace" for *Another Dimension Magazine* in 2014. It's essentially the prequel to "Jaded Winds" where I lay open the relationship between the married couple before her murder. There is betrayal on her part, so I use the good-to-bad-girl archetype again, but she's never able to escape her cruel husband while she's alive, so must wait until she is dead to exact her revenge.

> Clenching her fists, she kicked but couldn't move her legs. Xi struggled inside bindings. She fought for life, for the child growing inside her.
>
> Glowing white fog encircled her with the familiar embrace of the sea. Fabric had unfurled from her upper torso and ankles. The ends entwined and floated next to her as they rolled in the billows of an underwater current.
>
> Her last thought became a prayer to Chi Lang, the Seventh Son and demon of vengeance.
>
> Her last glimpse was of his decayed corpse in an ancient body of armor.
>
> "Ming will die." The demon's words were the last she'd ever hear.
>
> Xi accepted that she'd always been a water person, then opened her hands and let go. (Mason, 2016, p. 19)

I'm currently writing a short story titled "Earth Smothers Fire" which has to do with the relationship between four sisters. In it, I use Asian dragon metaphors, their colors and the meanings behind them, as well as the four directions, which comes from a range of beliefs that cross a multitude of cultures and religions. I make it clear that the main character has lost something of herself by way of Western influences, so in times of need, she doesn't know where to turn and becomes confused—becomes chaos. She struggles with the duality of the good and bad girl within her, looking for answers from the West where she has grown up. With nowhere else to turn, she listens to the advice she's given, which may not end well.

It isn't solely the story of Mae Nak that has influenced me, but it has had the most impact on my life with its duality of good and bad, loss and power, and the rebirth of fierce strength alongside the finality of female despair.

Mae Naak is both a malicious killer and a maternal guardian. She is a man's dream as well as his worst nightmare [...] the sole purpose of her physical and spiritual existence is for love, or more precisely to serve and care for her husband forever. After she dies Nang Naak metamorphoses herself from feeble victim to a fearful demon [...] in order to hold on to her husband. (Wong, 2000, p. 131)

Recently, I told my mom that I plan to tackle both a screenplay and novel about Mae Nak from the viewpoint of a Thai Westerner. She said to tread carefully and be respectful. Of course, I know this, but she has always made it a point to remind us that we are not "Thai" in the eyes of Thais who live in Thailand. We are *farang*—foreigner.

While my Western Thai family visited my oldest sister and her real Thai family living in Thailand in the late 90s, we did a whirlwind tour of the country in two weeks. I got used to hearing the word *farang*, and being the word, which was at first offensive and then strange because at home in the United States we've always used that term to refer to the *other* in our eyes. Then I reminded myself that everyone, somewhere, is the *other* but remembered that some of us are othered no matter where we go.

With the increasing popularity in today's horror market for J-Horror (Japanese horror) and K-Horror (Korean horror) with T-Horror (Thai horror) on the rise, I'm excited to read and see more versions of the southeastern Asian stories I grew up with and love rewritten from different perspectives. Mae Nak will always be an inspiration no matter what story I have to tell.

REFERENCES

Mason, R. (2020). The Ninth Tale. In L. Murray & G. Flynn (Eds.). *Black cranes: Tales of unquiet women.* (pp. 127-141). Los Angeles, CA: Omnium Gatherum.

Mason, R. (2015). Jaded Winds. In Bailey, M. (Ed), *The Library of the Dead.* (pp. 221-236) CA: Written Backwards Media

Mason, R. (2016). Fathoms' Embrace. In McCoy, A. L. (Ed.), *Another Dimension Anthology.* (pp. 13-19) Wiley Writers.

Wong, K. F. (2000) *Nang Naak: The Cult and Myth of a Popular Ghost in Thailand* (pp. 123-142) Bangkok: Chulalongkorn University Press.

BECOMING UNGOVERNABLE:
LATAH, AMOK, AND DISORDER
IN INDONESIA

NADIA BULKIN

If there is one Indonesian word you know, it's probably *amok*. As in children dressing in Halloween costumes and running amuck, amuck, amuck (that's a quote from the 1993 movie *Hocus Pocus*). The original connotation isn't cute, though. It's not playful. It's an episode of frenzied violence, a sudden mass assault (Hempel et al., 2000) in which a brooding individual with no apparent violent tendencies grabs a weapon and starts attacking everyone in sight. It happens, overwhelmingly, to men. Which is not to say that women weren't also going crazy in colonial Indonesia and Malaysia. They just did it in a different way: they became *latah*.

Like amok, latah is associated with frenzy and disruption. Unlike amok, latah isn't violent. It's just shocking for everyone involved: a person is startled and then enters into a trance-like state filled with profanities, screaming, boisterous laughter, echolalia, and echopraxia (Bakker et al., 2013).

This behavior may sound innocuous to a Western reader, but it's uncharacteristic for the average Malay woman, who is meant to grow from the sweetness of girlhood to the grace of motherhood without ever becoming crass or coarse. In *wayang* terms, she must always be *halus* (soft). She must never be *kasar* (rough). After my mother and I left Indonesia, my American teachers would comment on the deferential way I stood next to their desks when they asked to see me—chin down, hands clasped. Like I was about to get hit. I was just trying to be lady-like.

(The only teacher who ever hit me was a Western man in an international school. But that's neither here nor there.)

Latah and amok were originally classified as as-yet-unidentified mental illnesses by colonial Dutch psychiatrists in the early 20th century (Bartelsman & Eckhardt, 2007). Exotic diseases to go with the exotic people and wildlife, I suppose. They're still classified as "culture-bound syndromes," though Malays aren't the only people who experience them. There's the jumping Frenchmen of Maine, for example, and Arctic hysteria (*piblokto*) among the Greenlandic Inuit. Anthropologists call this the "latah paradox": the culturally unbound culture-bound syndrome.

Our cultural mental illness isn't how Malays understand latah or amok, unsurprisingly. Amok is traditionally attributed to an attack and possession by a powerful tiger demon (*hantu belian*). Latah is attributed to ... well, spiritual weakness as a whole. The afflicted are literally *lemah semangat*, weak-spirited, with spirit referring here to an inner strength that's both psychic and secular. Women are seen as more easily shocked, more prone to losing control, more "easily 'poked,' 'pierced,' 'invaded,' and 'taken over' by spirits" (Peletz, 1996, p. 177). They're more susceptible to suggestion, both human and inhuman.

It's probably important to note, here, that you don't need a whole lot of ritual to access the spirit world in Indonesia. I always tell people that you can feel it as soon as you step off the plane, though that's probably the humidity: the spirit world has constant access to you. Which isn't to say that spirits have nothing better to do than bother you, but humans are meddling in those waters, too. Spiritual energy can make you sick, cause you misfortune, steal your money, steal your spouse, steal your kid. It crashes planes and starts earthquakes and determines trial outcomes. It's the country's biggest, richest black market, and you're really better off not messing with it if you're not a spiritual elder of some kind. The one thing you can do to protect yourself from its impact is to be *kuat semangat*. Strong-spirited.

Hold on, you may be thinking: how can women be open to all this spiritual malware and also limited to quiet sweetness and light? Glad you asked. It's because women feel more shame (Peletz, 1996).

I'll be honest, I'm not very strong-spirited. I don't need a spiritual elder to tell me that. I don't know how much my parents really were, either, so maybe I can blame it on them—my mom would tempt fate by wearing green on a beach where a Spirit Queen drowns green-clad people (it's her favorite color, you see); my dad would worry about it, the same way he worried about everything.

"You have to pray for your parents," one of my babysitters once told me, probably when she realized that my father wasn't a very devout Muslim and my mother was, well, *nothing*—the greatest spiritual risk of all. When my father died, his friends urged me to "be a good Muslim" for the sake of his soul, but my mother's illness had already spread to me—I had already decided, by then, that I didn't believe in God.

I didn't believe in God because I didn't feel God—or didn't feel whatever other people claimed to be feeling, anyway. But you'd never catch me dead saying I don't believe in ghosts or demons or black magic. Being an atheist hadn't protected my mother from being attacked in a rental house by the ghost of the previous owner. An omnipotent, undepictable God was beyond my imaginative powers, but I took my religion teacher more seriously when he told us that jinn were lurking over our left shoulders at all times, urging us to sin. I could believe that I needed to say a set of magic words ("prayer," people call it) before getting in a car or going to the bathroom or going to sleep. I *believed* in danger. I could *feel* fear.

That's another thing about women, apparently: we worry more (Peletz, 1996). My experience has not backed up this generalization—as a small child I once wrote that "daddy is worried a lot"—but there's no doubt that I've followed in Daddy's footsteps in this regard. For most of my life, I've treated my anxiety—spiritual and otherwise—with a clench. Stomach or jaw or shoulders, curled and calcified into stone. I suspect that I've been trying to be strong, to be resilient in the way that Indonesians are quite proud of, even when it means survival at the expense of rebellion.

Grace under pressure, that's how former coworkers used to describe me. But under my placid exterior I was always screaming, see? Inside, I was swearing, flailing, running to the roof so that I could fantasize jumping off. And sometimes, when I was startled—really, genuinely startled, like that time I walked into my living room and saw the infamous German K-fee coffee commercial, the one where a relaxing scenic drive is suddenly interrupted by a screaming monster—I would feel the clench letting go, beckoning me to dive into what I can only describe as a lawless void where every bone and blood cell would be free to burst loose. I never went latah, though. I was too young for it.

I would just scream, and scream, and scream, even after the electric shock wore off.

One explanation for latah is that it's what happens when you can't hold the clench anymore. Many anthropologists have suggested—and let me tell you, anthropologists *love* latah—that latah is a "symbolic representation of marginality" or "a learned coping strategy in the form of a cathartic stress response" (Kenny, 1978, p. 209; Bartholomew, 1994, p. 331). Basically, latah provides a way for women—especially older, poorer, widowed women living on the social margins—to act out.

While women get access to emotional response through the nonsensical behavior of latah, men get access to emotional response through the anger and destruction of amok. There's no equivalent "amok paradox" because there doesn't need to be—we know this type of destruction is so viscerally understood as a lightning that strikes men, especially after a period of setback and depression. We know family annihilators. We know men who commit suicide-by-cop. We know berserkers. We always have.

How does the phrase go? Men are afraid that women will laugh at them; women are afraid that men will kill them?

This un-mystery of masculine madness has made amok a useful tool of the state. The fascist Suharto regime began blaming violent incidents on "amok" as soon as it made a run for power in 1965, a habit that Indonesian military and police continue to this day. It's not that troops and cops fired into a crowd of people—it's that the people ran amok (Bachelard, 2014).

It's easy to see why the state likes "amok." I can think of three benefits the state gets by blaming violence on "an impersonal force beyond human control" (Colombijn, 2002, p. 50): the state's hands are washed clean of blood, even as the military hands out weapons and paramilitary provocateurs bate crowds; it keeps civilians in a dizzy state of fear, worried their neighbors might go on a rampage at any moment; and it discourages any international inquiry into the true cause of the conflict. It actually *banks on* exoticism.

No, wait, four benefits: it also gives the state a pretext for bringing down an iron fist. Those angry people are out of control, after all.

Funny is the wrong word, so I'll say that it's *ironic* that a condition as frenzied and uncontrollable as "amok" gets used to enforce the social order of the fascist state. That includes punishing women who step outside of it. For years, the Suharto regime propagated a ghoulish story about Communist women killing six military generals in 1965 while partaking in "naked, sexual dancing," castration, and eye-gouging (Wieringa, 2011, p. 15). The story was a lie, but an enduring one. In the mass killings of millions that followed, members of the Communist women's organization were specifically targeted for attack, rape, and murder. Why blame women specifically? Because the fascist social order will always put a special priority on controlling women. Because in embodying the polar opposite of the Indonesian feminine ideal (Larasati, 2013, p. 39; Robinson, 2009, pp. 63-64), these shameless "Communist whores" represented a dangerous threat to the social order that had to be destroyed.

Despite all the ink that's been spent debating it in anthropology journals, the feminine madness of latah isn't actually much of a mystery, either. Like those jumping French lumberjacks, latah is best understood as a "culture-specific exploitation" of an exaggerated startle response (Simons, 1980, p. 195). Your startle response can get stretched out of shape by all sorts of stressors, including those common to marginal life in Indonesia. Hunger on the factory floor, for instance (Ong, 1987). Or the deaths of loved ones. Describing accounts of spirit possession in *Reason and Passion*, Peletz (1996) writes that "Mak Zuraini [...] was never subject to *latah* until she experienced the deaths of two of her children" (p. 177).

Maybe that's why consulting religious elders and healers—the go-to solution for most cases of spiritual affliction in Indonesia—doesn't seem to do much to "help" cases of latah. In his review of latah in Southeast Asia, Winzeler (1995) cites one man who claims to have stopped experiencing latah through "his own efforts and the Will of God" (p. 133), but notes that he should be considered an exception, not the rule. Many women who experience latah don't think salvation is possible, and wouldn't want it, anyway.

This sort of fatalistic shrug is a common sight in Indonesia, because hey, what else are you going to do? There are these melodramatic commercials that air on television around Eid—usually sponsored by oil companies and the like—about families separated by poverty or illness, that serve to explicitly remind the viewer to endure their trials with poise, to have *ketabahan* (faith) that relief may someday come.

Ketabahan is another traditional Javanese quality that I don't have much of. After my dad died, my mom gave me a necklace with a golden seashell charm that was meant to symbolize ketabahan—only for me to start a long, ugly, angry protest against the world as it spun, refusing to continue living while my father was dead. It took me many years to start believing people when they said *everything will turn out okay*, and more years with medication and therapy to subside the anxiety that used to make me feel like I was barely holding in a scream. These days when I'm startled, I shriek for a normal length of time. But Indonesia isn't known for its investments in mental healthcare.

On the other hand, latah isn't a true disorder in the clinical sense. It's a "disorder" that *causes* disorder, and intentionally so. It *disrupts order*. And that's the point: latah sets you free. Under spiritual suggestion, the shame that holds back your ferocity like a scold's bridle is lifted.

Latah lets you "respond in kind" to any teasing and abuse you may endure (Winzeler, p. 135). Latah lets you rebel against rules and bosses with other women (Bartholomew, 1994), because if women are inherently more suggestible—prone to spiritual influence, weak-spirited—then your friends can hardly be blamed for catching the "bug," can they? And latah gives you plausible deniability over whatever you may have done under its influence. *So sorry,* you can say, *I don't know what came over me.*

There are limits, of course, as there always are. I've never heard of latah being used for political purposes, or to disrupt a military action. At least not yet.

But I'm reminded of this piece of advice I started hearing in college, and many times since: that if you think you're being followed and you're on your own, you should act crazy. Flail your limbs like you're having a seizure. Sing a nursery rhyme in a loopy voice. Act possessed. *Become ungovernable.* Tap into whatever your culture perceives a madwoman to be and watch the berth you're given widen; watch the leash you're on extend.

REFERENCES

Bachelard, M. (2014, December 8). Indonesian military and police fire into crowd of West Papuan civilians, killing 5. *The Sydney Morning Herald*. Retrieved February 27, 2022, from https://www.smh.com.au/world/indonesian-military-and-police-fire-into-crowd-of-west-papuan-civilians-killing-5-20141208-122wf0.html

Bakker, M. J., van Dijk, J. G., Pramono, A., Sutarni, S., & Tijssen, M. A. (2013). Latah: An Indonesian startle syndrome. *Movement Disorders: Official Journal of the Movement Disorder Society, 28*(3), 370–379.

Bartelsman, M., & Eckhardt, P. P. (2007). Geestesziek in Nederlands-Indië–vier psychiatrische syndromen: amok, latah, koro en tropenneurasthenie [Mental illness in the former Dutch Indies–four psychiatric syndromes: amok, latah, koro and neurasthenia]. *Nederlands tijdschrift voor geneeskunde, 151*(51), 2845–2851.

Bartholomew, R. E. (1994). Disease, disorder, or deception? Latah as habit in a Malay extended family. *The Journal of Nervous and Mental Disease, 182*(6), 331–341.

Colombijn, F. (2002). Explaining the violent solution in Indonesia. *The Brown Journal of World Affairs, 9*(1), 49–56.

Hempel, A.A., Levine, R.D., Meloy, J.D., & Westermeyer, J.D. (2000). Cross-cultural review of sudden mass assault by a single individual in the oriental and occidental cultures. *Journal of Forensic Sciences, 45*(3): 582–588.

Kenny, M. G. (1978). Latah: The symbolism of a putative mental disorder. *Culture, Medicine, and Psychiatry, 2*(3), 209–231.

Larasati, R. (2013). *The Dance that Makes You Vanish: Cultural Reconstruction in Post-genocide Indonesia*. Minneapolis: University of Minnesota Press.

Ong, A. (1987). *Spirits of Resistance and Capitalist Discipline: Factory Women in Malaysia*. Albany: State University of New York Press.

Peletz, M.G. (1996). *Reason and Passion: Representations of Gender in a Malay Society*. Berkeley: University of California Press.

Robinson, K. (2009). *Gender, Islam, and Democracy in Indonesia*. New York: Routledge. pp. 63–64.

Simons R. C. (1980). The resolution of the latah paradox. *The Journal of Nervous and Mental Disease, 168*(4), 195–206.

Wieringa, S.E. (2011). Professional blindness and missing the mark: Sexual slander and the 1965/66 mass killings in Indonesia: Political and methodological considerations. *Asian Journal of Women's Studies, 20*(3), 50-76.

Winzeler, R. (1995). *Latah in South-East Asia: The History and Ethnography of a Culture-bound Syndrome*. New York: Cambridge University Press.

HOLY REVELATIONS

GRACE CHAN

"He who belongs to God hears what God says. The reason you do not hear is that you do not belong to God."

John 8:47, New International Version

On a still summer's night, the Holy Spirit descends. A campsite scattered with wooden cabins, surrounded by a whispering fringe of Australian natives. Amped-down electric guitars, casting wistful chords from the windows of the community hall. Within, it's dark. Only the multicoloured spots from a cheap disco light whirl over upturned faces. A forest of teenagers, straining towards Heaven.

The youth pastor torrents with prayer. The hall swells with *amens*. The shadows imbue me with rare confidence. I raise my arms a little higher, my hands almost level with my shoulders, reaching for absolution, for communion. I beg to feel, like the others, what I am supposed to feel—or even a humble portion, just enough to be deserving.

The girl in front of me has one arm high above her head. Her other hand is clutched to her chest. I know her. Not well, but we've both been in this church since we were toddlers. She's two years my junior. She sways harder, side to side. Her whole body starts to shake. A strange muttering flows from her lips.

Just as she bends into a Z, two youth group leaders rush forward and gently lower her to the floor. I see her mouth, still moving frenetically with spiritual tongues. Her limbs twitch against the scratchy carpet. Her eyes are squeezed shut in her pale and glistening face—her expression twisted in beatific passion, in virtuous and desired possession.

I, too, yearned for this overwhelming consumption. It seemed to be granted to others but not to me, and I wondered what I was lacking. I did everything the same as them. I'd attended Sunday services with my family since before I could even remember. I performed devotional time, most days—reading the Bible, praying, journaling. I even dragged myself to Bible Study Fellowship, an evening class divided by age groups, for the most Christianly of Christians. Therefore, the problem must be something internal, some intensity of faith I had yet to attain, a relinquishing of the ego I had yet to realise.

My parents didn't grow up Christian. They converted in their university years, and then joined our evangelical church shortly after migrating to Melbourne. The church was a newly established community. Most, like us, had moved to Australia in the eighties and nineties. Most, like us, were members of the Chinese diaspora who'd been in Malaysia or Singapore for several generations.

For the first few years, church services were held in Box Hill— one of several suburbs in Melbourne's eastern corridor that would become a second home to ethnically Chinese migrant communities in the late 20th and early 21st century (State Government of Victoria, 2021). I remember climbing a flight of narrow stairs, holding my mother's hand, to reach a musty chapel with white-painted walls and orange carpets.

Later, our church moved a couple of suburbs farther east. This site was much bigger and seemed, to my childhood eyes, incredibly grand and hip. There were three separate parking lots. The auditorium had a brick baptism pool and a multi-tiered stage for a band and a grand piano. There was even a separate chapel and a nursery and lots of smaller rooms where they ran the 'Kid's Church'.

After the service, the congregation would squeeze into a tearoom where the aunties spread out platters of homemade treats. Kueh lapis, its nine jewel layers I would peel apart with my teeth. Kueh talam, serimuka, and the blobby, bright orange angkoo filled with mushy bean paste that none of us kids wanted. If we were lucky, there were curry puffs, piping hot and crispy from the oven.

It was easy to get to the table first—kids could weave and duck between the adults, who stood around in warm-breathed clumps, talking loudly in a blend of English and Cantonese about how their children were doing academically and which high school they were hoping to get them into. Geographical zoning and scholarships and selection examinations.

They would pray for one another's families, they assured each other. They would even put the children on the prayer list in the church bulletin. In the end, it was all in God's hands. All blessings sprang from Heaven. You just had to have faith.

Christianity teaches me to hold paradoxes together in my head. Ours is a Trinitarian faith. We believe that there is one God who exists in three persons. God, our Father in Heaven, seems like a distant authority figure, holy and spotless and judgemental. Jesus the Son is more approachable, emanating compassion and humanity. The Holy Spirit is the most mysterious—I imagine a ghostly but warm aura, flying around and imparting divine power and forgiving sins. I picture the three persons separately and then all overlapping, melding into one divine being.

When I am five years old, repeating the words of a prayer that my mother speaks for me, I repent for my wrongdoings and accept Jesus into my heart. I imagine the Holy Spirit floating into my chest and wrapping itself around my own spirit, which is probably situated somewhere inside my ribs. I know that God will protect me from all the scary things in the world. My fears melt away.

At one time we too were foolish, disobedient, deceived and enslaved by all kinds of passions and pleasures... He saved us through the washing of rebirth and renewal by the Holy Spirit, whom he poured out on us generously through Jesus Christ our Savior...

Titus 3:3-6 (abridged), New International Version

The youth group organises an outing to the cinemas. We are going to watch Mel Gibson's *The Passion of the Christ*, with a steely-eyed Jim Caviezel portraying Jesus. I sit in the third row of the tiny suburban theatre and watch as Jim Caviezel is tempted by a beguiling, androgynous Satan, betrayed by Judas, flogged to a bloody pulp, and nailed to a wooden cross.

We are spellbound, horrified, unable to turn away. The glowing screen illuminates our tear-stained faces. A third of the way into the movie, I'm already sobbing. Afterwards, on the way home, I lean my head against the car window and let the cool breeze shake through me. My body feels entirely dehydrated and numb, but my soul is consumed by guilt and self-reproach and an intensity of worship that is perhaps a sort of love.

For days afterwards, images of Christ's suffering saturate my mind. I remember how the burden of bearing all mankind's original sin far outweighed the physical pain, and I weep again. How could I ever have doubted, and how could I ever doubt again? I will be better, I will be better, I will be better.

In her essay *Ecstasy*, Jia Tolentino (2019) writes, *"Spiritual matters felt simple and absolute. I didn't want to be bad, or doomed... I wanted to be saved, and good. Back then, believing in God felt mostly unremarkable, sometimes interesting, and occasionally like a private, perfect thrill."* (p. 132)

Ours was a Chinese church in the broadest sense. We were not affiliated with any particular country. Some of us spoke Cantonese; others spoke Mandarin, Hokkien, Hakka. The younger generation spoke English, shedding our parents' dialects. We were bound together by the shared experiences of breaking ourselves off from our old homes and attempting to assimilate into a new society that was frequently unwelcoming. We held hybrid identities, but we wanted to be Australian.

Initial hopes of a better, luckier future often did not pan out. In their new countries, migrants were cut off from their family and social networks, unable to find the sort of employment they had expected, abruptly forced into downward socio-occupational roles. Not only did they face language and cultural barriers, but they found themselves grappling with an unexpected loss of status and self-confidence, and feelings of guilt, regret, and loss.

The church became a way for uprooted families to regroup in a foreign country. At first, the support was practical and social: you could find a dentist, a handyman, and playmates for your children in the church community; you could network safely with other educated, socially conservative peers. But in the longer term, the church forged a path for migrants to rebuild a new identity as Australian Chinese (Wang & Piller, 2021).

The spiritual beliefs of the church provided a transformative comfort. Salvation was a balm against the anxieties of the world, dampening the fear of the unknown and the uncontrollable. Western society was an unfamiliar, hostile place—in the workplace, migrants were hounded and turned away; white people hurled abuse in the schoolyard and supermarket; right-wing politicians warned that Australia was being "swamped by Asians" who "have their own culture and religion, form ghettos and do not assimilate" (Australian Human Rights Commission, 1997).

But with the Holy Spirit indwelling, there was a way to arm yourself, like a warrior, against trials and tribulations. All suffering had a purpose: God was merely testing your faith. Wretched yet virtuous Job, who had everything taken away from him but still praised God, became our beacon of inspiration.

The evangelical faith brought order to a chaotic world. Christianity imparted a clear morality. Temptation and sin led to judgement. Repentance and obedience led to forgiveness, peace, blessings. There was a familiar, reassuring authoritarianism to the faith: God our Father, surrounded by a host of benevolent angels; the pastor at the head of the church, and a flock of associate pastors, ministers, deacons, and volunteers around him. As a member of the congregation, you had a place in this hierarchy. If you were baptised and ate of the body of Christ, you became part of the church.

Christianity became a bridge between two cultural identities. Wang & Piller (2021) write about "adhesive identities"—a "fusion of different national, linguistic and religious identities in Chinese migrant converts," allowing migrants to "find a comfortable space for themselves as first generation migrants in Australia."

As a Western religion, Christianity was an overt, acceptable demonstration of social acculturation. Our congregation took pride in the fact that our services were conducted in English and that the sermons regularly addressed current Australian socio-political issues. We were educated, white-collar evangelicals who served our communities and listened to American preachers on the radio.

Nevertheless, Christianity was also a vehicle for the continuation of traditional Chinese values in a less explicit form. The male figure at the head of the church and at the head of the home. Values like humility, obedience, self-sacrifice, and familial duty. Importantly for parents, the church provided an environment for their English-speaking, culturally divergent children to be nurtured in traditional values and sheltered from the 'negative' influences of individualistic Western society. In Kid's Church and youth group, their precious offspring—the very reason for their harrowing international displacement—would be surrounded by studious and clean-living peers, protected from the wild, dangerous temptations of premarital sex, alcohol, and drugs.

Satan (n.)

Proper name of the supreme evil spirit and great adversary of humanity in Christianity, Old English Satan, from Late Latin Satan, from Greek Satanas, from Hebrew satan "adversary, one who plots against another," from satan "to show enmity to, oppose, plot against."

Online Etymology Dictionary.

Temptation. It becomes a thrilling, taboo sort of word. The Bible is littered with archetypal stories of temptation, where Satan appears in a desirable mien and holds out one's deepest unconscious wishes on a silver platter. The first and most famous temptation, of course, is the temptation of Eve in the Garden of Eden. The serpent, sly and crafty, beguiles Eve with fruit from the Tree of Knowledge. I wonder what is so terrible about wanting to know good and evil, but I am taught that it's not so much about knowing—it's simply that God has forbidden it, and disobedience is a sin.

The temptation of Jesus is just as compelling. "Then Jesus was led by the Spirit into the desert to be tempted by the devil," it reads, in Matthew 4:1 (NIV). It is God's will, then, that this trial be endured. Satan tempts the starving, exhausted Son of Man with bread, pride, and all the splendorous kingdoms of the world. But Jesus resists, as we too are to resist.

We learn that Satan was once the most powerful angel, but he rebelled against God and fell from Heaven, along with a host of other wayward angels who became demons. These fiends present themselves in all sorts of ways: as false gods and idols, as the Antichrist, as infernal forces beckoning us towards sins like lying, greed, pride, praying to other gods, witchcraft, and sexual deviation.

I can recite all the books of the Bible from memory, but Revelation is my favourite, for its psychedelic visions of the end times. I devour the proclamations about thrones and elders, powerful scrolls, and mythological creatures. Seven trumpets release apocalypses: hail and fire mixed with blood; the sun and moon struck dark; an angel hurling a mountain, ablaze, into the sea. I am magnetised, alive. I am filled with visions of the fantastical-made-real.

I squirm, ready at any moment for the Rapture—the moment of Christ's second coming, when angels will descend and pluck true-believing Christians off the face of the Earth. I pray for it to occur during my lifetime, for my incredulous peers to see me rise anointed into the sky like a superhero.

He seized the dragon, that ancient serpent, who is the devil, or Satan, and bound him for a thousand years.
Revelation 20:2, *New International Version.*

The sea gave up the dead that were in it, and death and Hades gave up the dead that were in them, and each person was judged according to what he had done.
Revelation 20:13, *New International Version.*

There was a story that went around. I can't remember it exactly, but it was something like this:

A man and his wife migrate from Malaysia to Australia. They settle into their new community and move into a nice home. They convert to Christianity. But something isn't right. The wife falls ill and rapidly weakens. She is haunted by terrible nightmares and a constant feeling of dread.

The man calls their church pastor into their house. They pray and search the house from top to bottom. Eventually, the pastor discovers, in the back of a wardrobe, a box of belongings that the wife brought over from Malaysia. At the bottom of the box is a heathen object.

An *idol*, the pastor warns the couple with great gravitas. It is a way for demons to come into the house, into the wife. These false gods are powerful and devious. They can possess you if you are not careful. You can't just bring anything with you from overseas.

The pastor removes the idol, lays hands on the wife, blesses the house, and tells the man and his wife to pray for forgiveness. The wife quickly recovers.

Christianity provided a clear path for the Chinese Australian immigrant to navigate two enormities. To the rear, there was the loss of an old culture, with its once-familiar traditions, customs, beliefs, and social ties. To the fore, there loomed a new culture, complex and unfamiliar, difficult to navigate, fraught with its own invisible dangers.

To cling too much to the old would only be a hindrance to assimilation. It was vital to shed past attachments and habits to forge a new identity in this new country. Buddhism, Taoism, ancestor worship, household shrines, temples, superstitions, lucky charms, mantras, meditation—they were no longer relevant, possibly even dangerous.

Language, too, was an old skin that needed to be sloughed in gradual, flaking layers. Speaking too much Chinese, especially in white spaces, marked you as one of those non-compliant migrants plotting from ghettos to steal jobs and education from the innocent, hardworking white Australian. The Chinese language didn't have a function in this new world. Church services allowed recent immigrants to perform their English—singing hymns in English, listening to sermons in English, reading the bulletin in English—in a non-judgemental, culturally safe environment.

On a deeper level, Christianity soothed the grief of immigration. The trials of integrating into Western society were merely part of the mortal burden, commissioned by God as He had commissioned them upon Jesus. The disappointments and failures—job loss, financial hardship, family breakdowns—were reminders not to invest your hopes in worldly treasures, but to hold out for the promised, abundant rewards in heavenly afterlife.

The social structure of the church provided an additional ego-restoring function. Here, you could serve in a role according to your strengths, whether it be playing in the worship band, collecting offerings, or volunteering as a counsellor. You could be respected by other members of your congregation. You could become a person again, visible and worthy, no longer on the margins.

In my later teenage years, I visit a Pentecostal church. They are holding an evening service, which I think is incredibly trendy.

My friends and I weave across a big, bustling foyer and into an auditorium so large I can't grasp its proportions. I feel like I'm at a concert—the pews are sardined with worshippers, the lights are completely dimmed, and the massive stage whirls with colourful lasers. Whispering and nervous, we squeeze into a pew in the back corner of the hall.

Towards the end of the service, the pastor's impassioned sermon morphs into a wild prayer. He shouts for God's gifts to rain down on every member of the congregation. I've never witnessed something like this at our church, where the closing benediction is always chanted in grave, formal tones.

I watch as the Holy Spirit seizes people around me. One by one, they begin to speak in tongues: some muttering under their breath, others throwing their heads back and unleashing incomprehensible praises to the ceiling. Syllables trip over each other in breathless, unstoppable incantation, like an ocean geyser, like an ancient curse. I'm terrified and spellbound by their devotion. They have found their place in the universe. Every fibre of their being is aligned.

Teeth aching, I wait for my skin to evaporate, for the spirits of my childhood to wash through me. I am taken back to the times when I lay in bed and felt my mind open wide to Heaven. I'd been taught that God can see and know everything, and so can my deceased ancestors. I imagined them picking through my spread-out secrets. I felt dark with sin—I was a stain, an indelible inkblot moving through the world.

I wait to be swept into a higher plane, as I waited when I emptied my mind in meditation. I did this even though my parents and the youth group leaders had warned direly against it: when you meditate, you let your guard down and open yourself up to an invasion of Satan's legions. But by this time, I was already drifting. I breathed in and out and waited to be snared in a net of temptation, to be dragged down by vicious claws into the flaming circles of Hell.

God's gifts do not rain down on me this evening. I slip out of the auditorium, through the nearly empty foyer, and out into the parking lot. The air is edged with a hint of coolness. I walk around the side of the brick building and stand in a bed of bark chips, gazing out over a sea of parked cars and into the dusk-heavy clouds. Opposite me, a slender eucalyptus tree bows its head and twirls its veil of leaves.

I take a slow, deep breath. For years, I yearned to elevate my existence, to hear God's voice in my ears and feel the Holy Spirit tremble my bones. I wanted to walk the path laid out for me by my parents and by the pastors. I yearned to be cleansed, to belong.

But tonight, I am here. Just here. No spirits, dark or light. Only the air whooshing into my lungs and dissolving through my membranous insides. Only my skin, prickling pleasantly as the temperature drops and the night descends. I wait for the service to end, for my friends to emerge. But I'm in no rush. I'll leave in my own time.

REFERENCES

Australian Human Rights Commission. (1997, January 1). *The Racial Hatred Act: Case Study 3 Pauline Hanson's maiden speech.* Retrieved from https://humanrights.gov.au/our-work/racial-hatred-act-case-study-3-0.

Online Etymology Dictionary. (2022, February 20). *Satan (n.).* Retrieved from https://www.etymonline.com/search?q=satan

State Government of Victoria. (2021). *Melbourne's Chinese Community.* Retrieved from https://liveinmelbourne.vic.gov.au/discover/multicultural-communities/chinese.

The Holy Bible, New International Version. (1973, 1978, 1984). Grand Rapids Michigan, United States of America: International Bible Society & Zondervan Bible Publishers.

Tolentino, J. (2019). *Trick Mirror* (p. 132). London, Great Britain: 4th Estate.

Wang, Y., & Piller, I. (2021). Christian bilingual practices and hybrid identities as vehicles of migrant integration. Retrieved from https://www.languageonthemove.com/wp-content/uploads/2021/06/Wang_Piller_ChineseAustralianChristianity_preprint.pdf

HUNGRY GHOSTS IN AMERICA

VANESSA FOGG

On the day that my first book, a standalone fantasy novelette, is released from a small press, I am dropping off my eldest daughter at summer camp. My parents have come along to see their granddaughter off. I mention my book's release—I don't know why. I try not to talk about my writing around my parents. There must have been a reason that I casually let it drop. My first little book, released in both print and digital form.

My mother says to me, "Don't get excited about it. Don't—" She pauses. "Don't think about it too much."

Don't get excited; it's not a big deal, why make it a big deal, why are you wasting time on this?—is that what she's saying?

Or more likely, I think, looking back—*Don't get excited and you won't be disappointed. Don't count on having any success with your writing. Concentrate on paying work and family. Don't let this get to your head.*

Don't get too excited. Don't think about it. Don't dream too much.

In Buddhist tradition and Asian folklore, there are spirits known as "hungry ghosts." These beings sinned in their mortal life, often by displaying excessive greed and desires. In the afterlife, they are punished for such sins by becoming creatures of insatiable appetite. They are often depicted as monsters with huge, swollen bellies, long, thin necks, and mouths no larger than the eye of a needle. They feel the hunger pangs of starvation, but their mouths and necks are too small to ever take in enough food to slake their hunger (Rotman, 2021; Lions Roar, 2020).

When I first learned of the concept of the hungry ghost, I felt an instant resonance with it.

Like all parents, mine have hopes and dreams for their children. From the beginning, my sisters and I are made clear on some of these dreams. We are all to do well in school. We are all to go to good colleges. We are all to get good, financially stable jobs. To my parents, being a medical doctor is the best job of all: well-paying, secure, respected by everyone. It's a cliché, of course: the Asian immigrant parents pushing their American-born offspring toward medical school. Nevertheless, it's one that my Thai-Chinese immigrant parents fulfill.

Here's another cliché: the American-born children in rebellion, pursuing their own career dreams and paths. Their own hungers and desires, no matter how it breaks their parents' hearts. To various degrees, in different ways, my sisters and I fulfill that cliché, too.

In the middle of the night, the phone rings. My father answers it, and shortly after I hear the garage door opening: my father is driving off to work, to the small rural hospital where he staffs the emergency room in addition to providing inpatient care. On top of his hospital service, he runs his own solo practice in internal medicine, providing medical care in an office setting.

My father works late. He works weekends. His hospital pager goes off during dinner and school events. It's the 1980s in rural Midwestern America, and small communities like ours have trouble attracting physicians. That's why my father is on call every other weekend for years: because there are only two medical internists in town to share the burden. It's why most of my father's colleagues are also immigrant physicians from Asia—places like India, Pakistan, the Philippines. It's why we're here. Because white doctors don't want to practice in tiny, isolated three-stoplight towns like this, so immigrant physicians come to do the job.

My dad sinks into his chair, exhausted, after work. He snaps at us. And he and my mother both push my sisters and me to follow in his steps and become medical doctors, too.

He says that it feels good to help people. But mostly he talks about how being a physician is a well-paying, stable job. "It puts a roof over your head," he tells us. "It lets you take care of your family. We can go on vacations. Look at the good life we have."

Years later, I will appreciate the value of a stable, high-paying job and what it allows. But at this moment I'm young and idealistic and naïve. I want to have a *calling*. At the least, I want a job that I would enjoy. I'm squeamish; I don't like blood; I don't think I want to be responsible for people's lives.

"Nobody likes their job," my mother tells me. "You're not supposed to like your job."

I do well in school, especially English. My parents are proud when my writing is praised, when my essay wins an award. They think the idea of making a living as a writer is ludicrous.

"Hungry ghosts" are figures from Buddhist lore, originating in India. There, they are known as preta, literally "the departed" in Sanskrit. As Buddhism spread out from India and took hold throughout East and Southeast Asia, the stories of preta spread as well, and the preta changed, mutated, took on new forms and names. It is in Chinese that they took on the literal name, "hungry ghost" (饿鬼 ,"è guǐ" in Mandarin). In pictures, they are sometimes portrayed in flames— fire issuing from their mouths, blazing from their bodies. There are different kinds of hungry ghosts, and they have been depicted at various times in various traditions as having needle-sharp fur, bulging eyes and clawed hands, animal heads, or other deformities. They often have distended bellies and spindly limbs as well as thin necks (Rotman, 2021). In Japan, they are known as *gaki* and some of them have the ability to eat—but they can only eat repulsive and humiliating things, like human corpses, vomit, or feces. And even so, they are not able to eat enough (Meyer). They stay hungry. Hunger is the constant, the defining feature, across countries and cultures.

In Thailand, my parents' birth country, these ghosts are known as *pret*. They are most often described as tall and very thin, with a mouth the size of a needle hole. Throughout Asia, hungry ghosts can be doomed to their existence for a variety of sins. In Thailand, it's said that children who hurt and behave disrespectfully toward their parents will be reborn as pret (Chadchaidee, 2019).

I try to be a dutiful child. I know that I am sometimes disrespectful. Certainly disobedient. It's possible that I am being disrespectful now, at this moment, in even writing this essay.

For a long time, I do not understand my parents' obsession with financial security. As far as I know, neither grew up impoverished. My mother's family was not rich, but I don't have an impression of real hardship. She and her siblings all went to college. My father and his siblings, too, all have college degrees, and some have post-college degrees. My impression, in fact, is that my father's family was relatively well-off. After all, my paternal grandfather founded a successful construction company which has been passed down to two generations.

But there are always the stories of my grandfather's childhood. Of how my father's father grew up as an illiterate peasant boy in the south of China. The story of how he rose from nothing to something, from literal rags to riches. It starts with the day that he ran away from home. He'd been sent to collect money from someone on behalf of his own father. On the way home, he stopped to do some gambling and lost all his father's money. Terrified of the beating that surely awaited, he fled.

He fled all the way to Malaysia, eventually finding a distant relative who took him in. He learned carpentry there then struck out on his own once again—this time north to Thailand, to the southern city of Hat Yai where he would found his construction company and a large family of his own.

He was twelve when he first ran away.

How often was that little boy hungry, traveling all on his own? Did he go hungry on that sea voyage to Malaysia? Did he ever go hungry before, in his home village in China?

How hungry for knowledge was he, learning carpentry skills and the ways of a new country, absorbing what he would need to know to make a living? What hunger impelled him to move yet again, to cross another border to Thailand? There was ambition, surely, driving him in all this: in the establishment of a livelihood, a life, a successful business in a foreign land. There was surely hunger both metaphorical and literal.

How true is any of this family legend? Was he really only twelve? How did he do it? What is elided in this story?

I don't believe my father ever went hungry as a child. He seems to have been raised in a comfortable background. He's never spoken of personal poverty. But of all the things that he could hate, a picky eater is surely at the top of his list. He cannot abide wasted food. When I trim the fat from my meat and push it to the side, he scorns me for not eating it. He eats all the scraps that my sisters and I leave on our plates. A memory of him at the near-angriest that I've ever seen him: scowling and seething because a young cousin did not (in my father's opinion) eat enough, and not enough of the "high-value" foods, at an all-you-can-eat buffet.

I didn't think my father ever went hungry as a child, but … did he? Is this all the legacy of my grandfather's hunger, passed down to his children as story and thrift and respect for food? Is this just the standard cultural tradition of respect for food and scorn for waste, a tradition that most Asians are brought up in? What are the roots of that tradition? How long does hunger last?

I do not know of prolonged physical hunger, but we all have our hungers, after all.

It is the merciless hunger of the "hungry ghosts" that fascinates me so. The insatiable, unending nature of it. I'm an adult when I first learn of these ghosts, and I imagine a creature completely consumed by hunger, consumed until there is nothing left: the ghost *is* hunger. That's all it is: all mind and sense eaten away, until it is only pure hunger existing, craving.

I know little of my mother's family. Her father, too, was an immigrant from China to Thailand. He also came when he was young—perhaps only thirteen or so. He used to tell his children that he made the trip to Thailand by hanging onto the back of a boat.

"Of course, it can't be true," my mother laughs at this story. "How could he hang to the back of a boat all that way? In the water, all that time? Wouldn't he be eaten by sharks?"

My parents want me to be a doctor, but I want to be a writer. I love stories, I love fiction. I want to write my own. They say that I can major in English in college, but I should at least complete the pre-med curriculum.

The joke is on me. I take my first college course in molecular biology and fall in love with it. I switch my major to biology.

But the joke is also still on them, because I don't want to be a medical doctor. Now I want to be a research scientist, a professor— in either neurobiology or molecular cell biology. Perhaps both.

My parents are both bitterly disappointed. My father rages. "Do you know what 'Ph.D.' stands for?" he says. "Poor and Hungry Doctor."

(He's right. He's right and I won't understand for years, not until I see/experience for myself the instability of academia, the ruthless job market, the competition for grants. Getting into medical school is fiercely competitive, but if you can make it through with the M.D. degree and residency training you do, indeed, have an incredibly secure career).

Everyone, including my research science mentors, encourages me to apply for a combined M.D./Ph.D. program. "If the roof falls in," one of my professors tells me, alluding to the scientific grant funding situation, "you'll still be able to practice medicine."

I study and take the MCAT exams for medical school. I score well. I sit in front of my medical school applications. I look at the essay section, in which I am supposed to explain why I want to become a medical doctor.

I find myself unable to write a word.

I know little of my parents' personal hungers, their personal ambitions outside their dreams for their children. My mother went to nursing school in northern Thailand. I've never asked why she chose that field. She came to the United States in the early 1970s. As she tells it, she came for an adventure, a lark. In 1965, President Lyndon B. Johnson had signed the Medicare and Medicaid health care programs into law, and as coverage from these programs expanded across the U.S., the demand for health care professionals skyrocketed. Hospitals recruited nurses and doctors from abroad. My mother and father both came, separately, as part of that recruitment wave. My mother came with some of her nurse friends; she thought she would see America, have an adventure for a few years, and then go home.

She met my father at a party in Detroit, Michigan, where she was working, and he was completing his medical residency. They married. When my mother became pregnant with me, she quit her nursing career.

I know little of my mother's interior life. But even as a child, I sense her unhappiness in the early years of our family. She is raising three children almost entirely on her own, far from her friends and half a world away from her family. My father works long hours and isn't around much. She's an outsider, a foreigner, in our tiny Midwestern town. To even buy decent Asian groceries, we have to drive two hours to Chicago. She doesn't seem to have local friends.

My parents argue a lot. They argue in Thai, which I don't understand well, but sometimes I get the gist of a conversation. I hear her yelling one time, and she's asking my father why we can't move. Why can't we move to a bigger city, even if it's just to the college town forty minutes away—why can't we just move someplace bigger.

Hungry ghosts—like most ghosts—are generally invisible. Their suffering is unseen. They may be moving among us right now, begging for food from us, unheard (Gaki Zoshi, 12th cent).

What happens when hunger is unrecognized by others? What happens when it's unacknowledged even by the one possessing it? How long can you suppress your hunger? How long can you push it down, squelch it down, keep it down, and deny it?

I don't apply to medical school. Instead, I apply to graduate schools, and when the Molecular Cell Biology program at Washington University in St. Louis extends an offer, I accept it. The tuition is fully funded, and there's a modest stipend to live on. My parents are disappointed with my decisions, but they drive to St. Louis with me and help me move in.

I graduate. I also fall in love with a fellow scientist, and we get married. We start postdoctoral research positions in a new city. We have our first child.

Science breaks my heart.

The reasons are complex and also straightforward and entirely foreseeable. There are not enough tenure-track positions at research universities relative to the number of biology Ph.Ds. who want them. Balancing research and a new baby is hard. My postdoctoral research has not gone as well as I've hoped.

Pursuing one's dreams doesn't always end well. I'm not good enough. My parents were right.

My husband also leaves academia. Unlike me, he did what everyone advises: he finished a dual M.D./Ph.D. program. He's trained as both a medical doctor and researcher, with a medical fellowship now under his belt. He decides to give up the research and take a full-time clinical position. We move to a new city for his job. We have a second child.

In the years to come, I will focus on my family and also on trying to find a new career pathway. I'll be a stay-at-home mother. I'll explore scientific writing and editing. I'll dip my feet back into research for a time. I'll leave research again.

And along the way, I'll rediscover my old love for fiction writing.

My parents both took straight-line career paths. They wanted the same for their children. They wanted something *safe*.

The health-care field is what my parents both know. It brought them to this country. For years after my Ph.D., my mother keeps telling me that it's not too late to apply to medical school. She says this as I hold a wailing infant in one arm while trying to prevent toddler mischief with another. She says this even as I start to land well-paying freelance medical science writing gigs. She says this knowing that I don't *need* to work; I'm lucky that my husband can support us all comfortably.

Is she just worried about what might happen if my husband can't support us? If he should ever leave me, or become incapable of working? It's a risk, yes. But it's the same risk she herself took with my dad.

"I just don't you want you to be stuck at home, like me," she says. I hear the ghosts of past frustrations in her voice.

My parents don't understand what writing means to me. To be fair, most non-writers can't.

My father seems mostly bemused by my fiction writing. At least he doesn't nag me about finding a "real job." Perhaps he's just comfortable with the idea of my husband financially supporting me and the kids, just as he did for his wife and children.

My mother switches from pushing medical school to urging me to apply to pharmacy schools. She doesn't take seriously my freelance career in technical scientific writing, although at least she takes it more seriously than my fiction.

"You should focus on work while your mind is still sharp," she tells me, and by "work" she means the well-paying, technical kind. "You can do the other writing when you're old and retired."

She thinks mental sharpness isn't required for fiction? I think incredulously. But I say nothing.

Hungry ghosts can be fed. Throughout Asia, there are rituals and festivals at which food is offered to these ghosts. At the right times, by the right means, their suffering can be alleviated.

In the West, perhaps the best known of such festivals is the Chinese Hungry Ghost Festival, which falls during the seventh lunar month. It's believed that on the first day of this month the gates to Hell are opened, and ghosts are free to roam the Earth. The entire month is known as "Ghost Month" and throughout this time, families may offer food, "money" made of joss paper, and other symbolic paper offerings to the spirits of their ancestors. They may also provide offerings to any lonely, suffering ghosts who don't have descendants to care for them. On the day of the Hungry Ghost

Festival itself (the fifteenth day of Ghost Month, or the fourteenth in some parts of southern China), a large feast for ancestral spirits is traditionally served, with lavish displays of food offerings. This festival is observed in various forms by ethnic Chinese communities around the world, and similar festivals occur in Japan, Thailand, Vietnam, and other countries (Keaton, 2002).

One might say that it seems unfilial to assume that an ancestor has become a hungry ghost, through sin or ill circumstance. But it would be worse to let such an ancestor spirit go hungry, if that is indeed what they became. Better safe than sorry (Keaton, 2022).

I have some small successes with my fiction writing. I sell stories. Writers who I admire say nice things about them. I'm even longlisted for a prestigious award.

My mother downplays these events when she hears of them. She seems newly astonished, taken aback, every time I remind her that I do, in fact, get paid for my short stories.

I'm hurt. I don't understand why she acts like this. Why she tells me not to spend too much time on my writing. Why, when my first small book is released, she tells me, "Don't get excited."

Is she trying, in her own way, to protect me? To warn me against getting overinvested in an impossible dream? I've already had my heart broken by one dream. To my mother, pursuing a path in the creative arts must seem even more absurd than my attempt to pursue a career in academic research.

I inwardly rage at the scenario I've spun for myself. *Of course, I'm not taking my writing* THAT *seriously*, I argue with her in my head. *I'm not stupid. I don't expect to ever make a living off my fiction writing. I'm just doing this for fun.* I know I'll never publish a big-time novel with a big press. I know that I'll never really get anywhere. I know to keep my dreams small. It's just a hobby, that's all. I'm not stupid.

For so many people, pursuing a career—pursuing even a hobby or interest—out of pure love must seem an impossible luxury. I assume this held true for all four of my grandparents, who must have grabbed onto whatever would allow them to earn a living. I know this is how my parents look at life, even though they were raised in materially better circumstances.

I think that maybe the ghosts of hunger are passed down through generations, in ways that we don't understand.

I have scant memories of my grandparents: a few images from childhood visits to Thailand. My maternal grandfather in a hospital bed, near the end of his life. My paternal grandmother giving me cookies, or some kind of treat; I can't remember now what they were. Just her face wrinkling up as she smiles kindly at me, eyes creasing to crescent moons. She nods and I nod back, both of us wordless, unable to communicate across language barriers.

I know little of my grandmothers' lives. I know that my mother's mother was born and raised in Thailand, and that she seems to have separated from my mother's father at some point. She had five children, and ran a small convenience store to keep her family afloat. She was known as a great cook. She was famous for her *sai au*, a northern Thai-style sausage.

My father's mother came from China to Thailand when she was a teen. She left her family because she didn't get along with a stepmother. I don't know how she got to Thailand, how she met my grandfather, or how they got married. They had twelve children. My father doesn't tell family legends of her, as he does of his father.

I don't know what any of them dreamed of. I don't know my ancestors' hungers. I don't know what I would feed them, if I were to make an offering for them at the Hungry Ghost Festival.

I would like my parents' understanding and approval, their acceptance of my choices. But I think some hungers are destined to go unfulfilled.

It's Christmas Day, 2021. I'm in my parents' home in Las Vegas, where they moved after my father retired from over forty years in medical practice. The dining table is set: white tablecloth, decorative holiday runner, crystal glasses waiting to be filled with wine. A mix of American and Asian foods on the table: prime rib, mashed potatoes, rolls; a spicy tomato salad, a vinegary salad of wood-ear fungus, fried spring rolls stuffed with ground pork and glass noodles.

My husband and kids are with me. My sisters and their own families, too. Our mother and father. All of us gathered again for the first time in two years, for the first time since a pandemic hit American shores and COVID-19 precautions kept us all apart.

For tonight, at least, the conversation flows easily. Naturally. We avoid each other's sore spots, any topics of tension; no rough edges slow down the bright, quick stream of light chatter. My mother and father are both smiling. There's so much food. It's been so long since we were all together.

I ask my mother why her father left China for Thailand, and why so young. All these years, and I've never outright asked her before.

Everyone in his family died in the pandemic, she says, and my sisters and I are taken aback.

The pandemic? What pandemic? We've never heard of this before.

"The pandemic," my mother repeats. She can't explain exactly what pandemic, what disease, this was. She doesn't know. A disease that swept through his village, and all the neighboring villages. That wiped out his entire family, parents and siblings, leaving him alone: a child of only thirteen or so.

We puzzle at the nature of this pandemic. Was it the Spanish flu? Do the dates line up? Is "pandemic" even the right word—was it more of a local epidemic? What was this disease? There are so many things it might have been, in a poor region during a time of poor public health, so long ago.

We don't know. My mother doesn't know. The conversation moves on.

It may seem callous, but the past is unknown and we're here now, in the present. And although we're still in the midst of our own modern pandemic, we don't talk much of that either. Later, during this visit, tensions will flare; my mother will make a remark about my writing and I'll bite my tongue. But for now we're cutting up slices of mango cake. Food has always been my mother's language of love, and we've made so much food together these last few days.

There's so much unspoken among us. But not everything needs to be spoken aloud. The love in our family, for instance, never is.

I realize that it's okay to voice some hungers, even if it's only to myself.

I *do* take my writing seriously. I don't hope to earn a living at it. I know to keep my expectations low. But that doesn't mean I can't take it seriously as a craft, as a pursuit. That it's more to me than a frivolous hobby. That it's *important* to me.

There are the necessary hungers, the hungers for food, shelter, and safety. There's the hunger for love and family. I have it all. I have a husband who is the love of my life, and I have our children. I have my sisters. I have parents who care, even if they don't always understand.

It's okay to want even more. It's okay to recognize that. To stay up late while my husband and children sleep, to type out the imaginary worlds in my head.

Doesn't the denial of hunger just help it grow?

The hungry ghost is a spirit that has haunted me since I first learned of it. To me, it's a metaphor for all the desperate, yearning, unfulfilled hungers a human could have.

But humans are not literally hungry ghosts. *I* am not a hungry ghost.

Hungry ghosts can't feed themselves. If they feel any relief from hunger at all, it's only a temporary relief, given through the kindness of family or strangers, through ritual offerings made at the right times.

I can feed myself. I can name my hungers and take them seriously. I want my daughters to grow up to do the same. We are more than survival. And more than what others expect of us.

We can hunger, and we can feed that hunger, little by little, a bite at a time.

REFERENCES

Chadchaidee, T. (2019). *Thai ghosts and their mysterious power*. Booksmango.

Keaton, H.L (2002). Feeding hungry ghosts: Food, family, and desire in stories by contemporary Chinese American women (Publication No. 3040686) [Doctoral dissertation, The University of Tulsa]. ProQuest Dissertations Publishing &Theses Global.

Keaton (2002, 8) discusses this, observing that: ". . . it is important to note that, in practice, all deceased ancestors are treated as Hungry Ghosts, and surviving relatives pay homage to their souls through various rituals that include food and paper offerings. Strictly speaking, a Hungry Ghost can be a deceased person who has failed to become reincarnated due to unworthiness, an unresolved attachment, or relatives' lack of attention to the death rituals. However, according to Welch's The Practice of Chinese Buddhism. "It would have been unfilial to suppose that" one's descendant "had deserved to be reborn as a hungry ghost, but it would have been even more unfilial to neglect the appropriate measures" just in case the deceased was one."

Meyer, M. (n.d.) Gaki. *Yokai.com*. Retrieved from https://yokai.com/gaki/

Rotman, A. (2021). *Hungry ghosts*. Somerville MA: Wisdom Publications.

(Late 12th century) *Gaki Zoshi (Scroll of the Hungry Ghosts)* [Painting]. Kyoto National Museum, Kyoto, Japan. https://www.kyohaku. go.jp/eng/syuzou/meihin/emaki/item03.html#:~:text=Through%20 words%20and%20pictures%2C%20this,water%20in%20a%20 temple%20cemetery

This painting by an unknown artist provides a striking illustration of the desperation of hungry ghosts, and of how they are invisible to regular humans. In one section (Image B), three gaki are seen kneeling and begging amidst a bustling temple crowd, unseen by the humans moving around them.

What are Hungry Ghosts? (2020, August 27). *Lion's Roar*. Retrieved from https://www.lionsroar.com/what-are-hungry-ghosts/

100 LIVERS

K.P. KULSKI

In 1984, during the early hours, on a lonely stretch of Highway Five—the dashboard of our car crumpled into my mother's chest and killed her instantly. I was five years old. It would be the first monumentally defining experience of my life. A turning point that would rob me of more than just a mother, but well-being, family, culture, and identity. When one parent is an immigrant, losing them is additionally complicated, and for me, grief and trauma fused with memories. Things I cling desperately to—half-remembered scents, the cadence of Korean in my mind, flavors of soups, and the texture of rice cakes. The echoes that permeate my life. An entire connection based on loss. A yearning and hereditary grief without defined shape. All these years without my mother, she's always been in the corners, in the shine of tears, the burn of disappointment, and the heartbreak of grief.

Before we embarked on this road trip, one that had been meant to return us to our home in the woods of Washington State, my mother piled traditional Korean blankets onto the back seat, forming a makeshift bed. These blankets, long ago made from real mink, now mostly made of faux fur, are known for their exceptional heaviness and warmth and, in the age before seatbelt laws, created a whimsical mini-landscape for my imaginative mind. My adult older brother planned to drive overnight, so the blankets served exactly as intended, an on-the-road bed.

I had been fast asleep when my exhausted brother lost control of the car, careening, and crashing us into the highway guardrail. While my mother's lungs were crushed by the impact, I had been thrown onto the floormat behind her passenger seat, hitting my head along on the way. Her body took all the force of the collision, diverting it from me. The blanket she had so carefully arranged protected me from the sight of her death, piling over me, like a cocoon. I would stay this way until I returned to consciousness. Convinced I was dead, I wept in confusion until pulled out by my weeping and bloodied brother. My brother would, years later, commit suicide over the trauma and guilt related to the accident. He left behind three beautiful children, two of whom my mother never had the chance to meet. Loss compounded by loss. Grief compounded by grief.

My mother's death became the starting point of an involuntary erasure, establishing a tragic history that has greatly defined my life. A pain forever attached to love and longing of what was and what could have been. An invisible weight intensified by life as a biracial girl in America where the bewildering journey for identity is forever coupled with mourning.

Identity can be a brutal thing, and, for me, oddly correlates to Korean stories of the fox spirit, *kumiho*. The fox spirit appears across many Asian mythologies, most known are the *huli-jing* of Chinese lore, or the *kitsune* of Japanese mythos. In each, the stories describe a shapeshifting fox who usually transforms into a beautiful woman. But the goals of the spirit vary, at times sinister and others benevolent. However, in Korean mythologies the kumiho embodies a particular and consistent malevolent edge. Dark and bloody, the original kumiho is a thing of nightmares, a sinister being, almost always female, who feeds upon human flesh.

"Her beauty and desire, together with deceit, have to be seen in analogy to the behavior of a beautiful woman standing outside societal norms." (Uther, 2006, p. 140).

"The kumiho, the fox demon spirit, always takes the shape of a woman, like a young bride, or a daughter who will consume her family." (Yun, 2012, p. 89).

Yet she embodies something further, a depth and a key to deconstructing identity ... and the lengths required to obtain it. This is because some kumiho stories surround the fox spirit's desire to become human herself. That while she can take the shape of a human, she seeks to truly become human, not only in appearance. She pursues genuine identity.

Child,
A hundred-year-old fox devours one hundred humans
And becomes a woman.
I, a woman poet, devour one hundred fathers
And become a father.

(Kim, 2006, lines 1-5)

The necessary "work" required to achieve human-ness varies. Often this can be achieved through killing and consumption of a requisite number of human livers, usually 100. Of course, the dark nature of the kumiho plays a part in my personal intrigue with her, but there's more; I understand intrinsically what it means to strive for an identity that appears to be mine yet can be stolen at any point. To be a product of two worlds and be dimorphic in presentation. My own sense of self continuously struggles to embrace both halves without canceling one in favor over the other. A drive to be recognized as valid in either form, but internally questioning it in perpetuity. A painful journey exacerbated by brutal loss ... to ultimately hunger for identity.

Yun (2012) points out in her story, "Kimchee", how the Korean language overflows with emotion, how the act of communication is much greater than words. She goes on to explain that in Korean saying, "I am hungry" implies more than physical hunger, but means something greater, an emotional and spiritual yearning. The ache of emptiness that longs to be filled.

When separated, I talk to my sister almost every day. When we're both hungry, we whisper the hunger rolling into our empty stomachs. We speak poetry over the phone.

"I want *kkadugi kimchee* with *bap* and *galbi.*"
"I want *kimchee bocumbap.*"
"I want *naymeunggook.*"
"*Kimchee jjigae.*"
"Oh yes, *kimchee jjigae.*"

Korean reveals exactly what you feel and forces you to feel what you say. You speak and your feelings are revealed. When I speak *kimchee jjigae* into the phone, I am saying I am more than hungry. I have hunger." (Yun, 2012, pp. 87-88).

My favorite kumiho story is that of "The Fox Sister" (Fenkl, 1999). The story begins when a farmer and his wife, who have three boys, long for a daughter. The wife becomes pregnant and gives birth to exactly that, a girl, and they are jubilant at the news. Unfortunately for the family, the daughter isn't a human child but instead a demonic fox spirit. They do not yet realize this. Of course, such a thing is destined for disaster. When the child reaches six years old, odd things begin to occur. Cows are found each morning, dead and mutilated in the field.

The father charges his oldest son with investigating. The oldest son hides himself and stays up all night watching the field. In the darkness of the wee hours of the morning, he sees his little sister emerge from the house. She approaches a cow and shoves her small hand into the animal's side, piercing its hide; pushing past flesh, muscle, and sinew, she reaches in until she has found the animal's liver. This she rips out and consumes on the spot as the maimed cow flails at her feet and dies. The brother, stunned and horrified, hurries to report all this to his father.

His father, however, who adores his daughter, accuses his son of jealousy. Subsequently, the father throws his son out of the house. He then charges his second eldest son with the same duty, to investigate and report on what is happening to the cows.

The second son stays out all night, hidden and waiting. Sure enough, the same thing happens: he sees his beloved little sister emerge from the house, go to a cow, and pluck out its liver. Again, she eats the liver on the spot as the cow dies at her feet. The second brother is also horrified by this. In the morning, he goes to his father and tells him everything. The father is again angry, accusing this son of much the same sin as the eldest and throws him out of the house.

The father charges his last son with the same duty, and this son, after witnessing what happened to his two elder brothers, decides that he won't be reporting anything negative about his sister no matter what he sees. He stays out all night and goes to his father in the morning and reports that the moon killed the cows.

The two elder brothers wander the countryside for a long time and one day decide to return home. They arrive to find the house empty except for their little sister who tells them that everyone has died from illness. After they agree to stay with her, she cooks an elaborate meal for them. The two brothers eagerly eat their fill, and there is a contentment among the three. In the middle of the night, the second brother is woken by the sound of chewing. To his horror, he finds his sister standing over the dead body of their eldest brother.

> *Globules of gore-thickened-blood fell to the wood floor, slogging into the crevices. A lump of viscera so fresh and slick that when little sister hungrily raised it to her mouth, it seemed that against the night, it made a death shaped hole of shadow. This girl he'd adored, only a few years before, lifted as she giggled with abandon upon his shoulders, now rent with her small teeth the liver of their older brother. Slowly, to his horror, she turned to him, eyes glistening with excitement.*

> *"Only one more, big brother. I need only one more liver and I will finally become human."* (Kulski, 2022)

Initially, this seems to be a wonderfully dark tale about a murderous creepy child. The fox sister exemplifies a sinister creature, preying on opportunity, even upon her own family, relying on deceit to achieve her ends. But there's more here, a deeper commentary about identity and the lengths one must go to find it. When one does not intrinsically fit, what can be done?

"How was it possible that I existed outside of the racial order of the census forms in my grade school, and what would I have to do in order to correctly fill in the answer to my racial puzzle?" (Thompson, 2000, p. 172).

Just as the fox sister must murder to achieve identity, for those who are biracial, identity has its own emotional brutality. It comes at a cost, the expunction of one heritage in order to fit into a monoethnic category.

"I did spend a great deal of energy rejecting my Chinese heritage, which I thought would certainly differentiate me from my white classmates. I would not allow my mother to teach me Chinese, which she attempted to do; I made fun of the Chinese food in restaurants where she would take us; and I identified more and more with my father whose side I would take when he belittled my mother's culture and 'superstitions.' I thought if I did not speak Chinese then I could use that as proof I really was white ..." (Thompson, 2000, p. 173).

Another striking element in the story of "The Fox Sister" is that the kumiho does not come from outside the family but from within. She is a daughter and sister, the youngest and well-loved member of their family. Yet she is not granted humanity as a birthright, instead she must strive for it in the darkest of ways—through the murder and consumption of her own family.

As I crumpled into the floor of our car, at five years old I had crossed an invisible threshold. After my brother pulled me out, after the ambulance ride alongside the last thing left of my mother, her purse, my father would pick me up and finally I would go home. Or so I thought, because home had transformed into a place almost unrecognizable and cold without my mother's presence.

For objectionable and selfish reasons, my white-American father would cut off all communication with my mother's family. Taking me across the country without leaving any contact information. A heart-rending action. My *immo*-aunt would later, after laying eyes on me again after fifteen-plus years of separation, sob and tell me over and over, "I thought I lost my niece forever."

Like the fox sister, I am the youngest and only daughter for my mother. Also like the fox sister, I have three older brothers, in my case half-brothers who are full Korean. The separation would rob me of my brothers, nieces, and nephews, as well as the entirety of my mother's family. Cousins, whom I once spent afternoons playing alongside, suddenly gone. Next, I would lose my mother's language. I no longer heard, or interacted with anyone who spoke Korean, my first language. Soon, the words and sounds would slip away into an ocean of regret and half-recalled memories.

My new household would be made up of my frequently-out-to-sea or bar-hopping father and paternal grandmother. Later it would be my father, his girlfriend, and her two children, later again, it would be my father and his new wife. I was an unwelcome addition: the Asian girl in a white family. The third wheel that my father had long ago emotionally left behind.

Home became a place where I acutely did not belong. A place where my fiercely New England grandmother would clutch me and proclaim that she'd knock "the slant out" of my eyes. The place where later, my stepmother would request that I did not display photos of my mother. With some exceptions, until high school, I was often the only Asian kid in schools that were predominantly white. To kids who were Asian, I was, in their view … not Asian and definitely not one of them. I lived in a limbo world, between two places and not fully belonging to either.

> For a long time I had tried to belong to America, wanted and wished for it more than anything, but in that moment all I wanted was to be accepted as a Korean by two people who refused to claim me. You are not one of us, Kye seemed to say. And you will never really understand what it is she needs, no matter how perfect you try to be. (Zauner, 2021, p. 107).

I desperately wished to belong to someone. I desperately wished that I too could be human. I longed for golden hair and blue eyes—if not that, then for the unmistakable black hair and eyes of my mother. To be undeniably the child of either of my parents. I studied my face, limbs, and food preferences for proof of where exactly I fit. I weathered the unrelenting and tiring question from children and adults, "what are you?"

> There was something in my face that other people deciphered as a thing displaced from its origin, like I was some kind of alien or exotic fruit. "What are you, then?" was the last thing I wanted to be asked at twelve because it established that I stuck out, that I was unrecognizable, that I didn't belong. (Zauner, 2021, p. 95).

The worst part is that I never really had an answer. What is the Fox Sister? If she is monstrous, it is not because she kills; it's that despite her parentage she is *not* human.

> The full moon called to the blood in her stomach, and while her family slept, the daughter went to the cattle they kept … and in the palm of her hand was the cow's liver, completely intact. Pressing her nose against the organ, she bared her teeth and took her first bite. Still hungry, the Fox Daughter pushed her arm into the cow again and again, removing the organs one by one until the cow fell to its side, completely empty, like a solid ghost on grass. (Yun, 2015, p. 85).

While I do not harbor murderous tendencies and nor am I a fan of liver in any form, I can't help but feel empathy for her. A sense of sisterhood. I know that for those who are biracial, belonging is something that must be pursued. A performance to convince and demonstrate authenticity. A losing race to be whatever qualifies me as American enough, or Asian enough, then other times too much of either.

> I had spent my adolescence trying to blend in with my peers in suburban America and had come to age feeling like my belonging was something to prove. Something that was always in the hands of other people to be given and never my own to take, to decide which side I was on, whom I was allowed to align with. I could never be of both worlds, only half in and half out, waiting to be ejected at will by someone with greater claim than me. Someone full. Someone whole. (Zauner, 2021, p. 107)

I am told that when I was born, my mother seemed mystified that she could give birth to such a white-looking child. Later, it would not be unusual for my blond-haired, blue-eyed father to jokingly and rather convincingly disavow that he was my father because of my dark hair, dark eyes, and Korean features. But how does one get to become "enough" to be part of the very family that gave you life? Fox Sister must simultaneously destroy her family and collect organs in order to do so. I like to pretend we don't know the ultimate end of the story. I prefer to assume she killed her brother and ate his liver as well. Not because of the violence of it or the concept of familial murder as an acceptable gateway, but that the intent, effort, and ultimately sacrifice could lead to clarity.

If she had done so and completed her quest, I want dearly to know—was it enough? Whatever curse had been laid upon her, did it lift her from the floor of a crumpled car with a dead mother? Did she, at last, reunite with her family, reclaim her culture and therefore her humanity? Did America finally embrace her as one of its own daughters?

Did she at long last—belong?

Or is the lesson, that belonging is really a brutal thing that only destroys and leaves us with nothing to belong to in the first place? That for those of us who are biracial, we will exist forever in the spaces in between, yearning for completion but forever denied it.

Perhaps her brother pulled her out of the crumpled car and embraced her. As he wept, maybe he told her that she was enough just as she was, that there would no need to search. He would say, "it's us now; we are left." Then he would never give up on her, his children, and himself.

But the truth is, the little girl probably still sleeps somewhere on Highway Five—under a pile of mink blankets, dreaming of all the possibilities and refusing to look at the cruelty of reality.

A caterpillar
devours its own path
and paves the way of a cabbagewhitebutterfly.
It uses all its might to eat up
the green path
to go alone up to the sky
where there is no one.

(Kim, 2006, lines 32-38)

REFERENCES

Fenkl, H. (1999). *Fox Wives and Other Dangerous Women.* https://web.
archive.org/web/20061111095249/http://www.endicott-studio.com/
rdrm/fordangr.html

Kim, H. (2006). An Automatic Film Processor. *Anxiety of Words* (p. 113)
(Don Mee Choi Trans.). Zephyr Press.

Kim, H. (2006). Father is Heavy, What Do I Do? *Anxiety of Words* (p. 111)
(Don Mee Choi Trans.). Zephyr Press.

Kulski, K.P. (2022). Unpublished fiction.

Thompson, B. Y. (2000). Fence Sitters, Switch Hitters, and Bi-Bi Girls: An
Exploration of "Hapa" and Bisexual Identities. *Frontiers: A Journal of
Women Studies,* 21, pp. 171-180.

Uther, H-J. (2006). The Fox in World Literature: Reflections on a "Fictional
Animal". *Asian Folklore Studies, 65,* pp. 133-160.

Yun, N. (2012). Kimchee. *Fourth Genre: Explorations in Nonfiction, 14,* pp.
79-91.

Zauner, M. (2021). *Crying in H Mart.* Alfred A. Knopf.

PLANT A CHERRY TREE
OVER MY GRAVE

KIYOMI APPLETON GAINES

When I die, plant a cherry tree over my grave.

I always expected to be a mother. In our society, there's an expectation of parenthood. Neither a question of want nor intent, but default. Research shows childless people are viewed with suspicion and hostility. For years, I carefully didn't correct assumptions that I'm not-a-mother-yet, so my intentions wouldn't prevent opportunities. I've seen it happen to others without "a family." My days have been sprinkled with the casual, and sometimes aggressive, assumptions of my impending motherhood since my girlhood. It was an assumption I had made, too—and I *did* want it—ever part of "the five-year plan." Until I was closer to forty than thirty. Until it wasn't.

The idea that I might want to be a parent in future years was never compelling enough to become one. I have a family, and different choices, and different priorities. Are they less worthy?

People choose not to have children for many and varied reasons, none of which are anyone else's business. That's not what this is about.

Monster (n.) an animal of strange shape, abnormal in form or structure, one who deviates from normal or acceptable characteristics, a threat. From the Latin *monstrum*, a divine omen indicating disaster/misfortune, an abomination; derivative of *monere*, to remind, to admonish, to instruct; a warning.

Our cultural imaginings hold an ancient trifold concept of womanhood—Maiden, Mother, and Crone. One transitions neatly from one to the next. There isn't a fourth option. Anything else is an animal of strange shape.

Noriko Reider (2019) says that ideas of the Japanese mountain witch, *yamauba*, sometimes called Yamanba, solidified in the middle ages as new ideas of Buddhism were brought from the continent; ideas of an ideal woman that still hold sway today.

Of course, it is the strange that we fear most. Those most likely to be accused of witchcraft have been women who didn't quite fit into a neat category of womanhood. Such female figures are non-women, mistrusted, unvalued, banished from the community. Over years, transformed and corrupted into a monster.

It's hypothesized that stories of yamauba come from periods of famine when the old, infirm, and very young—those not likely to survive anyway—would be brought to the mountain. While there's little historical evidence of the practice, such stories abound across cultures. Periods of anxiety always see a scapegoating and ousting of the unlovely and unlovable—the ones who are strange.

I didn't set out to be a witch either. But here we are.

There remains, always, a leeriness of that strangeness. In friends who, laughingly, do not let the baby fall into my awaiting arms. If you don't want children, you must not like them. And what do the stories tell us, after all? Witches eat children.

> **Oni** (n.) hiding, invisible, secret; malevolent; an outsider, other; the invisible soul or ancestral spirit, both benevolent and punishing. (*Often translated as "demon" in English.*)

The thing that has defined yamauba, and many monsters, is that they eat the flesh of humans. This has been the accusation, the justification, for witch-hunts of all sorts. For the good of the community, to chase out, even kill, that which was strange, monstrous.

It's suggested—in literature, film, art, articles, and even in person—that there's a lack of wholeness in the absence of parenthood. That pregnancy itself conveys some magical completion of womanhood on the female form. The act of birthing brings with it new maturity and generosity of spirit. The childless are often labeled either pitiable, for hopes unrealized, or selfish.

Headline: Pope Says Choosing Not to Have Babies is 'Selfish and Diminishes Us.'

Along with the assumption that little girls will grow up to be mothers, is the implication that those who don't become mothers don't grow up. At least, not fully. We have no space for women who don't want children.

Diminish (v.) to make or become less; to break into pieces.

Demonish (adj.) one with the characteristics of a demon; a monster.

I have nibbled my share of baby fingers and toes.

Along with blowing raspberries on laughing bellies, changing diapers, giving baths. I'm not incompetent with children, for not having given one a name. I shouldn't complain. I can, after all, "give them back."

More women are childless by choice, but my friend exaggerates it. *I don't know anyone who's pregnant. Everyone I know says they don't want kids.* She looks to her husband, wide-eyed, for validation. *We're the ones who are the minority now,* she insists, and he nods.

Later, our group of friends, mothers and future mothers all, will gather around her and I will find myself closed out of the circle.

My father called me Oni when I was little, an affectionate nursery version of my given name. It has perhaps become an unintended prophecy. A paternal benediction has always been a thing of power.

I hang out with the men. It seems easier for them. Women still do the bulk of childcare, even with the rise of stay-at-home dads, involved fatherhood, and co-parenting. With different societal expectations and physical realities, they seem more comfortable with knowing they either do or don't want children, without any moral judgment attached to the choice.

I stand with them and talk about things other than children and childcare. But before long, there are proposals of "guys nights," from which I am specifically disqualified. You know what they say about women with more male than female friends.

Women without children, who don't want children, are dangerous.

There's always adoption if you want to be a parent, he says. Everyone says.

Parent (n.) one who produces offspring; a person who brings up and cares for a child.

Parent (v.) to act as a caregiver to a child.

No, I don't want to adopt. I don't want a child.

We can just be aunt and uncle to our friends' kids then. Go to their school things, pick-ups, drop-offs, drive them around, buy them things. We can just be on-call—

No! If my life is going to revolve around a child, it's going to be my own child!

Fine! Then let's have a baby!

I don't!

Want!

A baby!

I am raging, shrieking like a wind tearing down a mountainside. I can feel the transformation.

"Yamanba's intense thoughts to manifest herself in a tangible form cause her to appear in the form of an oni-woman." (Reider, 2019, p. 415)

You're gorgeous, he says.

I can feel the smirk twisting my mouth up. I feel ancient. *You do know how makeup works, right?*

I am thinking: what happens when I'm not anymore?

"Her eyes were sunk deep in her head but still her eye-balls protruded. She had a big mouth, and fangs from her lower jaw almost touched the edges of her nose. That nose resembled a bird's beak, and her forehead was wrinkled up." (Reider, 2019, p. 414)

Baby doesn't want to have children, my sister told me. *She was worried because she thought she had to. I told her, Auntie Kiyomi doesn't have children, and she felt better.*

It made me proud for a moment, to give my nieces a different example of womanhood.

I need you to be an example for my kid! The wheedling, placating tones of others somehow makes it different. It feels sticky and ill-fitting. I will show them that *other* women don't have children.

I'm not an example, but a warning.

Children are a sign of God's blessing on a marriage, my cousin informs me around baby three or four.

The soft curve of flesh between my hips stays—stubbornly—blessedly?—empty, shrunken, barren, and my breasts remain unused for nourishment.

Later in the story-cycle, Yamanba, a variant of yamauba, transforms from mountain witch to beloved protector. She's welcomed back, no longer a monster. She is beautiful, erotic, and embodies all the feminine virtues. She finds this redemption only in conformity, only through becoming the mother of the folk hero Kintaro.

Apparent (adj.) readily seen or understood, manifest to the senses.

Aparent (adj.) having no interest or involvement in parenting; of no parental significance.

Witches and non-women notwithstanding, it's still largely an uncharted path. Every woman in my direct line of descent has been a mother. I know only a few women who aren't, and because of the deeply personal reasons behind decisions about reproduction, I have never asked—why? Is this what you wanted, or intended? How did you come to your choice? Was it hard? Are you like me? Was it sad for you, too?

Descendant (n.) a person, plant, or animal originating or coming from an ancestral source.

Ancestor (n.) a person from whom one is descended. From the Late Latin *antecessor*, literally "fore-goer." Derived from the Latin *antecedere*, to go before.

When friends announced their impending parenthood, I smiled and cheered.

Then cried for two days.

Decorating the Christmas tree with the ornaments that my mother sewed while she was pregnant with me—soft and colorful cloth toys, safe for little hands—that I always assumed I would, one day, give to my own child, I cried.

I am sorry that I will never bring the love and joy and sense of community to my loved ones that I have experienced with the birth of every child in my circle. I'm sorry my parents won't come specially to meet the new most important person in our shared world. I'm sorry I won't ever have that special connection with my mother—that I've read about—that happens only when a daughter becomes a mother herself. I cried at these and other realizations of things—other assumptions—that will never be.

It can be surprisingly heartbreaking, letting go of an assumption.

When my grandmother died, I felt I'd lost a part of myself, bereft and broken in a way I hadn't anticipated and wasn't prepared for. I had dreams of her for the first couple of years after, until she was sure I'd be okay, I suppose. She knew I would be.

Kiyomichan, Kiyomichan, she would sing my name.

There is evidence that long ago—*mukashi mukashi*—mountains were regarded as a place of rest, a place for the dead to be buried.

In Buddhism, as in many religions, a corpse is impure. The women relegated to the mountain—who tended the mountain, and perhaps the dead—would have borne this impurity and strangeness.

In Japan, Buddhism traditionally teaches that a woman should be subject in all things. Meek, quiet, industrious, submissive. A woman should submit to her father until married, and to her son once widowed. Growing up in a conservative Christian yet distinctly Japanese household, that Christianity was an Eastern religion long mistranslated and misunderstood was not lost on me. Nor the parallel tracks that guided the one good and right way to be a woman.

As expectations solidified around ideas of what a woman should be, those whose natures did not conform to such binds were hazarded in predictable ways: forced to suborn until they broke, or died, or fled, or were pushed out.

The women in my family are notoriously possessed of a brash stubborn streak.

Forgo (v.) to give up the enjoyment or benefit of; to forsake.

It is not a default, nor by accident. It is a considered, informed, intentional choice.

But, not easy. Not for me, anyway.

Why am I so sad about not having a baby that I don't want?

I don't know. But there it is.

What would you say if I told you I wanted a baby? I tell myself I'm joking, feeling hostile.

A pause. *If you want a baby, we'll have one.*

I laugh, because despite myself—knowing, yet not knowing quite what I was looking for—it's the right answer. Tell me you love me without telling me you love me.

I don't, I say. I'm playing games, I will admit, cringing, only later. *Kokoro no oni.* The oni of the heart. Monster.

He says, *I figured.*

And that brings with it a question of my very right to feel this way. Who am I, after all, who presumably could have a child if I wanted to, if I weren't actively preventing it, to be sad about the success of my aims? After years of expense and fighting doctors' offices over their haphazard approach to granting my access to birth control, after all that effort, why should I be sad? As legislators continue to tighten restrictions on family planning, the ability to choose not to have a child is becoming as much a point of privilege as the private schools and extra-curricular lessons of those who have them. What right do I have to feel sorrow in that?

I thought I would be a mother. I chose something different. There's loss in all the selves we decide not to become. Yet this choice, this not-becoming, is weightier than others. Perhaps the approximate weight of a pregnancy.

I never wanted to be a mother, my mom told me over the years. *I never thought I'd be good at it.*

I think she was good at it. But I also saw how much she gave up in order to be so.

My grandmother's picture is in our homes now, and on the altar in Japan.

Noriko Reider (2019) notes, "A popular belief dictates that a religious service should be held for the departed souls of one's ancestors so that these ancestors will protect their descendants. On the other hand, unattended souls are thought to roam in this world to do harm to people as oni."

I can see middle-age from here. And suddenly, what was always a decision of not now, of maybe never, of choosing my own life, the life I could make, will no longer be a choice. It becomes permanent. As permanent as a baby.

I won't have anyone to remember me.

In the stories where she is not redeemed, yamauba's grave is marked—by the priest who kills her, as a warning for others—with a cherry tree.

The family story is that she lost a baby, and then another. They were both what was then called a "blue boy." So, a neighbor, fictive-kin, gave her baby to my great-great-grandmother, until later my great-aunt was born. She never had children, either.

As time passes, I begin to realize:

It's not about a baby. It never was. It's about dying.

REFERENCES

Reider, N.T. (2019) Yamauba and Oni-Women. *Asian Ethnology, 78*(2), 403-427

*Definitions in this text are the author's own compilations, drawn from multiple dictionaries, readings, and understandings of the words.

BELONGING TO FEAR

FRANCES LU-PAI IPPOLITO

My grandmother haunts me best at night when the kids have crawled into bed and are fast asleep. Alone in the dark, I hear Popo's breaths behind my chair—airy and hissing—drawing closer with each second ticked away of the quiet night. Like algebra, she approaches me asymptotically. Me being the straight living line that my grandmother curves infinitely to approach but can't intersect from death.

Still, she tries. A cool, moist air tickles the nape of my neck and ruffles the fine fuzz over my earlobes. I know she's reading over my shoulder, right off the pale flickering screen, while I struggle to weave, purl, and tuck the threads of a broken story together. I'm usually exhausted when she visits like this. The low-hanging words long harvested and consumed. When she gets to the unfinished sentence and the blinking cursor, there's a click of her tongue. It's a noise easily mistaken for the radiator shuddering awake, but this is the sound Popo makes when she's impatient. Having planted the story spores in me decades ago, she's tired of waiting for the plants to grow.

Sometimes, I worry that I will fail her. That, despite my best efforts, I can't recollect the stories she wants me to tell. When that happens, I close my eyes and sink into that liminal space where night stretches long like a cat's spine. In that pause, I hear Popo's fear— her sharp gasps, muted squeals, and my favorite way she switched to our mother tongue, exclaiming "Ah-you! Ah-you!" when she was frightened enough to cover her eyes with her hands but also curious enough to peek through the V of her fingers.

These sounds of her fear always guide me back to the page and to the purpose. The purpose to write for her, and give her a voice even after she's gone. Because more than anyone else in my life, my popo belonged to fear—her sense of self and community all bound and entwined to that utmost primal emotion for survival.

The burs of fear hooked into her early, at seven years old, when she and her family abandoned their home in the forested mountains of Anhui Province to escape the Japanese Army as they pillaged and raped eastern Chinese villages during the Second Sino-Japanese War. Those seeds sprouted on the last train out of Guangxi during World War II, where she clung to the metal posts of an overcrowded train car that had no walls and only flimsy planks of bamboo to support her feet. The sprouts strengthened and flowered in a Cultural Revolution that vivisected our family by geography and ideology. And then it bore wild, fragrant fruit, ripening like the mango, litchi, and passionfruit of the Taiwan she left behind to graft herself into the fresh soil of a new country—one where she didn't speak the language or understand its people.

Growing up in America, I experienced the resilience of Popo's fear in two dominant flavors. The first was her unwavering love of 80s American horror movies. The second, the paralyzing anxiety she felt at the othering of our existence on the road to Americanization.

The first flavor was my favorite, one that I tasted in the summer of 1985. By then, it'd been a little over a year since we'd immigrated to the United States. My grandparents, mother, and an aunt and uncle lived together in the tight quarters of a 900-square foot two-bedroom apartment with a single bathroom. The deep south of Tuscaloosa, Alabama was not, perhaps, the obvious choice for newly arrived Chinese Americans, but there was an opportunity to run a Chinese restaurant there, and my family decided this was the best entrée into American life. It turned out later that the Moon Gay Inn was haunted, and our stay would be short after a foolish attempt to reason with the malevolent dead. However, that is a story for another day: one that I heavily fictionalized as "Qian Xian" in Flame Tree's *Asian Ghost Short Stories*. (Ippolito, 2022, pp. 135-141)

Back in our apartment, we didn't own much, abandoning furniture, clothes, books, and toys for the international passage. What we did have was a wood-grain-finished 19" CRT color TV and a black, blocky VCR. This was by all accounts an unusual splurge for us, but one prompted by the advice of a well-meaning neighbor who told us TV was the best way to become a "real" American.

"It'll help you pick up English," the elderly woman with frizzy dandelion white hair said at our gathering in the hallway. Then she pointed a gnarled, arthritic finger at me.

I shrunk farther behind my mother's hips. My mother was on her mid-day break from the restaurant and the scents of Americanized Chinese clung to her waist—eggrolls, Moo Goo Gai Pan, and sweet and sour chicken—food that we never ate at home.

"Can she read and talk English?" the neighbor asked.

My mother shook her head.

"You should only speak English. Using two languages confuses her," the woman concluded.

Brow furrowed, my mother gave me a worried glance. In our culture, seniority in age and knowledge were supremely respected assets. While "Aunt Sue" was neither family nor Chinese, my mother valued the woman's seventy years' worth of life experience.

Aunt Sue was right that dropping a home language was fashionable at the time. Back in 1981, Senator Samuel Hayakawa (R-CA) introduced an amendment to the Constitution entitled, the English Language Amendment (ELA). (Leibowicz, 1985, p. 519). If passed, the amendment would have designated English the nation's official language.

Senator Hayakawa, a Canadian immigrant of Japanese ancestry and linguist himself, was quoted in the congressional record saying, "The ability to forge unity from diversity makes our society strong. We need all the elements, Germans, Hispanics, Hellenes, Italians, Chinese, all the cultures that make our nation unique. Unless we have a common basis for communicating and sharing ideas, we all lose." (Mujica, 2012, p. 4). The amendment ultimately did not pass, but Senator Hayakawa went on to found U.S. English in 1983, which still exists today, as do renewed attempts to pass the ELA; most recently in 2021. (GovTrack.us., 2022; Mujica, 2012).

Though the ELA did not, on its face, expressly seek to displace a heritage language with English, the sentiment that English was an intractable necessity compelled many immigrant friends of ours to adopt an English-only approach.

In all the years since that hallway conversation, I have been grateful that my family was incapable of doing the same. Their English too "broken" and anemic to fully commit. It kept us off that narrow, slippery plank to assimilation and sustained my linguistic connection to Popo. Instead, my family bought the TV and VCR, thereby ensuring that the first English phrases I learned were along of the lines of: "the price is right," "no whammy," "1, 2, Freddy's coming for you," "the power of Christ compels you," and "you son of a bitch, you left the bodies, and you only moved the headstones."

I was excited by the TV, having watched shows in Tampa, Florida, where my married aunt, Black American uncle-in-law, and mixed-race cousins lived during my uncle's stint in the military. I, however, had never seen a VCR. It was a mesmerizing thing—heavy and sleek, smoothed metal edges and square buttons marked with white hieroglyphic symbols that actuated it to life. For sure, I decided, there had to be magic in this creature fashioned out of metal carapace, wired innards, and a corded tail. Not any kind of ordinary magic, but portal magic, akin to the metal plane that delivered me from Taiwan to the United States. One that I could activate as long as I fed it through the rectangular flap.

Popo also recognized the potential. Truthfully, she and I had a lot of time to contemplate the possibilities. For most of the day, we lived quiet lives. My uncle and aunt hurried off after breakfast to English classes at the state college, while my mother headed to work at the restaurant. Stuck at home, Popo and I found ways to occupy our time. There were the domestic rituals—cutting floral print fabric to sew our clothes, knitting sweaters for the fall when school started, and the washing of rice and chopping of daikon, carrots, and garlic for our lunch. Once all that was done though, Popo would tap me on the shoulder from where I sat at the kitchen table, drawing and coloring ducks (I had a fascination with catching ducks at that age).

"Xiao-qi." She called me by my Chinese nickname. "Ba dianxi da kai." Let's turn on the TV.

That was my favorite part of the day. I cleaned up the scrawled birds, put away my crayons, and joined Popo in the living room where she sat, perched at attention on our tan couch. Popo's face seldom expressed big emotions, characteristically uncharacteristic in its schooled inscrutable calmness like the mirrored surface of a placid lake. But when she held out the hard plastic video case to me, a frisson of excitement radiated off her wheat-colored skin—a palpable energy that flowed over the raceway of her wrinkles and buzzed like a bumble bee in a zig-zag path from her slipper-clad feet to the tight black curls of her cropped, permed hair.

Memory is elastic, but after so many years, it's impossible for me to remember all the movies we watched together. I do, however, know for certain that we watched every *kǒngbù diànyǐng* (horror movie) my uncle was able to find on the shelves of the local video rental store. While other five-year-old girls dreamt of unicorns and ponies, I had nightly visions of possessed puppets, murderous men, great white sharks, cornfield demons, *mogwai*, and a hockey-masked man who silently chased long-legged, buxom blondes through moonlit woodsy paths.

As an adult, I've often wondered why Popo loved American horror so much. Her dedicated consumption filled me up on horror tropes that I earnestly believed were "real" American truths:

- Don't get into a transportation device with a fly.
- Don't eat after midnight.
- Dolls wake up at night.
- Only virgins survive.

For the longest time, I believed Popo loved these stories because horror gave her a connection to a community for which she shared no lived experience or frame of reference. Because the fundamental human instinct to stay alive is naturally ubiquitous, Popo may have related to the plight of chase, the terror of death, grief of loss, and glimmers of survival that played through straightforward dialogue, easy-to-follow plotlines, and exciting soundtracks. Maybe these stories gave Popo a sense of belonging when she felt unmoored and uprooted in a new culture, community, and country. After all, Fear is universal and transcendental, capable of crossing cultural barriers and bridging linguistic gaps. And it made the most sense that she would lean into this emotion more than the others. Fear had always been her loudest companion.

Nonetheless, there's another, much darker, way to explain Popo's fascination with these American stories. An explanation tied to the second flavor of fear she shared with me. A flavor spiked with trauma.

Sometimes, the passing of intergenerational trauma comes in big, sweeping gestures, like tall waves that slam into the shore. In my high school freshman year, my grandfather's anger became just that, buffeting straight into me. Until then, he'd been stern, but never harsh or mean. However, he yelled at me when he learned that I enrolled in an elective Japanese language class. I loved Sailor Moon, the whiny, underestimated, crybaby that managed to "Mary Sue" her way out of everything. Despite her blonde hair and western features, she was an Asian-adjacent character to me, anime being one of the few non-American media options I had access to in the 90s. But Wai-Gong was incensed and accusatory. Why had I chosen *that* language? I gave him my reasons, but he never gave me his, refusing to tell me why hearing the polysyllabic language flow from my lips made him rageful. He probably wanted to spare me the details, and at thirteen, I had no conception that the exaggerated squeals of *kawaii* girls awakened in him buried memories of death, war, and occupation.

Other times, the transfer of intergenerational trauma can be silent and stealthy; muzzled but motile. Popo never told me about her traumatic childhood experiences. This knowledge came later, long after her death, from conversations I had with my great aunt who recounted the gist of the family history and timeline, but still refused to dwell on the painful specifics: like what it was like to lay in a muddy ditch hiding from a road of marching soldiers; the last time Popo saw her father alive; her brother's suicide; and the boat ride to Taiwan over a tempestuous sea.

These deliberate acts of omission were attempts to erase or forget traumatic memory. But the lingering effects of unspoken events remained in that voiceless void, manifesting themselves as social anxiety in our new country. Because, however much Popo was scared and thrilled by the fiction we watched on screen, she was for decades genuinely terrified of leaving the house, using the phone, or answering the door by herself. Whenever there was a knock at the door, she placed her finger over her lips as she crept to the peephole to look out. She hardly ever opened the door to anyone outside the family, even for the people we knew. When she did, it was only a crack, a sliver to fit in a whisper: "No English." She would give a strained smile, too, a demurring kind that never reached her eyes.

The people on the other side usually pressed their case. "I'm fundraising for my school. Would you like to buy some chocolate?"

"Have you found Jehovah?"

"Can we come in for the repairs?"

"Sorry, no English." She apologized as if not knowing a language she'd never needed or been taught was her fault.

Hidden from the door gap, Popo's hands would clench into fists behind her back. I watched her discomfort, unable to do much at that point because my English hadn't been much better. It unsettled me to see her distressed, and I wanted more than anything to speak for her, to use my voice. But, instead, I turned mute because the same fear had nested in me—a realization that I was now othered and marginalized for the price of American admission.

My fear, like hers, manifested into social anxiety, particularly an extreme telephobia. Even when I could muster the wherewithal to answer a call, my voice shook, stuttered, or cracked, instantly making me unintelligible and awkward. The simple act of ordering pizza was an eternal nightmare that family members asked me to repeat because my English soon outstripped theirs. And, I was ashamed, so much so that I hid under the table with the phone, dragging the cable like a plastic vine down the wall and over the carpet. All to practice dialing for the time.

With this in mind, I wonder if Popo watched American horror

movies to find relief from this bitter second flavor of fear she had in her mouth. In the movies we watched, she and I seldom saw ourselves represented on the screen. There was the mystical grizzled Asian man in an odds and knobs thrift shop, Kungfu man, dragon ladies, and Phoebe Cates who I learned years later is a quarter Chinese. The lack of representation bothered me because no one who looked like me had adventures. On the other hand, for Popo, it may have been a small mercy to see bad things happening to people who did not look like her. She had seen too much real violence to want to see herself represented in the pretend kind. Afraid to answer the door, pick up the phone, or go outside, I recognized over time that my grandmother did not belong to China, Taiwan, or America. She belonged to the state of Fear. And in American horror, she found a respite from her own terror. If she had to be othered in this new "safe" country, then at least she wasn't the only one suffering.

Though my grandmother kept her real fears sealed in, she was a storyteller in her own right and shared freely the Chinese horror folktales and ghost stories of her youth. I think she mostly meant these stories to be entertaining and titillating, but also, I believe, she wanted to warn me. Women, especially non-conforming women, inevitably got screwed.

One story that she told me was Hua Pi, 画皮, or The Painted Skin. There are many English translations that I've read since Popo's telling, too many for me to successfully detangle from her version. (Pu Songling, 2010). Nonetheless, the basic components are the same. A demoness blends into human society by wearing a beautiful woman's skin. When Wang, the son of a rich family comes upon the disguised demoness crying in the road, he's immediately enamored and seduced by her beauty. He offers her safe refuge at his spare home where he studies for civil service exams. He promises no one will bother her, especially his boorish, uneducated wife who stays at the main house and tends to the housekeeping.

The demoness proves to be an intelligent and affectionate companion. In the main house, the wife is unhappy but resolutely virtuous and dutiful despite her husband's neglect. Things carry on well enough for Wang, for several years in some versions of the story, until a Taoist priest sees Wang at the market and tells him that he is surrounded by an evil spirit that he must exorcise with a fly whisk. Wang doesn't believe the priest but returns home with the whisk and secretly spies on his beloved side piece, who has peeled off the human skin to retouch the paint. Without her beautiful costume, the demoness is hideous. That night, the man rejects the woman when she comes to his bed, revealing what he discovered about her. In her anger, she rips out his heart and leaves. Eventually, the priest hunts down the demoness and kills her.

That should be the end of the story, but it isn't. You see, this story has always stood out to me because the wife becomes the hero. The long-suffering and submissive wife begs a mystical vagabond to bring her husband from the dead. He beats her and tests her to prove her absolute conjugal devotion by swallowing his coughed-up phlegm. She swallows it. When she does, he laughs and disappears. Humiliated, the wife goes home to weep over her undeserving husband's corpse. Then, the phlegm turns into a new human heart that she vomits into her husband's empty chest. He lives again and has learned from his errant past to love the virtuous wife versus lusting the untrustworthy, sexy vixen.

In many ways, this story is a lesson of forbearance for young women. The male lead fades off-stage, and the quiet wife wins in the contrasting juxtaposition of two strong female characters. "Hew close to the wife," is the apparent moral. Because suffering ensures survival.

I, however, have always identified more with the demoness than the wife. As a Chinese American kid, I experienced a costuming of myself, upon arrival to the United States, that was commiserate in scope to the donning of a painted skin. This task was executed in two parts. First, I scrubbed off my obvious Chinese-ness as best I could (like a layer of dead skin at a Korean Spa)—the accent, fragrances of my homecooked lunches in the elementary school cafeteria, bowl-cut hair and blunt bangs, and the bright floral pants that Popo had sewn by hand for me. Second, I coated and oiled myself with things distinctly American—He-Man/Smurf references, crimped hair (this was the 80s), pizza and PB&J sandwiches, and glitter (so much glitter). I, like the demoness, was dressing myself up for consumption, a meal fit for an American palate that spat out anything too foreign or ethnic. And, like the demoness, I sought refuge in a new home where safety was given in exchange for artifice.

Of course, I am aware that this metaphor is too general and simplistic, and possibly dangerously inaccurate for a discussion of something as complex as, say, the Myth of the Model Minority. But, as a child, the rules were easy. Bullies came after you if you weren't American enough (or even if you were). Teachers pulled you out of class for ESL if you didn't use perfect English. Strangers on the street called you "Chinky" and told you go back to your country if you wore the well-loved clothes you'd brought with you from overseas. Grocers spoke louder and slower to you because by being shouty about broccoli and cauliflower they converted your foreignness into deafness. And thus, for me, I have never seen the Hua Pi demoness as the cause of Fear in this Chinese story, but a belonging of Fear, the property of it, just as much as my grandmother and I belonged to Fear—all three of us uneasy guests trying to sustain a welcome in someone else's home because that welcome has always been temperamental and revocable at a moment's notice.

On March 16, 2021, that welcome was revoked for six immigrants of Asian descent in Atlanta, Georgia by twenty-one-year-old Robert Aaron Long who purchased a gun and ammunition for $460 from Big Woods Goods in Holly Springs, Georgia and then proceeded to open fire on three massage spas in the Atlanta counties of Cherokee and Fulton. (Stevens, 2021). There was a total of eight victims—Soon Chung Park, 74; Hyun Jung Grant, 51; Suncha Kim, 69; Yong Ae Yue, 63; Delaina Ashley Yaun, 33; Xiaojie Tan, 49; Daoyou Feng, 44; and Paul Andre Michels, 54. (Nieto del Rio, G., 2021). Most of the Asian victims were women, who from their family photos in news articles had the skin and faces of my Popo's, my mother's, and myself. (Nieto del Rio, G., 2021).

I saw the Atlanta shootings as an express and immediate revocation of residency, a permanent eviction from a belonging to an America that has frequently gaslit or reframed violence against Asian Americans as something justifiable. Indeed, before the bodies of the victims cooled, Long, an evangelical Christian, claimed he targeted massage parlor workers because he blamed them for his "sexual addiction." (Dickson, 2021). And before Long's words fully escaped his lips, I heard a collective sigh of relief. *This wasn't racism. Don't we all know how tempting those exotic women are?* Cast as sexual ne'er-do-wells, these women, like the Hua Pi demoness, secured their own demise. Except they didn't have an opportunity to rip out a heart before they were brutally shot down.

When I write stories that lean heavily into my Asian American heritage, I focus on these victims, Popo, my daughter, and the other women of my family. We, as a loose, diasporic collective, have had, continue to have, and will always have an ample share of macro and microaggressions. According to a new study from the Center for the Study of Hate and Extremism at Cal State University San Bernardino, in 2020, Anti-Asian hate crime increased 146% across 26 of America's largest jurisdictions that comprise over 10% of the nation's population. In New York City, reports of anti-Asian hate crimes increased 223% in early 2021. However, these are *reported* crimes. For my own experiences, I know most incidents aren't reported. There is a cultural tendency, at least in my family, to stoically bear suffering and to be that virtuous wife, daughter, mother, sister, aunt, and girl that Hua Pi promises will survive.

But what if we stopped caring about merely surviving? How would we then live our lives? What would we say? What stories would we write if in the end all that mattered were the words left behind and the memories of how we treated each other? Would I then feel comfortable enough to embrace #VeryAsian and never question, as I do now, whether my work is acceptable and relatable to the Majority's gaze? And what if we, like Audre Lorde (1978) in her poem "Litany of Survival," accepted that:

For those of us
who were imprinted with fear
like a faint line in the center of our foreheads
learning to be afraid with our mother's milk
for by this weapon
this illusion of some safety to be found
the heavy-footed hoped to silence us
For all of us
this instant and this triumph
We were never meant to survive. (p. 255)

I am afraid of failing Popo. I am afraid of failing myself. I am afraid of hate. I am afraid of fickle love. I am afraid for my children. I am afraid for all of us. I am afraid of all of you. I am afraid of myself. I am afraid when I speak. I am afraid when I am silent. I am afraid that this Fear will consume me. I am afraid to consume it.

And I am ashamed to always feel this burdensome weakness. Yet, Fear does that. It stuns you, pushes you down, and tries to smother the life out of you—pinning you to the pavement with a knee on your neck until you finally forget how to breathe.

For now, through a sisterhood of women, I can borrow breath to finish the stories Popo reads over my shoulder. To share with my daughter and son. To share with you. To break open your chest. To rip out your heart. To make you feel and understand. To put you back together. To forget about my own individual survival and focus on the survival of us all through our stories, our narratives, our pain, and our joys.

And from there, to join my voice to the chorus of unquiet roars.

REFERENCES

Ippolito, F. L-P. (2022). Qian Xian. In L. Murray (Ed.), *Asian Ghost Short Stories*, (pp. 135-141). London, UK: Flame Tree Press.

Mujica, M. E. (2012, August 24). *English can unify America.* POLITICO. https://www.politico.com/story/2012/08/english-can-unify-america-080054

Leibowicz, J. (1985). The Proposed English Language Amendment: Shield or Sword? *Yale Law & Policy Review, 3*(2), 519–550. http://www.jstor.org/stable/40239199

GovTrack.us. (2022). S. 678 — 117th Congress: English Language Unity Act of 2021. Retrieved from https://www.govtrack.us/congress/bills/117/s678).

Pu, S., 1640–1715. (2010). *Selections from Strange Tales from the Liaozhai Studio.* pp.168–179. Beijing: Foreign Languages Press.

Stevens, A. Songling. (2021, July 27). Spa shootings: A timeline of events that left 8 dead in metro Atlanta. *The Atlantic Journal Constitution.* Retrieved February 23, 2022, from https://www.ajc.com/news/spa-shootings-a-timeline-of-events-that-left-8-dead-in-metro-atlanta/UH5ZJVXV3FCY3LUPW4T6CUCSC4/

Nieto del Rio, G., Sandoval, E., Berryman, A., & Knoll, C. (2021, May 11). What We Know About the Victims in the Atlanta Shootings. *The New York Times.* Retrieved February 23, 2022, from https://www.nytimes.com/2021/03/19/us/atlanta-shooting-victims.html

Dickson, E. J. (2021, March 25). The Atlanta Spa Shootings Are Fueling Far-Right Attacks on Porn and Sex Work. *Rolling Stone.* Retrieved February 23, 2022, from https://www.rollingstone.com/culture/culture-features/atlanta-spa-shootings-asian-women-sex-addiction-1146368/

Center for the Study of Hate and Extremism at Cal State University San Bernardino Organizational. (2021). Report to the Nation: Anti-Asian Prejudice & Hate Crime New 2020–21 First Quarter Comparison Data.

Lorde, A., 1978. *A Litany for Survival by Audre Lorde | Poetry Foundation.* [online] Poetry Foundation. Available at: <https://www.poetryfoundation.org/poems/147275/a-litany-for-survival> [Accessed 23 February 2022].

THE DEMON-HAUNTED GIRL

THE POWER OF THE PONTIANAK MYTH IN A PATRIARCHAL WORLD

CHRISTINA SNG

"In Southeast Asia, legend has it that a man out alone at night must never look directly at a beautiful woman, because she might be a ghost that rips his guts out." (Kreems, 2018)

The 1980s was a golden age for horror, and I was born just in time to experience the first rumblings of the retro era. In Singapore, horror was all the rage, and I grew up devouring every brand of horror, including the intriguing stories of our own South-East Asian vampire ghost—the Pontianak—the long-haired beauty who waits by dark, unlit roads, haunts banana trees, and eats the organs of evil men. As a child listening to these whispers and tales, I was never afraid of her. After all, in these whispers and tales, she never harmed women or children, but got the revenge she sought. She was my hero.

In this beautifully diverse part of Asia, we have embraced the cultural stories and folk tales of our shared history. The Pontianak stands out in our collective memories as the ghost we admire and fear the most. Stories are passed down from parent to child, peer to peer, like wisps in the forest. There are flickers of light but never the whole story.

From my childhood memories and ghost stories shared at the back of my grade school form room between classes, the Pontianak was described as a beautiful woman with a pale face and long black hair who leaves a lingering scent of frangipani wherever she goes. Taxi drivers often told of the woman in white who wandered dimly lit roads at night, waiting for someone to stop and offer her a ride (Loh, 2018). In the car, she would use "her dagger-like nails to tear open their stomachs and devour the organs in a bloody feast"

(Kreems, 2018).

In my poem "Pontianak" published in *Tortured Willows: Bent, Bowed, Unbroken* (2021), a collaborative poetry collection with Lee Murray, Gene Flynn, and Angela Yuriko Smith, I explore an encounter with the Pontianak:

PONTIANAK

She stood by the road alone
In her white flowing dress.

The night was moonless,
The streetlight, broken and bent.

The wind promptly picked up,
Gently billowing her hems.

Twin headlights blinded her—
The car stopped by her side,

And a man popped his head out,
Looking at her appreciatively,

He asked, licking his lips,
"Do you need a ride?"

Her mother always told her,
Never get into a car with a stranger.

She nodded, fearless this time.
The worst had already happened.

Leaning over,
He let her into the passenger seat,

Immediately asking her
All kinds of intrusive things

That she ignored
And deflected.

Enraged, he stopped the car,
Locked the doors, and grabbed her.

That was how she died.
The first time, anyhow.

This time,
She turned to look at him

And he scrambled away, screaming,
Unable to unlock the car in time.

She sank her long blood-red nails
Into his lily pale neck

And extended her jaw
To let her needle-sharp teeth

Clasp his head in her mouth,
Biting it off clean.

Brain was fat and juicy, she decided.
The rest of him, useless, tasteless.

She turned off the headlights
And walked into the night.

One down, many more to go.

In the poem, I include a backstory for the Pontianak because hers is a story that should be told, especially during these times when women are fighting for our right to live, work, and be respected as equals in the eyes of the law and in society. Having read many such stories in real life, this is my version of her backstory.

Most origin stories of the Pontianak focus on a woman dying in childbirth (Duile, 2020). This does not seem to logically leap to the transformation of a mother into a vampire-like creature who haunts and tortures men. When I dug deeper, I found the darkest and most plausible version, which would be just cause: "Pontianak (Kuntilanak in Indonesia) is always female. In some narratives, it is said that she is a victim of rape who fell pregnant and was eventually killed by her rapists." She later "appears here as a traumatized ghost seeking revenge against men." (Duile, 2020, p. 286) Despite the fact that "she is undead … and a gruesome and dangerous vampire, with white clothes and long black hair", she is "also a woman subjected to the traditional roles of womanhood. She becomes the latter when caught and a spike or a nail is driven into her head or the nape of her neck" (Duile, 2020, p. 286), becoming a "good wife" again. It is note-worthy to consider the "phallic" symbolism behind the spike.

> "When human, Pontianak is a beautiful and subordinated woman. However, when the spike or nail is removed she turns into a ghost again. She is then uncontrolled and symbolically depicts the inappropriate aspects of female behaviour." (Duile, 2020, p. 286-7)

'Inappropriate behavior' of a woman, controlled only when she has a phallic nail in her brain or spinal cord—this describes a call for women to be subjugated by men, casting women in dichotomous roles of monster versus saintly mother, both versions forced to behave according to the rules of men—a call for women to be subservient, to be property. This ideology goes back 12,000 years when humans began farming (Ananthaswamy & Douglas, 2008). Before the agricultural era, the sexes were more egalitarian.

According to anthropologist and primatologist Sarah Hrdy at the University of California at Davis, "For most of our history, we have been hunter-gatherers, and patrilocal residence is not the norm among modern hunter-gatherer societies. Instead, either partner may move to live with the 'in-laws', or a couple may relocate away from both their families. A degree of egalitarianism is built into these systems. If they reflect what prehistoric hunter-gatherers did, women in those early societies would have had the choice of support from the group they grew up with, or the option to move away from oppression." (Ananthaswamy & Douglas, 2008)

After humans began farming, life began to look less egalitarian for women. "With the advent of agriculture and homesteading, people began settling down. They acquired resources to defend, and power shifted to the physically stronger males. Fathers, sons, uncles, and grandfathers began living near each other, property was passed down the male line, and female autonomy was eroded. As a result, the argument goes, patriarchy emerged." (Ananthaswamy & Douglas, 2018)

In many places around the world, women are still treated like property and suffer all forms of abuse. Domestic violence is too often swept under the carpet as a family matter. Family members frequently accuse battered women of lying and trying to break up the family. Neighbors pretend not to hear men beating their wives, and the police try not to get involved, for the same reason. Punitive measures are inadequate or completely absent (Lim, 2019). In addition, women are frequently victim-blamed by those around them, particularly and most significantly, by family and friends.

"The women who face domestic violence from husband and in-laws have no way out, because the system considers these acts of violence as acceptable." (Niaz & Hassan, 2006) If women try to ask for help to escape from abusers, there is often none, and the results can be fatal (Women's Action). Social support agencies offer some help, but the truth is, there is little a personal protection order (PPO) can do against a man hellbent on killing his wife for leaving him. In fact, filing a PPO may offer him that last spark of fuel to finish the job.

Cultural attitudes in many places are still entrenched and steeped deeply in patriarchy, where male children are valued over female children with devastating results to the girls.

> ...very often young unmarried girls and women suffer tremendous physical and psychological stress due to the violent behavior of men. The nature of violence includes wife-beating, murder of wife, kidnapping, rape, physical assault, and acid throwing... Customs and traditions are often used to justify violence... Finally, the recent economic reforms in South-East Asia have been accompanied by a rise in the incidence of reported domestic violence, rape, and alcohol abuse. (Niaz & Hassan, 2006)

While feminism and liberalism have helped to mold egalitarian and enlightened views in many countries, others have much catching up to do (World Population Review, 2022). If we consider that these myths likely originated as a response to women suffering unspeakable crimes and violations, but finding themselves ostracized and unable to fight back, the Pontianak's role as an avenging angel becomes clear.

"The Pontianak, who has endured violence and suffering, avenges the real-life crimes women living in misogynistic societies experience on a daily basis: the femicide, rape, and domestic abuse." (Kreem, 2018) She serves as a warning to men who act cruelly against women, much like the boogeyman prevents children from getting out of bed at night. Yet, her efforts may not be sufficient to enact real change.

"The Pontianak's murderous violence…is only viewed as legitimate because she's dead. It says a lot about Asian society that we cannot grant agency to living women but only when they're undead," says Dr. Alicia Izharuddin, senior lecturer in gender studies at the University of Malaya. (Kreem, 2018)

Fear of women, of our bodies, of how different we are compared to men. Menstrual blood and our fluctuating moods are frequently made light of during this most painful and discomforting time. Finally, our ability to create and grow life within our bodies, something a biological man can never experience, is something we are often resented for.

Patriarchal views are still rife. Despite the efforts of some governments to equalize women in society (Lim, 2019), inherent beliefs are invariably passed down from parent to child, and society to child, and they are almost impossible to eradicate. (Sundar, 2021)

With these ingrained attitudes, resentment builds over the helplessness against such power and the symbolism it creates. Consider how the backlash against feminism and #MeToo gave birth to the movement of incels. Adherents to patriarchy do not want women to speak out against mistreatment, to say no, or to transgress in any way. This is reflected in the prevalence in the Pontianak myth.

In his December 2016 paper, "The Villainous Pontianak? Examining Gender, Culture and Power in Malaysian Horror Films", Yuen Beng Lee Adrian writes about "how the employment of female monstrosity articulates male fears around female empowerment and suggests a broader challenge to a sense of normality, cultural and religious beliefs." (Lee, 2016, p. 1431)

Going further, authors like Chandranayagam suggest the myth emerged to warn young men to leave women alone, an admission that the cause of rape is a rapist: "The Pontianak ghost is said to usually appear as a beautiful woman walking along a lonely road. As such, this story might be told to discourage young men from disturbing women when they are walking alone along a lonely road." (Chandranayagam, 2008)

In South-East Asian cultures, there exists a deep-seated fear of beautiful pale-faced women with long black hair who wear flowing white dresses. She is pregnant, or has lost her child, and seeks to avenge the wrongs men have done to her.

The men in these stories know they have done something terrible, but the point of view of the woman is often missing, dismissed. In death, as a ghost, she can enact revenge on the men who brutally abused her while she was alive. But she is only powerful when she is dead. (Kreems, 2018)

Nevertheless, it is satisfying to see justice for a battered woman, even in death, in a world where everyone else fails her. For humans, the concept of fairness is deeply important, and the failure to receive justice for a lifetime of abuse can destroy a person.

As Lee says, "The empowerment of this female figure through its ability to return from the underworld in order to exact her vengeance on those who have wronged her articulates a sense of fear about the empowerment of women." (Lee, 2008, p. 1442)

The Pontianak does what we cannot. She is a symbol for justice. For those who decry her means of exacting justice as cruel and unnecessary, they fail to remember what some men have done and gotten away with.

If we consider one of the other things that makes the Pontianak so frightening, we can look to Loh, who says: "What makes her so scary? It is her classic backstory of tragedy and revenge, which taps into our primal, social and cultural fears. Asian horror tropes are typically about cause and effect, misfortune and retribution—all of which lean into something all the more real and frightening." (Loh, 2018)

Domestic violence is the most underreported crime in the world (The Crime Report, 2017; Paul, 2018; UN Women, 2022; World Health Organization, 2021) and even the rare cases that make it to court far too often see rulings in favor of the aggressor. Survivors retraumatize themselves to bring their abusers to account only to be victim-shamed and abused all over again.

What would the Pontianak do? Come back from the dead, cut him open, and eat his organs? Is that *just desserts*? Is it enough?

Here is where the Pontianak becomes our avenging angel, our role model, and shines as someone women would like to be when we grow up:

> "The Pontianak does not play the role of a submissive housewife, nagging mother-in-law or a scantily dressed female character with a low IQ or as sexual prey. She is instead portrayed as a figure of authority and intelligence who can think, manipulate and cunningly presents the threat of castration towards her nemeses who are often men who have wronged her in the past." (Lee, 2008, p. 1441)

Perhaps this is why little girls see her as a hero, as I do.

The winds of change arrived in the wake of the #MeToo movement and did monumental work to highlight incidences of sexual assault and battery against women worldwide. We are beginning to say no, despite beatings, despite everything. And people are listening.

Once, in our world, over 12,000 years ago, women were revered and respected without exception, in a time before property laws, in matriarchal societies, in peaceful societies. When will we achieve this again? I don't know but now that we have found our voices, we will not stop shouting this message:

Women are people. We feel. We think. We bleed. We dream.

We are not property.

When that day arrives, I imagine the Pontianak turning to show her true face to the world and nod with approval. After all, her blood-thirst was not born only from men's fear of women, but from millennia of injustice and rage screaming from the beaten, battered bodies of women who never got a chance to live free.

REFERENCES

Ananthaswamy A. & Douglas, K. (2008). The origins of sexism: How men came to rule 12,000 years ago. *New Scientist.* 18 April 2008. Retrieved from: https://www.newscientist.com/article/mg23831740-400-the-origins-of-sexism-how-men-came-to-rule-12000-years-ago/

Chandranayagam, D. (2008). Southeast Asia: The Power of the Pontianak. *Global Voices.* 1 November 2008. Retrieved from: https://globalvoices.org/2008/11/01/south-east-asia-the-power-of-the-pontianak/amp/

Duile, T, (2020). Kuntilanak: Ghost Narratives and Malay Modernity in Pontianak. *Bijdragen tot de Taal, Land en Volkenkunde 176,* Indonesia. pp. 279–303.

Kreems, N. (2018). Southeast Asia's Vengeful Man-Eating Spirit Is a Feminist Icon. *VICE.* 14 September. Retrieved from: https://www.vice.com/en/article/kz5evx/pontianak-spirit-ghost-malay-man-eating-southeast-asia

Lee, Y. B. (2016). The Villainous Pontianak? Examining Gender, Culture and Power in Malaysian Horror Films. *Pertanika Journal of Social Science and Humanities. Vol 24* (4). pp. 1431-1444. Retrieved from: https://www.researchgate.net/publication/310698456_The_Villainous_Pontianak_Examining_Gender_Culture_and_Power_in_Malaysian_Horror_Films

Lim, J. (2019). The Big Read: Some men just don't get it—more awareness but abuse of women in S'pore still a problem. *CNA.* 02 April. Retrieved from: https://www.channelnewsasia.com/singapore/abuse-women-psychological-physical-singapore-harm-men-gender-882966

Loh, G.S. (2018). Halloween doesn't scare us. We're Asian—we've got the pontianak all year round. *CNA Lifestyle.* 12 October. Retrieved from: https://cnalifestyle.channelnewsasia.com/entertainment/halloween-pontianak-asian-horror-stories-superstitions-219021

Niaz, U & Hassan, S. (2006) *Culture and mental health of women in South-East Asia.* https://www.ncbi.nlm.nih.gov/pmc/articles/PMC1525125/

Sng, C. (2021) Pontianak. In A. Y. Smith & L. Murray (Eds.). *Tortured Willows: Bent, Bowed, Unbroken.* (pp. 100-101). Independence MO: Yuriko Publishing.

Sundar, D. (2021). Household and care responsibilities a source of stress for more than half of mums: Study. *The Straits Times.* 6 May. Retrieved from: https://www.straitstimes.com/singapore/community/household-and-care-responsibilities-a-source-of-stress-for-more-than-half-of

The Crime Report (2017). *Report: Nearly Half of Domestic Violence Goes Unreported.* https://thecrimereport.org/2017/05/03/report-nearly-half-of-domestic-violence-goes-unreported/

Paul, D. (2018). *U.N. finds the deadliest place for women is their home.* https://www.washingtonpost.com/world/2018/11/26/un-finds-deadliest-place-women-is-their-home/

UN Women (2022). *Facts and figures: Ending violence against women.* https://www.unwomen.org/en/what-we-do/ending-violence-against-women/facts-and-figures

Women's Action (n.d.). *Violence.* Retrieved from: https://www.womensaction.sg/article/violence

World Health Organization. *Devastatingly pervasive: 1 in 3 women globally experience violence.* 2021. Retrieved from: https://www.who.int/news/item/09-03-2021-devastatingly-pervasive-1-in-3-women-globally-experience-violence

World Population Review (2022). Gender Equality by Country 2022. Retrieved from: https://worldpopulationreview.com/country-rankings/gender-equality-by-country

THE AGENCY OF MODERN KUNOICHI
THE WOMEN OF NINJA STEALTH AND PERSEVERANCE
TORI ELDRIDGE

Everyone has their own idea about *ninja*. They envision assassins in black pajamas scurrying across the rooftops of castles in feudal Japan or, perhaps, the cartoon turtle warriors they loved as kids. More recently, the word ninja has been appropriated to mean anything cool or executed with astounding skill. We have ninja Techs, ninja Bloggers, ninja Warriors, but none of them refer to the dedicated practitioners of the ninja arts. We exist. And you'll find us all over the world.

Fewer people have heard of *kunoichi*, which is not surprising considering the secondary place women have occupied in Asian societies. And yet…we also exist.

The term "ninja" is relatively new, but the shadow warriors originally known as *shinobi* have appeared in recorded history since the 6th century. Both names are written with the same *kanji* (character) and translate to mean "one who moves in stealth or perseveres." This meaning has added significance to me as a woman.

From earliest times in history, Chinese women have been subservient to and defined by their relationship and duty to men. The Sāncóngsìdé 三从四德 Three Obediences and Four Virtues, a Confucian set of moral principles and social code of behavior, defined a woman's duty in relationship to men at each of the three stages of her life: to her father before marriage, to her husband during marriage, and to her son after marriage in widowhood. The female virtues of chastity, modest speech, appearance, and womanly work—including her ongoing obligation to provide matrimonial-restricted sex—were equally beneficial to men and designed to confine a women's life and influence to the home.

When Confucianism came to Japan, The Three Obediences and Four Virtues came with it, taking away the relative freedom Japanese women were permitted during the Heian Period, between 794 CE and 1185 CE. During this time, women were allowed to divorce, remarry, and hold property in their own right if they were born to families of high rank. Not only were they allowed to be educated, it was expected of them. Japan had developed its own system of writing during that time. Although men of high rank were still required to use Chinese calligraphy, the Japanese kanji system was used by everyday people, including women, many of whom wrote beautiful works of poetry in gracefully written calligraphy.

Fifteen years ago, when I was tutoring my youngest son for an Asian history exam, I learned about *The Tale of Genji*, written by noblewoman and lady-in-waiting Murasaki Shikibu in the early 11th century and is widely considered to be the world's first novel. I was astounded. The world's first novel was written by a woman in medieval Japan? I was further astounded when I spotted the Penguin Classic version of *The Tale of Genji* facing out on a bookshelf at my local Barnes & Noble the following week. I was astounded but not entirely surprised since my ninja training involves the ability to attract and recognize coincidences as part of a heightened attunement and manifestation. More on this magic later.

With all signs pointing to this historically significant literary masterpiece, I bought the 1,216-page novel and raced home to read it. Royall Tyler's translation of Murasaki Shikibu's epic yet intimate tale captivated me with its poetic prose and nuanced complexity of courtly life in medieval Japan. It also illuminated the confines under which noble women and their ladies-in-waiting lived. Although the story slowed for me around page 800 when—spoiler alert!—the title character dies, the novel continues to be the most beautiful work of literature I've ever read.

Whether Asian women found beauty and meaning within the confines of gilded cages or through hard labor in roles similar to slaves, they have influenced men and society behind the metaphoric *shoji* screens in subtle and not-so-subtle ways. There have also been women, like Murasaki Shikibu, who have made their mark in history, not as muses or behind-the-scenes influences for men, but by their own self-directed agency.

Chinese warrior Liang Hongyu (c. 1100-1135) was such a woman. Liang Hongyu grew up on her father's military base and, after a time as a courtesan, married a junior officer and fought with him in battle. They both attained the rank of general, and she was awarded the title, "Lady Defender." There were other notable women warriors during this time, but Liang Hongyu and Mulan—who many scholars have verified as an actual person who lived and fought during the Han Dynasty (206 BCE–220 BC)—are the most beloved by girls and women in China.

When I was a girl in Honolulu, my first impactful introduction to the history of my Chinese heritage came through *The Good Earth* by Pearl S. Buck (1931), set between the 1880s and 1930s in a farming village in East Central China. O'Lan's life was hard and cruel from her time as a servant through her marriage to farmer Wang Lung. As he grows more prosperous, he becomes less satisfied with her tireless work and shrewd practical mind and becomes infatuated with a tea-house girl with exquisite lotus feet. This was my first introduction to foot binding, made even more horrifying since this subjugation and mutilation was conceived and perpetuated by women.

Foot binding is said to have begun during the Song Dynasty reign of Li Yu between 961 and 975 CE, when he became entranced with his concubine Yao Niang who broke and bound her feet into the shape of tiny crescent moons then danced on her toes with delicate beauty in a bejeweled golden lotus. Court ladies followed suit, and soon the practice became the means by which brides were measured in the most literal sense of the word, from the most desirable three-inch "golden lotus" feet to the unappealing "iron lotus" that measured five inches or more. The fact that teetering on bound feet also changed a woman's gait to rely on her thighs and buttocks undoubtedly added to the appeal. Although China banned the practice in 1912, some women continued to bind their feet in secret. The last factory that made lotus shoes didn't close until 1999.

Yet despite gender limitations throughout history, Asian women have broken through the norms to become warriors, rulers, artists, scholars, and the *samurai* women who fought in battles and to protect their homes throughout the Sengoku Period in 15th and 16th century Japan. It was during this period that the kunoichi—the name given to female ninja formed by the *ku, no,* and *ichi* strokes for the kanji character meaning woman—first appeared.

All kunoichi can trace their roots to the legendary folk hero Mochizuki Chiyome, who used her ninja heritage and female advantage to serve her daimyō (lord) after her husband was killed in battle. So it is told. And so I choose to believe. Whether Chiyome lived as an actual woman or only in legend, she empowered women to rise, like a lotus flower, out of the muck and bloom.

The lives of Asian women have and, to some extent, continue to be shrouded in female-diminishing limitations, expectations, and stereotypes. We are seen as pliable, accommodating, and self-effacing; women who understand their place and will put up with unpleasant conditions out of duty and obligation—women who persevere, often in stealth or behind the scenes.

Although my white American father taught me to speak out and expect equality from men, his relationship with my Chinese-Hawaiian mother reflected ingrained perceptions and attitudes he wouldn't have recognized or been able to admit.

The same could be said for my mother who was far more Chinese in her thinking than she ever believed. While she hid her resentments behind a gracious façade, her true feelings erupted in bursts of anger and, more typically, through inscrutable silence. It wasn't until my adulthood that I realized the cultural significance of her grudging acceptance for the path her life had taken. Whether in truth or only in her perception, she had subordinated her will and dreams to a man.

My mother was an adventurous child and an independent young woman who journeyed to Tokyo from Wailuku, Maui at the end of WWII. But despite her rebellious and courageous nature, my mother would never have pursued the ninja arts. She grew up in a time where women worked behind the scenes and aspired to attract men. It wouldn't have occurred to her that she could be powerful in her own right.

Mochizuki Chiyome believed she could do both.

As the story goes, history's first kunoichi was the daughter of Mochizuki Izumo-no-kami, a renown ninja from the Kōga region. She married Mochizuki Moritoki, a distant relative and samurai lord in the Shinano Saku region who was killed in the fourth and most severe battle of Kawanakajima. After the battle, Daimyō Takeda Shingen was said to have asked Chiyome to form an underground network of female spies to infiltrate his rival warlords.

In keeping with her ninja heritage, Chiyome hid her mission behind the illusion of what people expected to see. She recruited her spies under the guise of a magnanimous noblewoman wanting to help women and girls rise from poverty, prostitution, and other misfortunes in life. She trained them in a variety of roles where they could blend in with society and gain intimate access to their targets. No matter what the roles her spies assumed—*geisha*, servant, prostitute, wandering Shinto priestess—Chiyome's kunoichi used their feminine wiles and expected societal positions to gain access and build trust in ways their male counterparts couldn't have achieved.

Chiyome also taught her kunoichi how to fight with brutal effectiveness by exploiting female expectation and using their smaller size and restrictive wardrobe to their advantage. Modern-day kunoichi do the same.

When I was actively training and teaching as a fifth-degree black belt in To-Shin Do ninja martial arts, I excelled with my ability to slip inside an attack and use my agility to disrupt balance and strike in unexpected ways. Since I was easy to pick up or throw, I learned to fight while suspended in the air and by accelerating the momentum of my attacker's force beyond their intent or control. I turned the restrictions of my clothing and footwear to my advantage and considered all of my accessories as a potential tool or weapon. As with Chiyome's kunoichi, I and other contemporary kunoichi have learned to capitalize on what others perceive as weakness.

The ninja arts encompass martial techniques that include strikes, kicks, chokes, holds, joint-locks, pressure points, throws, and grappling as well as strategies for breaking balance, structure, directing energy, and other effective methods of winning a fight. We train in classic and archaic weaponry as well as modern 20th and 21st century weapons and tools that can be used in everyday life. There have also been lineages focused exclusively on the many aspects of espionage, invisibility, disguise and impersonation, stealth, horsemanship, water techniques, geology, meteorology, and spiritual refinement. I do not exaggerate when I say that the ninja arts are the most all-encompassing martial art in the world. As a 5th degree black belt, I have only tapped the surface.

What I have always found most empowering about my own training is the way fighting techniques and strategies can apply to and promote emotional, mental, and spiritual wellbeing.

For example, the concept of disrupting an opponent's skeletal alignment can be applied to disrupting their emotional alignment as well. Conversely, the methods for aligning one's self, physically, can be used to find emotional balance and a calm and solid center from which to operate in the world. From the simplest strike to the most complex fighting scenario, almost every physical technique and principle I've encountered can be applied to daily non-violent life.

The ninja arts can also empower lives through esoteric study, practices, and rituals. Through meditation, hand gestures, and recitation of empowered words and phrases, the ninja can cut through disillusionment, influence actions, create a field of protection, align themselves with nature, and increase the likelihood of success. Much of this can appear to be magical, mystic, or superstitious. In some ways, perhaps it is. Certain practices are tied to the Shinto religion or Tendai Buddhism. Some of the rituals were also practiced by samurai, such as the recitation of power words while finger sword-cutting the *kuji* grid in the air then sealing it by air-writing a significant kanji. All these practices can be used to calm the mind, empower the spirit, and focus intent.

Aligning ourselves with natural forces and becoming more

attuned to the energy around us has a way of attracting what we need and/or recognizing it more clearly when it appears—as exemplified by the "coincidence" of my finding *The Tale of Genji* a week after discovering the mention of it in my son's Asian history textbook. The more we attune ourselves to these occurrences, the more frequently they appear. Or perhaps, the more adept at manifestation we become.

Through the protagonist in my Lily Wong thrillers series— *The Ninja Daughter* (2019), *The Ninja's Blade* (2020), and *The Ninja Betrayed* (2021)—I share my knowledge and impressions of the ninja arts as authentically as I can. Many of Lily's fighting techniques and esoteric practices mirror my own. The wisdom she discovers through self-reflection or through her *ninjutsu* teacher are inspired by valuable life lessons I hold dear. In this way, I hope to open my readers' perceptions beyond the stereotypical mystical black-clad assassin of feudal Japan and show a positive and empowering version of contemporary ninja.

"I thought about the wisdom and lessons Sensei had shared with me over the years. Every bit of our physical training had an emotional, spiritual, and moral component, and all of it guided me along a higher path toward enlightenment. The unattainable goals were always the most important of all." (Eldridge, 2021, p. 190)

As *The Ninja Daughter* title of the first book declares, Lily Wong is a ninja *and* a daughter not the daughter *of* a ninja. This distinction is important. As in Ancient China and Japan where the Three Obediences and Four Virtues mapped out a woman's behavior and social standing in relationship to the men in her life, this tendency continues today whether consciously or not. At first glance of the title, the popular assumption is that Lily is descended from a male ninja and will come into her own under his dedicated tutelage. How many books, movies, and television shows perpetuate this theme? In how many titles is the woman described in relationship to a man? Like any person of skill, she has had teachers guiding her way. But I wanted Lily to make an impression on readers as an independent kunoichi with skills and agency of her own.

REFERENCES

Buck, P. S. (1931) *The Good Earth*. New York: John Day.

Eldridge, T. (2019) *The Ninja's Daughter*. Hoboken, NJ: Agora Books.

Eldridge, T. (2020) *The Ninja's Blade*. Aberdeen, NJ: Agora Books.

Eldridge, T. (2021) *The Ninja Betrayed*. Aberdeen, NJ: Agora Books.

Murasaki, S. (2003) *The Tale of Genji*. Royall Tyler (translator). USA: Penguin Classics.

GHOST MONTH IN TAIWAN

BENEBELL WEN

I learned about demons before I learned about angels, and of *preta*—hungry ghosts—before I heard of buddhas or bodhisattvas. One childhood summer my sister brought home from Taiwan our dead uncle's demon, the demon he inherited from Grandpa. Maybe it was my fault. Over the years I've gotten creative with how I convince myself it wasn't.

Summers in Taiwan press against the skin until you sweat—a suffocating heat that disorients my two sisters and me, who have just arrived in Tainan, nestled in the deep south of the island, in the heartland of Taoist mysticism. We're towed in line by our mother, who has returned to her hometown. Her childhood friends come out onto the narrow cobblestone street to greet her.

The cobblestones were first paved during the Qing Dynasty, and a fortune-teller squatting in front of a street-side shrine still uses copper coins from the Qing to divine the future. Constructed of red granite and golden glazed cylindrical roof tiles guarded by two stone lions, it is a shrine to Guan Di, the god of war, justice, retribution, and loyalty to one's family.

Upon seeing my mother approach, the fortuneteller beams brightly, teeth missing, cheeks like hide toughened by the tropical sun, and shouts out my mother's childhood nickname.

"Avi!" the woman exclaims. "Let me see how much you've changed!" Then she proceeds to read my mother's palm. When they're done, Mom introduces the fortuneteller to us as Auntie Su, then says it's time to go see Grandpa.

We enter a temple where urns of the dead are kept. Auntie Su hands each one of us a red candle and lights them for us. We're taught how to bow. A plaque in front of Grandpa's urn bears his name in calligraphy. We burn paper money.

"I'm home," says Mom to the urn, through tears. "I hope you've been resting well. Father, come meet your granddaughters."

My sister, Ci, the middle child, leans in close to me to whisper. "This place gives me the creeps."

"Don't say that. That's disrespectful."

She's defensive. "I'm not trying to be disrespectful. I'm telling you this place gives me the creeps. And it's freezing cold in here."

But I'm not cold at all. I'm still sweating. Ci shivers from a chill that no one else can feel.

We walk from the temple to my mother's childhood home.

"The creeps are following us," says Ci.

I'm annoyed. The heat and humidity have shortened my temper. "What are you talking about?"

When we get to the front gates of Mom's old house, Ci stops in her tracks. She looks behind us, across the street at the corner, fixated on that intersection.

Auntie Su is also a psychic medium. She turns to look at the street corner. Auntie smiles. "What do you see?"

"Grandpa and a woman that's not Grandma."

I roll my eyes, embarrassed. My sister is making things up again.

We've never met our grandfather. He died well over a decade before we kids were born. So, of course, I interrogate Ci in front of everyone. "How do you even know what Grandpa looks like?"

"He told me he's Grandpa," is her answer.

Mom and Auntie Su switch to Taiwanese, a dialect they know my sisters and I won't understand. Mom shrugs and nods, like she's approving.

"Your Grandpa is finally with his true love," says Auntie Su.

"Grandma wasn't Grandpa's true love?" asks a confused little Ci.

The fortuneteller pats my sister on her shoulder. "His mistress was a good woman."

"Grandma!" I exclaim loudly, with intention, throwing my arms open for the embrace. My sharp tone is to let the fortuneteller know that she needs to stop talking. But Auntie Su is still prattling on with my sister. *It's all right. You're just sensitive to what has happened in that house. Many tragedies. It's all right.* Ci must be talking about the creeps again.

Grandma, Mom's eldest brother whom we call Big Uncle, his wife Jo Ma, and an infantry of cousins welcome us with smiles and open arms. We enter the courtyard of the old house, a structure built in the late 1800s. There are three buildings linked by canopied walkways, raised on platforms of pounded earth, with arched doors and lucky red Fu talismans hanging on every window panel. It's Ghost Month, the seventh month of the lunar calendar, and the Fu talismans ward the home from unwanted spirit intruders.

Ghost Month is the one moon cycle every solar year when the gates between the worlds are left open. Spirits of both Heaven and Hell visit the human world to be among the living. Paranormal activity heightens. Mothers instruct their children to stay out of the waters. Malicious spirits, empowered by the *yin* of water, can pull you under and drown you.

Night is also *yin*. That's why mischievous spirits are most active after sundown. Come home before dusk. Take the long and winding path home to confuse and lose any spirits that were tailing you. Do not whistle after dark and do not speak their names, because that attracts their attention. And do not kill butterflies, moths, or grasshoppers, as ancestors take on their forms to come visit us.

And under no circumstances should an altar of offerings left for the spirits be disturbed.

During Ghost Month, close all windows at night, and ward the home with talismans to keep out the demons and hungry ghosts. Buddhist and Taoist demonology come with a motley hierarchy of devils and fiends. Demons are monstrous creatures from Hell, while hungry ghosts, akin to the Hindu concept of *preta*, were once human, but as punishment for serious wrongdoing, they lose their inner divinity—the good in their humanity. They are reduced to take on the form of their inner beast.

My sisters and I are escorted to the room we'll be staying in.

Three structures face each other, surrounding an open courtyard.

The place houses four generations and three extended families with no guest rooms to spare. Jo Ma puts out tatami mats in the ancestor altar room where we will be sleeping. A resin statue of Guan Di, the family's patron god, stands on a raised platform above a table spread of offerings, ritual tools, memorabilia, sentimental knick-knacks, and framed black and white photographs of deceased relatives. The largest and most prominent centerpiece among the photographs is Grandpa in a dark blue *magua*, a traditional formal jacket with a mandarin collar and knotted buttons. Close to Grandpa's portrait is one of a much younger man with slicked James Dean hair and a bomber jacket, posing for the camera with a movie star smile.

Mom checks in on us, making sure my youngest sister, who is only five, is tucked in. She examines the clasp on the window panels to make sure it's secure.

"Why do we have to sleep in here?" Ci asks. "I'd rather sleep in the living room."

At nine, Ci is terrifically imaginative, seeing fairies and magical creatures, ghosts with names like Kitty and Miss Darling, orbs of light, vivid dreams, time travel, and past lives.

"Nonsense." Mom tucks a stray lock of hair behind Ci's ear and smooths out the blankets. "Now go to sleep."

On her way out, she tells me not to open the window.

But unrelenting humidity persists through the night. At three a.m., unable to sleep, I rise from my tatami mat, unclasp the lock, and throw the window panels open. Finally, a cool breeze. I return to bed.

The next morning all three of us girls seem to have caught colds, with fevers, headaches, and bone chills. I quickly shut the window and reclasp the lock before my mother finds out.

At the breakfast table, it's clear that the three American girls have come down with something. Big Uncle, Mom's brother, remarks that maybe their father has descended from the spirit world to visit his granddaughters. After all, this would be the first time he is seeing all three of them together, and we were sleeping in front of the ancestors' altar. Not to mention it's Ghost Month. The gates between the spirit and human realms are open. Grandpa's able to move around freely.

"It wasn't Grandpa," says Ci. "It wasn't human."

"Hungry ghosts?" Jo Ma's eyes widen. Jo Ma is the bubbly aunt who believes in everything. She turns to Big Uncle and the two speak in Taiwanese. It's a pattern now, among the grown-ups. If they need to talk about something the American kids shouldn't know about, they switch to the dialect.

Mom turns to face me. "You kept the window closed all night like I told you to, right?"

"Of course."

Ci gives me the side eye. The next question out of Ci's mouth will stun the grown-ups. "Who died here?" she asks.

After a prolonged moment of cousins shifting anxiously in their seats, Jo Ma speaks. "Hungry ghosts called upon a demon to take your grandfather's life." She points behind her, over her shoulder.

We look in the direction and see nothing but a boarded-up wall plastered with Fu talismans and, on the floor in front of it, an aging incense burner coated with ash.

"There used to be a bathroom over there. He drowned in the tub." Jo Ma sets her chopsticks down, hastening to chew up her last bits of food to launch into the story. It's one I've heard before, but my sisters have not.

When Mom was still very young, her father died in a bathtub under unexplained circumstances. Probably a stroke or seizure, and then he drowned. Accidental drownings in bathtubs are not uncommon.

"But that would be the medical explanation for the supernatural," says Mom.

Whenever Grandpa comes up in conversation, Mom gets sad and distant. She was her father's favorite. I look over at Grandma just then and, in contrast to Mom, Grandma's fine. Her wrinkles are set in a smile, eyes twinkling because nothing will ruin the good mood that her youngest daughter's homecoming has put her in. Grandma grins at me and, with her chopsticks, plucks the choicest beef roll from the platter and drops it in my bowl.

Grandma, who had a twin sister, was torn away from her family and sold to Grandpa's family when she was eight. She was their servant until she reached the age of sixteen, and then was wed to Grandpa in an arranged marriage.

It was as much of an arranged marriage for Grandpa as it was for her, because he already had a true love, and protested the arrangement every day until their wedding banquet and every day after. He spent as much of his time away from Grandma as he could, and gave everything he had to that true love of his, a woman Jo Ma has described, in hushed whispers, as gentle and kind, ashamed of the pain she caused the family, and earnestly devoted to Grandpa.

Late into the night, Grandma would make the tofu and soy milk. She'd brew healing herbal tonics and, as they simmered, paint labels onto the bottles. The names of those medicines and the petitions she'd inscribe on talismans would be the full extent of Grandma's literacy. She'd go to sleep, alone. Then Grandpa would return home before sunrise, pack the foods and homemade medicines onto a pushcart to then peddle out onto the streets to sell. At sunset he'd return, give half of his day's earnings to Grandma for the kids and keep half for his true love.

Such meager earnings are not meant for keeping a wife and mistress, not even enough to feed his five children with Grandma, so he also sold magical amulets and charms, specializing in curse removal. He'd cast spells and read fortunes.

Grandpa was—to put it in terms of convenience—a witch doctor. Some of the tonics he sold probably worked, like the cough syrups. Other concoctions were love potions, or elixirs that promised to increase virility, intelligence, attract wealth, and even ward off evil.

Grandpa was also a medium who brokered deals between hungry ghosts and those desperate enough to see a witch doctor. He negotiated on behalf of the *preta* until a deal was struck—an ingot of gold and three chickens to cure your son's illness. But to reverse a generational curse, two ingots of gold won't be enough. Bring a third and the curse that has plagued the family for decades will be lifted. These offerings of gold ingots and chickens he brokered were intended for the *preta*, but instead of sacrificing them for the spirit's reward, he'd keep it for his family and his mistress.

One unusual summer night, Grandpa came home after his work day and didn't leave. He stayed with his wife. She drew a bath for him. It was the seventh lunar month, and yet Grandma opened the window panels. She leaned out and called to the moonlight, whistling a melody, then headed to the kitchen table to count the day's earnings. The earnings are then logged into a ledger she keeps by her bedside. This night, she puts all, not half, of the coins in her sandalwood chest.

Second Uncle, an adolescent, unwittingly walks past the closed bathroom door. He knocks to check on his father. No answer. He goes to fetch his big brother. When enough time and silence passes to cause alarm, the two break open the door and find their father has drowned.

Grandma rushes in and screams out at her boys. "Don't touch the body!" But she is too late. Second Uncle is cradling his father's head.

A widowed woman with five children would be a misfortune, but by then, her eldest son, Big Uncle, was in his early twenties, sinewy and strong, loyal to Grandma—through and through a family man. Grandma continued making the tofu and soy milk, but stopped with the potions, and in the mornings it was Big Uncle who latched the pushcart onto his bicycle and headed out to market. Every night he returned with his earnings and handed every last coin to Grandma.

Though Guan Di stood upon the family altar as Grandpa's patron god, after his death, Grandma spent more money than she could afford on an elaborate statue of Kuan Yin, the bodhisattva of mercy, and placed it in her bedroom. She became devoutly Buddhist, carrying prayer beads with her at all times, thumbing them and reciting mantras to Kuan Yin.

Mom, a teenager at the time, started to have dreams of her father aimless and wandering through a dank and dark cave.

"Avi," he would call out to her, "help me. Your father is very hungry. Your father is very cold. Baba is begging you."

Before she could reach out to him, she'd hear a rumbling and the ground beneath her father would quake. As the rumblings intensified, a beastly figure would come into view, galloping their way. Every time she had this dream, white feather plumes of a *fenghuang*, a phoenix, would appear in that moment and lift her away. She would try to leap off the feathers, try reaching out to her father, but the *fenghuang* won't let her stay.

As she floats apart from him, he'd say to her, "If you can't help me, then at least help your brother. Help him so he won't end up here like me."

Second Uncle wasn't the same after Grandpa's death. Where Big Uncle toiled from morning to evening to support the family, becoming a father figure to my mother, Second Uncle dropped out of school, pursued dead-end dreams of becoming an actor, and even stole money from Grandma and Big Uncle for liquor and cigarettes. Hours after Big Uncle had peddled off for the day's hard labor, Second Uncle rolled out of bed hungover and groggy. Grandma cooked him lunch and after he came back to life, he took to the bottle again, tumbling through the night drunk and basking in cigarette fumes.

Grandma could not bring herself to scold him, because she didn't blame her son. She blamed herself.

But Big Uncle wasn't so lenient. The brothers argued and at times broke into fist fights. Mom had to run out of her room, dash toward them, and only when their baby sister stood in between did they finally stop, for as angry as they were with each other, neither would risk hurting her.

As the years passed, Big Uncle raised his own family there, under that roof, in one wing of the home. Second Uncle got a woman pregnant, so she and the baby girl moved into an opposite wing. Mom still lived at home, too, a college student at Tainan University.

Superstitious or not, anyone who met Second Uncle would have said he was haunted.

Of Grandma's children, he has always been the more sensitive one.

Demons and hungry ghosts prey on the sensitive.

When Jo Ma tells the next part of the story, she does so with much animation and drama. Mom's version tries to spare us the details. But Jo Ma looks into our wide eyes and gives us every last delicious spine-tingling bit.

The screams begin around three a.m. Big Uncle and his wife Jo Ma leap out of bed and come rushing out. Our mother was already running toward the screams, to Second Uncle's room. His wife is pacing the floor, frantic and teary. When the three approach, the wife rushes to them and pleads, *You have to help him.*

Grandma comes racing in and instantly wails with fright at the sight of her precious second son. Big Uncle orders Jo Ma to get Grandma out of there, but Grandma runs forward and clings on to Second Uncle, who is tossing deliriously, yelling at the ceiling, pointing a shaking finger at the walls. *Leave me alone! Stop! Stop! I'm not going with you!* The amber lampshades cast an ominous dim glow around the room.

Mom steps forward. Second Uncle goes quiet all of a sudden. He freezes in place, as if listening intently. A deranged smile comes over his face.

He turns his full attention to Mom. "Avi! Quickly! Come closer! Dad's here! The demon's got him, too. But it's afraid of you. Come closer and scare it off!"

Before Mom can move, Big Uncle shoves her back and stops her.

"You're going crazy," he says to his brother. "Leave our little sister out of it."

"Avi! Avi!" Second Uncle continues to cry.

Mom's older sister—one of our aunties—is a Buddhist nun at a monastery just a short distance away.

"He's possessed by a demon," Mom tells her big brother.

In the moment, he isn't quite sure what his sister means by that.

"It's all my fault." Grandma continues to wail, beating her fists on her chest.

Big Uncle hollers an order to his wife, Jo Ma. "Get my mom out of here!"

Jo Ma tries once more, but Grandma wrestles free.

"Go get Sister," says my Mom to her brother. "She'll know what to do."

At a loss for a better solution, Big Uncle listens. He jumps onto his bicycle and makes a break for the monastery to fetch his sister the nun. It's pitch black out and hours before sunrise. He'll have to climb over a locked gate and sprint around the nun's quarters like a madman, yelling out his sister's name.

Mom's older sister, the nun, who I don't call Auntie but call Shi Fu—Master Teacher—follows Big Uncle into the room where the family has gathered around Second Uncle's bed.

"Avi!" cries Second Uncle, still turbulent and churning in bed.

Big Uncle tries to stop my mother, but she pushes him aside.

My mother speaks in a commanding tone, one that surprises Big Uncle and Jo Ma. She glares at the foot of the bed. "Reveal yourself!"

Shi Fu uses the sleeve of her kasaya robes to wipe away Second Uncle's sweat.

"Reveal yourself!" Mom says again.

She repeats the command. Her voice comes to a crescendo and that's when everyone in the room sees it. Jo Ma gasps. She points at the foot of the bed, but there is no need—the vision is clear to all. A towering shadow shows itself between the foot of the bed and the wall. A putrid smell like rotted eggs fills the room. By its side— Grandpa as a hungry ghost, looking pale and emaciated, hunched and destitute.

"Dad!" Mom cries out.

Shi Fu grabs a hold of her littler sister's hand to calm and steady her.

The gesture works. Mom sheds her fear. She puts herself between the creature and the bed. Summoning an authority she did not know she had, Mom calls out the names of bodhisattvas, invoking them.

Together, Mom and Shi Fu recite Kuan Yin's Great Compassion Mantra. The room fills with the tumult of their voices and Grandma's cries. Jo Ma scampers over to her husband's side. Big Uncle holds on to her protectively. The door to the room is shut and locked behind them, to keep out any awakened children.

Every relative present that night swears that upon Mom's last command to the demon, just before the break of dawn, the windows burst open on their own. Second Uncle exhales a final breath. His face unwinds and gives way to serenity. Shi Fu continues the recitations of the Mantra.

Through her sobs, Grandma hears her late husband's voice. Mom hears the voice, too.

No one blames you.

There is light. Day has risen. The atmosphere is tranquil.

"Kuan Yin has personally come to receive him," says Shi Fu, trying to reassure her mother. Big Uncle and Jo Ma guide Grandma out of the room. "He is safe now, and finally free. The demon did not take him."

Mom falls to her knees, sobbing, crying with relief. A disquiet that had entwined itself around her heart faded away that night. Her father was finally free.

In his dealings as a witch doctor, Grandpa had angered one too many hungry ghosts. Seeking retribution, the slighted hungry ghosts enlisted a demon for help in taking Grandpa's life, every last bit of his vitality to pay for his spiritual debts to the underworld. The accounting of offenses and ill-timed death caused him to become a hungry ghost, imprisoned by the demon. When Second Uncle touched his father's dying body, cradling Grandpa's head in the bathwater, a *yin* conduit for spirits, the demon imprinted upon the boy.

Comforting my mother, Shi Fu picks her younger sister up off the floor. "It's your *Ba Zi*," she explains. "You weaken them."

Ba Zi is the Four Pillars of Destiny each person is born with. Some people's *Ba Zi*, like Second Uncle's, make them more susceptible to spirit attachments. My mother's *Ba Zi* predetermined a natural gift for exorcism. And that night was only the beginning of a life-long path of spirit encounters and hungry ghost banishings.

Mom is a seer, a form of traveler between worlds. Through dreams, she can journey to regions of the celestial kingdom and regions of the underworld. She brings back messages from the dead. When a family loses a loved one, they'll ask Mom to check in on the deceased—Is he okay? Where is he now? Does he need anything?

Jo Ma has finished telling the story. I know, because that's the point where Mom always ends it.

But then Jo Ma continues. "According to Shi Fu, your Ma scared the demon away, but didn't banish it. You have to exorcise the demons, or else they just find another to attach to." My aunt turns to my mother. "Shi Fu said you've set the demon loose."

"Jo Ma," I ask. "Which one was Second Uncle's room?"

"The altar room," Jo Ma answers. "When we rebuilt this place, we converted Second Uncle's old bedroom into the ancestors' altar, since no one else would want to inherit a bedroom in which a death occurred."

Ci leans in and whispers in my ear. "That's why that room gives me the creeps."

That night, after both of my sisters fall asleep, I get up and approach the altar, picking up the framed photograph of Second Uncle.

Mementos from each deceased loved one is kept next to the photographs. For Grandpa, there's an ornately carved precious jade piece. Next to Second Uncle is a brass flint-and-wheel oil lighter—one of his treasured possessions.

Ghost Month coincides with typhoon season in the South Pacific. Winds will launch dust storms. Furious, relentless rains cause flash floods and landslides, burying cars under mud, knocking down food stalls and carrying them off for miles. Trees fall, blocking roadways. The power goes out and families scramble to light candles and salvage food.

That summer a super typhoon hits land days before the Ghost Festival. The Ghost Festival begins on the midnight before the seventh month's full moon until the midnight after. According to Mahayana Buddhist scripture, a monk with occult powers used his abilities to locate the soul of his dead mother and found that she had become a *preta*, or hungry ghost, because of the sins she committed in her mortal life. No matter how the monk tried, he could not help her, so he sought the Buddha's guidance.

The Buddha revealed that on the fifteenth day, the eve of the full moon, of the seventh lunar month, the gates between the worlds would be left unattended. The guards would have wandered from their posts to cavort on Earth, on their one day off every year. The monk's astral spirit would be able to pass the gates and into the underworld to retrieve his mother's soul. The monk followed the Buddha's guidance and saved his mother from damnation as a hungry ghost.

Ashen clouds and barricades of rain put us in a state of perpetual dusk. It's our summer vacation and here we are, stuck indoors. Ci and I have been exploring every nook, back door, and storage closet in the house. After board games with our cousins, we retreat to our room.

The glow of the altar candles entrances me. For Ghost Month, a more elaborate spread of fruit and flower offerings are placed on the table in front of the ancestors. I can smell the citrus with the musky notes of sandalwood incense, mingling with the scents of platters of fried scallion cakes, steamed buns, and braised pork belly.

"You really believe that Mom, Jo Ma, and everyone saw the same monster that night?" I ask aloud.

"I see monsters," Ci says, a little too matter-of-factly.

"No, you don't." My tone is curt and condescending, perched atop that big sister arrogance.

Ci has no comeback. She retrieves a comic book from under her pillow and pretends to read.

Feeling vicious for no rightful reason, I snatch the comic book from her hands and provoke her by tearing one of the pages.

Ci tries to grab it back from me. I leap out of the way, grinning. She chases me around that tiny room, but I'm too fast for her.

"Liar, liar, pants on fire," I keep chanting.

She screams for me to stop. I don't. Ci then crashes into the altar table, knocking over a dozen bowls of offerings, the incense, and candles. One collision causes another.

"Liar, liar ..." Before I can finish the chant, a blanket is in flames.

We scream for Mom. The adults rush into the room and put out the fire, but not before everyone is given a good scare. It's pouring out. We can hear the rainstorm pattering on the roof while we sweep up the broken dishes, having to toss all the food offerings Jo Ma painstakingly cooked earlier that day.

As punishment, Ci and I have to kneel in front of the ancestor altar for the rest of the night. What could be salvaged is placed back on the upright table.

Kneeling there, idle, impatient for the hours to pass faster, Ci speaks in a rhythmic sing-song voice. "The creeps— the creeps—"

This time, I don't rebuke her. I feel the creeps, too.

I grit my teeth and push back against the slithering shadow. Silently, I mouth the words. *Stay away.* I think back to Mom and Jo Ma's story. *Come any closer and you'll regret it,* I threaten the shadow.

It's then that I notice that Second Uncle's brass cigarette lighter is gone. Perhaps Grandma or Jo Ma took it when they were cleaning up the mess.

Our stay in Taiwan comes to a close. The whole family, along with Auntie Su, walk us to the end of the cobblestone road. But when Auntie Su goes to my sister, she grips onto Ci and leans in close, peering into her eyes, examining her pupils. The fortuneteller calls out to Mom. They exchange words, but they're speaking in Taiwanese again.

On the airplane, I notice that my sister is clutching something in her little hand. I ask to see it and she brushes me off. I pry it from her. It's Second Uncle's brass lighter.

"I can't believe you took this!"

"He told me I could."

"Who told you?" I shake my head. "You can't keep that."

She doesn't answer. Ci opens her palm at me. "Give it back."

Being older, I want to refuse, to assert my rank. "I'm telling Mom."

"No, you won't." There's a smug confidence to my little sister that I had never seen before.

The brass lighter tingles ominously in my hand. I immediately hand it back.

Ci slips it into her pocket, looks straight ahead, and smiles.

I feel the creeps. It is like knowing a bur has hooked onto her shirt sleeve, but it is stubborn, stuck on there, poking anyone who tries to remove it.

Through the years, Mom would remark rather casually about how her daughter, my sister Ci, seems to have taken on the qualities of her late brother, of Second Uncle. Ci blossomed from an introvert to a charismatic extrovert, the life of every party, bold if not reckless with the ways she teases at danger.

Three decades later, while visiting Ci's apartment, Mom would go searching for a pair of scissors, open a drawer, and discover her brother's brass lighter.

Of Mom's children, Ci has always been the more sensitive one.

Demons and hungry ghosts prey on the sensitive.

It's the night before our youngest sister's wedding. She's the baby of the family. Ci and I are bridesmaids. We've been instructed by the bride-to-be to get ample beauty sleep and show up early the next morning, fresh faced, ready for hair and makeup.

The wedding is happening in the seventh lunar month of the

year. Mom is not happy with the timing, but our baby sister—who really isn't a baby anymore—doesn't care. She's not superstitious.

At three a.m. an inebriated Ci stumbles into my hotel room and passes out. Her face is flushed, and she smells of whiskey and cigarettes. When I put my hand on her back, my blood runs cold and I'm shivering.

A well-known enigma in the line of work that Mom does is that seers like her can spot demons and hungry ghosts anywhere ... except when they're right under their noses.

tethered chokeholds

DOUNGJAI GAM

We all grow and blossom at different paces. One can plant a daffodil bulb and garlic at roughly the same time—depending on your zone—and the daffodil will have come and gone by the time the garlic is ready to be harvested. Some of us reach puberty later than others. We peak at different times in our lives, and some will never live long enough to achieve any sort of greatness.

I've always been a bit of a late bloomer—a procrastinator, day late and dollar short, and so on. My mother's side of the family is something I've wanted to learn more about. My mom would tell me some stories, but as far as learning more about our culture, I was often left on my own. With all that I've learned, I realize there's still so much more to delve into and I reckon that I'll never truly gain a full understanding. Having said that, I will continue to keep at it.

The Nariphon (Thai: นารีผล) is a tree from Buddhist mythology that is said to grow in the mythical Himaphan forest, said to be at the foot of the Himalayas. This tree bears fruit shaped like young women; their heads attached to the branches. Men, overcome with lust, would cut the fruit from the trees and consume them.

I was born in Nakhon Ratchasima in 1976. My mother is Thai, and my father is an Eastern European mix, born and raised in Connecticut. He saw several parts of the world while in the United States Air Force. They met while he was stationed in Thailand and married in a small ceremony before he came back to the States, having been assigned to McGuire Air Force Base in New Jersey.

On Valentine's Day 1977, my mom and I arrived in the United States. We took a plane from Bangkok to New York City. My mom had bundled me up in a snowsuit, hat, and booties, while she wore a light dress and sandals. My brother was born two years and two days after me. Not long after that, my dad retired from the USAF and we moved from the Air Force base to a small borough in Connecticut, two doors away from my dad's mom, who had become a widow less than two months before my brother's birth.

Growing up, I believed I was a Thai-Eastern European mix. It wasn't until my early twenties that my mom casually dropped in conversation one day that her side of the family is ethnically Lao but had moved to Thailand in the 1940s. Over the course of the next fifty years, they moved west and eventually settled in central Thailand, outside of Nakhon Sawan. Looking back now, it wasn't quite the earth-shattering revelation I thought it was at the time, but it did add another layer into trying to figure out the side of me I knew so little about.

Identity is not something I've written much about in my fiction, and I only began to tackle it head-on when I wrote my chapbook *watch the whole goddamned thing burn* (Nightscape Press, 2019). The main character, Sammi Hayes, is a Thai-American girl who grew up within a damaged family. She's an only child who takes care of her mother, whose mental illness spiraled after the death of her husband:

The door was shut. She knocked gently.

"Ma? You awake?"

Nothing. She knocked harder. This time she heard a grunt.

She's alive. That counts for something.

She opened the door and crept in. A small, jagged square of light splayed across the blankets, a stark contrast to the perpetual darkness in the room. Ma lay on her right side facing the window. It grew harder by the day to register her slight frame under the mess of blankets.

"Ma, *sawasdee ka*. I made you some tea."

No response.

"I'll leave it on the nightstand for you. Please remember to take your pills with them, okay?" She picked up yesterday's mug and placed the new one down. It didn't appear that her ma had taken so much as a sip of the herbal tea she'd asked for to go with her evening meds.

She turned back as she was heading out the door. "Ma, we're getting low on groceries. I'm gonna take the car and go into town for a few things." She paused to give her a chance to talk and when there was no reply, she went on. "Do you need anything?"

The faint figure shifted in the bed. Sammi was about to give up when she heard her ma's raspy voice.

"My pill. You get my pill please?"

"Sure, Ma, I get your pills." She closed the door and went back to the kitchen. She dumped the cold tea in the sink and made a note on her list to stop at the pharmacy. (gam, 2019, pp. 22-23)

In her foreword to *Black Cranes: Tales of Unquiet Women,* author Alma Katsu wrote, "Perhaps no cultural norm weighs more heavily on Asian daughters than our obligation to our parents, particularly in old age. It's this inescapable expectation that often makes the last years of a parent's life something to be dreaded. Knowing that you are expected to sacrifice your life in order to care for aging parents is enough to curdle anyone's love into resentment, and the bulk of this invariably falls to daughters." (Katsu, 2020, p. 5)

I don't remember exactly when it began, but the expectation that I was to care for my parents when they became elderly was instilled in me at a young age. I accepted this notion of filial piety without issue. I never questioned my mother about how or why she shirked her duties towards her parents.

she was a maiden
one of many
fruit of the nariphon tree
sliced away
consumed
the remains composted
in new soil
blooming anew
bearing fruit

the servitude continues

I've wondered how life would be under an alternative narrative.

Would it be different if I were a male? Certainly—for one thing, I wouldn't be a part of this collection. Would it be different if I weren't the firstborn? Not at all. Would it be different if I had sisters? I think maybe I would have had more shoulders to help balance the weight.

Listen: fantasizing about alternate timelines does nothing but create false stories in one's head, and the longer one lingers there, the sharper the knife of reality becomes.

No matter what my birth placement or gender was, the duty of becoming a caretaker to my parents ended up solely in my lap when my mother found her only son dead in March 2016.

not all seeds bloom
not all fruits will be sliced open
to reveal sweet bounties
it might look ripe
but the juice is poison

In July 2021, my father had a stroke. It wasn't his first one. He'd made a full recovery from the previous one, but that wasn't the case this time around. There were some complications, including a nasty UTI that required two trips to the emergency room while he was in rehab.

Initially, my mother suggested I come over every single day after work to help them out once my father got home. Spending an extra forty-five minutes to an hour driving back and forth wasn't an option, and I managed to get that down to once a week on the weekend. I ordered supplies for them when needed, and when I came over, I would handle the things my mom relied on my dad for, like balancing the checkbook and paying bills.

Since then, my life has changed drastically. Simple tasks I was mostly on top of began to slip through my grasp. There was no writing or reading to speak of. Hobbies I had taken up during the pandemic brought me no joy. 2022 started off rough with constant health issues and the death of my beloved cat Oona Toona. I felt like

I was slowly going to rot. Thankfully, things have begun to improve, but it's still a work in progress. Because of the love, persistence, and help from my partner, I don't feel as if I'm drowning as much anymore.

In Southeast Asia, much of each country's folklore is adapted from Buddhist mythology. The Nariphon tree can also be found in the *Vessantara Jātaka*, one of many folk tales about the past lives of Gautama Buddha. According to this particular jataka, twelve of these trees were planted by the god Indra to distract the hermits and yogis who lived in the Himaphan forest and lusted after the wife of Vessantara. The Nariphon trees grew fruit shaped in the image of Indra's wife, and the men of the forest would cut the fruit from the tree and bring them to their homes to consume them.

The Nariphon also makes an appearance in the Lao epic poem *Sang Sinxay*, written by Pang Kham somewhere between the mid-16th to end of the 17th century. While on a quest to rescue his aunt, Sang encounters the tree, which is guarded by a class of celestial beings known as the *phanyathone*. As part of his journey, he enjoys the fruits of the tree and fights the phanyathone.

For countless generations, women have been consumed over and over in the service of men and society. They have been uprooted and planted in new soil. My maternal grandmother went from Laos to Thailand, my mother and I from Thailand to the United States. Despite the radically different climate zone, much of the old elements remain.

If my mother were to have her way, my partner and I would be living with her and my father in the condo I grew up in. I would work and do my part in caretaking, but I wouldn't dare do anything like pump my own gas or (gasp) bring my car in to get my oil changed—the man takes care of those things. We almost had an argument one day in the waiting area of an emergency room—she could not understand why, when we were out the previous week, I filled the gas tank while she went inside to pay and my partner sat in the back seat. She has her expectations of how things should be done, and I have mine—like the title of that Bob Dylan song goes, the times, they are a-changin'.

The reason why I have a fierce independence streak and hate the idea of accepting help is because of my mother and her reliance on my father. I don't want to be under someone's control. I watch now as my mother struggles to learn these new concepts, and that's a position I don't want to be in, ever.

I've watched for decades as she let my father take care of the finances while she worked and took care of all of us. I know it wasn't easy for her. It wasn't easy being a mixed minority back then, and it's not that much easier now. People were rude to her, making fun of how she talked—even now, over four decades later, her accent is still heavy, and she talks fast and in a low register. I still seethe when I think of the grade-school classmate who wanted me to come to her house and refused to take no for an answer. I put my mom on the phone so she could tell her no, I couldn't come over. That phone call ended with this girl getting frustrated and repeatedly telling my mom to shut up. As you might have guessed, there was no friendship to speak of after that.

I'm not sure if I picked it up from my mother, or if it was a result of living in a household where communication was not great and yelling was a common occurrence, but I've always tried to make everyone else happy and maybe even like me a little bit. Part of it stemmed from being lonely—I didn't have a lot of friends growing up, and the ones I did have weren't always long lasting. I wasn't like the other kids—I didn't look like them. I didn't wear the same brand-name clothing. My jewelry came from the Avon catalog.

They were vivid-colored dragon fruit, and I was a nariphon that would seemingly never ripen.

Some of you have surely lived this story and are probably still living this story.

Over time, the demands and expectations weigh you down and force you to walk hunched over. Your innards and creative juices dry up and you're left with a nasty leathered husk. A shell you've outgrown. A piece of fruit that feels mushy and when you open it—because, admit it, you're curious—it's all gross with spots of rot and slime.

We can only give so much of ourselves to others before we shrivel up.

I flourish from seed
bloom tall and proud
with seductive curves
I encourage them
to pluck me
devour me
or hold me close
with hopes
I can bring them
success or luck
or maybe they just need
happiness
I can't stray far
tethered to this tree
in time
I shrivel
wither
my outer shell
a grotesque husk

my innards
rotting.

There have been times in my life where I've felt lost, like I didn't know who I was looking at in the mirror. I wondered if I were to open myself up, would there be anything left inside. In my collection *glass slipper dreams, shattered* (Apokrupha, 2018), I had a story called 'dead weight' about a man who discovers his wife has turned into a husk. She gave until she could give no more:

> Once upon a time, she had been a loving and affectionate partner. As the years passed, her passion ebbed and they fought frequently. Her kisses were perfunctory; sex became a chore. The words "I love you" were difficult to say, like phlegm you can't dislodge no matter how hard you cough. (gam, 2018, p. 32).

That husk could have been me.
I uprooted myself and replanted in new soil.
A fresh start.
I will continue to thrive.
I am mine.

REFERENCES

Nariphon. (2021). Wikipedia. Retrieved 13 January 2022 from https://en.wikipedia.org/wiki/Nariphon

Buddhist mythology. (2021). Wikipedia. Retrieved 15 February 2022 from https://en.wikipedia.org/wiki/Buddhist_mythology

gam, d. (2019). *watch the whole goddamned thing burn*. Mount Juliet, TN: Nightscape Press.

Katsu, A. (2020). Foreword, in Murray L. & Flynn G (Eds.) *Black cranes: Tales of unquiet women*, (p. 5). Los Angeles, CA: Omnium Gatherum.

gam, d. (2018). *glass slipper dreams, shattered*. Lexington Park, MD: Apokrupha.

gam, d. Unless otherwise stated, poems in this text are the author's own previously unpublished work.

SIGHTINGS

GABRIELA LEE

1. ESCAPE

Source: https://www.nbcnews.com/news/asian-america/74-asian-american-women-experienced-racism-year-new-report-says-rcna18626

When I was first getting ready to move to the US to study for my Ph.D., a lot of my friends were understandably concerned.

What will you do all by yourself?

Aren't you scared of all the Asian hate?

Are you sure you'll be safe?

I understood everyone's concern. It was in the middle of the pandemic, and I was traveling half a world away to live in a country that wasn't exactly known for its tolerance and understanding with people who looked like me. My first purchases from Amazon, when I arrived, were a small canister of pepper spray and a portable alarm. I have a baseball bat in my apartment right next to my bed in case someone decides that stealing from a grad student is a great idea. (It's not; we don't even get paid minimum wage.) Whenever I walk from the bus stop to my apartment building, a distance of about two blocks, I keep my keys within easy reach, slipping each serrated edge between my fingers like stumpy Wolverine claws, hoping that the shadows behind me are not being made by some crazy masked serial killer ready to attack a chubby five-foot-one-inch girl with a heavy floral-patterned backpack.

I understood everyone's concerns. When a guy lives alone, everyone assumes that they're safe because of their gender. Their penis protects them from all manner of attacks. They can walk around without a shirt on, and the shortest of shorts, and they'll be fine. They can leave their door open and if someone walks in, they'll apologize for entering the space.

But when a girl lives alone, everyone knows that they're unsafe. Their breasts and vagina make them open to any attack. They can walk around in four layers of clothing and still get cat-called. They need to triple-check their locks every night, make sure that they have an escape plan in case an intruder breaks into their home.

Even in the home of our own minds, women are unsafe. I grew up being told that I was too sensitive, that I took things too seriously, that I overreact. In Filipino, we use the word *pikon* to describe someone who can't take a joke, who can't seem to join in the fun. I was called pikon a lot of times—usually when I was being bullied by cousins or classmates. It seemed like an indictment: why can't you participate in your own destruction? Why aren't you having fun at the expense of your own self? Why are you trying to stand up for yourself—no, no, lie down, we want you to take this abuse without flinching. Nowadays, we understand that this was a form of gaslighting. Back then, it was thought of as good, clean fun.

My escape plan whenever I experienced this was to retreat into silence. Nothing bad could get to me if I kept my mouth shut. I decided that being quiet would be my superpower. I would pay attention to everything around me, but I wouldn't say anything. As far as I was concerned, escaping into imaginary worlds inside my head was far more convenient and much easier compared to literally running away. Say whatever you want, but I can keep quiet. It was how I escaped.

That's also the thing, isn't it? Children should be seen and not heard, and especially if you're a girl, you're not supposed to do anything but be pretty, like a vase. It was considered the height of disrespect to answer back to someone older. So I don't say anything when my older relatives ask me why I'm such a nerd. I don't make eye contact when I'm asked why I'm so fat, especially compared to my thin, statuesque cousins. I bite back a retort when I'm told that nobody is going to love me for looking like a whale in a dressing gown. I am too busy escaping inside my own head.

But when you get used to being quiet, you forget sometimes that you can speak up. When you're quiet, you end up becoming a ghost.

2. GHOST

Violence against women and children

BY ATTY. DENNIS GORECHO · MARCH 10, 2022

2

Dennis Gorecho

LEGAL BYTES

Violence and other forms of abuse at home are most commonly understood as a pattern of behavior intended to establish and maintain control over family, household members, or intimate partners.

Physical violence is only the most visible form of abuse. Psychological abuse, particularly forced social and economic isolation of women, is also common.

Source: https://businessmirror.com.ph/2022/03/10/violence-against-women-and-children/

One of the most famous hauntings in Manila is the legend of the White Lady of Balete Drive. White Lady stories were pretty common urban legends, especially if you attended a Catholic girls' school, which I did. There were always ghost stories that proliferated by word of mouth, from a friend of a friend of a friend. In third grade, one of my classmates proceeded to tell us that the canteen bathroom—located in a dark corner of the cavernous building—was haunted by a White Lady, the ghost of a nun who had hung herself in one of the stalls. Another classmate contradicted her—the canteen bathroom was haunted by a nun who was murdered by the Japanese troops during World War II, which was why we could hear echoes of her voice in the bathroom. And yet another version, shared by an older student, said that the nun was killed trying to protect the students from the soldiers who wanted to rape them, and that the prayers she muttered turned into screams if you stayed in the bathroom long enough. We all gasped at that version. Murder was one thing, but rape—

Well, our minds couldn't comprehend that. Not yet.

White Ladies are usually the ghosts of women, pure and virginal, who die under the most horrific of circumstances. But the White Lady of Balete Drive seemed to have made a strip of residential road her home. Some stories say she was a young woman violated by Japanese soldiers. Other stories say she was murdered by a jealous lover. And yet others say she was raped and left for dead by an evil cab driver. Whichever the case may be, she was always violently assaulted and then discarded. But the most common variation of the story I know is this:

One night (it's always night in these stories), an empty taxi cab stops to pick up a passenger. A young woman in an elegant dress enters his vehicle and gives her address on Balete Drive. She's unusually beautiful, ethereal. The driver complies and tries to make small talk with his passenger as she sits in the back. Sometimes, people say that she replies. Other times, she's just silent. As the cab moves down Balete Drive, the cab driver senses something amiss. Sometimes, the woman is just no longer in the back seat. Other times, the driver sees her, bloodied and bruised, her mouth open in a soundless scream. No matter the case, the driver usually hightails it out of there, with a story to tell his friends the next day.

The White Lady of Balete Drive legend was common enough that local ghost hunters would frequent the street looking for signs of the White Lady, disturbing the residents. Balete Drive itself is located in a more genteel part of Quezon City, in the northern part of Metro Manila. My grandparents' house, where we had Sunday dinners regularly with my maternal extended family, was near Balete Drive. Sometimes, whenever traffic along major thoroughfares became too bad, our cab drivers would take a shortcut through the haunted street.

When I was younger, I would always squint hard to see if there were any ghosts hiding behind the trees that lined both sides of the road. It seemed to me that the street was different to the adjacent roads. The trees created a canopy, blocking out most of the sunlight. The houses—mansions, really—were behind high cement walls or elaborate gates that allowed a peek into their crumbling, ruined glory. Some of the homes even had balete trees, old and gnarled and draped with ropey vines, growing behind the walls.

The balete tree is a favorite hiding spot for many creatures in our folktales: it houses the cigar-smoking giant known as the kapre in its branches, as well as the trickster tikbalang, who enjoys making travelers lose their way. The dwarfish nuno sa punso makes its home inside the mounds of soil between the massive roots, and the eel-like batibat spirits sleep inside its hollow trunk. To me, it made sense that if you were going to haunt a particular place, you might want to stay close to a place with a lot of balete trees. I understood the need to stay close to a place you might have favored in real life, of wanting to be near the place you felt most at home.

3. HAUNT

Why we are living in 'Gothic times'

By Hephzibah Anderson 14th March 2021

There is a surge in goth-lit that channels our fears and anxieties. Hephzibah Anderson explores how the genre's past and new stories delve deep into disorder and darkness.

"We live in Gothic times," declared Angela Carter back in 1974. It's a theme Carlos Ruiz Zafón took up several decades later: "Ours is a time with a dark heart, ripe for the noir, the gothic and the baroque", he wrote in 2010. Both authors had good reason. The Gothic has always been about far more than heroines in Victorian nightgowns, trapped in labyrinthine ancestral homes, and along with the supernatural, its imaginings probe power dynamics and boundaries, delving deep into disorder and duality.

Source: https://www.bbc.com/culture/article/20210311-the-books-that-are-channelling-our-fears

The idea of a haunting, of spirits remaining bound to a physical place, is more than just a horror trope. In classic Gothic literature, for instance, the haunting of a place or a person is usually a sign of guilt in the character, of some horrid past that they could not escape. The home is a haunted place in many ghost stories. Haunted characters usually harbored some deep, dark secret that is only revealed at the end of the story. For instance, consider the unnamed narrator in Edgar Allan Poe's "The Tell-Tale Heart" (1843), Mr. Rochester in Brontë's *Jane Eyre* (1847), or Sir Percival Glyde in Wilkie Collins' *The Woman in White* (1859). In all these stories, these characters are haunted by misdeeds, which eventually result in consequences that affect their lives. Read within a historical context, the Gothic tradition can also be read as a kind of haunting of history, in which it "functions as the mirror of eighteenth-century mores and values: a reconstruction of the past as the inverted, mirror image of the present, its darkness allows the reason and virtue of the present a brighter reflection" (Botting, 2012, p.15). I always think of ghosts and their places of haunting, not as something that is necessarily fearful, but a hidden melancholy that is only uncovered when the whole truth is revealed.

The many truths of the White Lady of Balete Drive also show up in various stories, plucked by writers in the Philippines. For example, in Dean Francis Alfar's "A Field Guide to the Roads of Manila" (2015), the personification of Balete Drive speaks about the spirit that still haunts his road. Similarly, in the *Trese* series of comics created in 2005 by Budjette Tan and Ka-jo Baldisimo, the White Lady is a presence that continuously haunts Balete Drive, specifically the intersection between Balete and 13th Street (an actual street that intersects with Balete). In the story, the White Lady was made corporeal and murdered a second time, and by the end of the narrative, another spirit had taken her place, implying that there has always been a presence haunting that space.

But perhaps my favorite version of the White Lady of Balete Drive has to be Nick Joaquin's surreal pastiche of a children's story titled "The Mystery Sleeper of Balite Drive" (1983) in which elements of the Snow White fairytale are woven together with elements of the White Lady urban legend. Here, the character of Blanca, who is both Snow White and White Lady, is both haunted and haunting: she is haunted by the magical curse that made her an orphan, and in turn, she haunts the dreams of the men who love her. Like many of Joaquin's stories for children, "The Mystery Sleeper of Balite Drive" borrows from Philippine folk beliefs but twists the story to make an incisive commentary on contemporary social and cultural issues.

It is also interesting to note that it is usually women who haunt the home, passively hidden in the shadowy closets and abandoned attics of a house, silent and present, as if waiting for another person to simply listen to them, to allow them the grace to be at peace. Ghosts are never about what the spirit had done while she was alive; it is always about what was done to her while she was alive, and how that violence, that injustice, tethers her to the world of the living, even though she is already dead.

4. SPIRIT

International Women's Day protests amplify feminism in Asia

MARCH 8, 2018 / 5:15 AM / AP

Source: https://www.cbsnews.com/news/international-womens-day-march-8-protests-amplify-feminism-in-asia/

Sometimes, though, there are days when I recognize myself in her, in the weight of her silence and sadness at witnessing the terrible things that happen to her—that lack of hope in her story, that whoever the perpetrators are, they will never come to justice. Filipino-American writer Anna Cabe (2019) describes the haunting of the White Lady in her own fiction, saying that "[w]hen I say that I write the White Lady, I am trying to imagine a life and afterlife for her that isn't engulfed in wrath and drowned in sorrow" (Queen Mob's Tea House). And it's true—there's no happy ending for the White Lady of Balete Drive. Her story is a warning to young women—do not go home alone, always have someone with you or make sure that someone else knows where you are going. Her story is also an ending for young women—for the hundreds of thousands of women throughout history who were silenced, whose spirits continue to haunt the collective awareness of humanity.

In her 2014 book *Ain't I a Woman*, bell hooks traces this violence through centuries, perpetrated by a patriarchal system to exert power over another body: "The female slave lived in constant awareness of her sexual vulnerability and in perpetual fear that any male, white or black, might single her out to assault and victimize"

(p. 24). To be a woman is to be constantly conscious of that "sexual vulnerability" and "perpetual fear" that is intertwined with the female experience. This is another kind of haunting, but unlike the separation of spirit and body, the living woman cannot separate her femaleness from the home of her body, and is therefore followed by the fear and vulnerability accompanying the very existence of being a woman.

Even the Gothic literary tradition of haunted women holds up a specific type of femininity meant as an example to readers in order to avoid a deadly fate: that of obedience, purity, and virginity. Botting (2012) observes that in these stories, "[e]xamples of virtuous and vicious conduct were held up for the emulation or caution of readers, good examples promoted as models while, in clear contrast, immoral, monstrous figures were presented as objects of disgust, warnings against the consequences of improper ideas and behavior" (p. 19). This is why the White Lady serves as a warning—after all, good girls don't go out late at night, all alone.

But is this really our fate? Should we be silenced even before death? Are we meant to be ghosts our entire lives, forever living in the spaces between fear and violence, with one hand always in our pockets, ready to fight or flee?

I don't know the answer, to be honest. There are days when I walk from the bus stop to the apartment without paying attention to my surroundings. There are nights when I double-check my doors and windows, making sure that everything is double, triple-locked, before I go to bed. There are days when I have to set aside my phone, sickened by the news that another woman was murdered by her husband, her brother, her father because she had defied their terrible notions of what a woman should be. There are days when my heart weeps when another woman who looks like me is pushed in front of a train, or followed to her apartment door and brutally murdered, or violated in a hundred different ways before being silenced. There are days when becoming a White Lady seems inevitable.

But then, I am also reminded of the spirit of persistence, of the tenacity of women's stories. I am heartened watching women who are brave and unafraid of using their voices to fight back against the violence and depravity that surrounds us. I am reminded that the spirit is not just a silent reminder, a haunting of the awful things that have happened in the past. The spirit is also something that animates us, that moves us to be better and stronger and braver than we are now. Maybe that's the story behind the White Lady: she is a reminder that we can speak up, that we are not invisible all the time, that even without the body, the memory—the spirit—will remain.

REFERENCES

Alfar, D. F., (2015). *A Field Guide to the Roads of Manila.* Philippines: Anvil Publishing.

Botting, F. (2012). In Gothic Darkly: Heterotopia, History, Culture. In D. Punter (Ed.), *A New Companion to the Gothic* (pp. 13–24). Blackwell Publishing Ltd.

Cabe, A. (2019, February 22). On Hauntings: Rewriting the White Lady of Balete Drive. *Queen Mob's Tea House.* Retrieved February 17, 2022, from https://queenmobs.com/2019/02/on-hauntings-rewriting-the-white-lady-of-balete-drive/

Hooks, B. (2014). *Ain't I a Woman: Black Women and Feminism* (2nd ed.) [E-book]. Routledge. Retrieved December 1, 2021, from http://ebookcentral.proquest.com/lib/pitt-ebooks/detail.action?docID=1899877

Joaquin, N. (1983). The Mystery Sleeper of Balite Drive. (pp. 17-33). In *Joaquinesquerie.* Philippines: Cacho Hermanos.

Tan B, & Baldisimo K. (2005–). *Trese.* Philippines: Alamat Comics.

TEARING OURSELVES APART:
THE NUKEKUBI

ANGELA YURIKO SMITH

I've just finished reading the essays in this collection, and I'm crying. Each story told is true and individual. Some overlap topics, but none are the same. These are individual perspectives, unique voices, and personal losses, but if I were asked what the common thread was, I would say sacrifice.

These are stories of women who have given themselves away in pieces. We've made cutlets and chops from self-respect, ambitions, and dreams so that others may feast. This collection is our invitation to partake of the meal we have served of ourselves. We gather on these pages to serve a potluck dinner, a sum of our parts. Our purpose, this time, is to nourish our sisterhood.

For my dish, I bring a *nukekubi*, lightly steamed in anger, and marinated for fifty-three years in briny weeping. A nukekubi is the best part of a ghost, in my opinion. Prepared correctly, she activates all five of the flavor receptor—sweet, sour, bitter, salty and *umami*. It's appropriate that a Japanese ghost would utilize umami, the most recently discovered taste modality. We can credit Dr. Kikunae Ikeda with broadening our flavor palates, but I'm not concerned with him at the moment. I am here to talk about her: my nukekubi.

A nukekubi, meaning "detachable neck," is a *yokai*, or ghost, more specifically, the head of a ghost. By day, she blends in with everyday people. At night, her head detaches from her body to roam the Earth, searching for victims. She attacks by screaming to immobilize her victim with terror, and then biting.

Many believe she is just another cultural story like the Slavic folktale of Baba Yaga or the Adze, a vampire that travels as a firefly in the legends of the Ewe people of Ghana and Togo. She has been picked up with creative license to haunt modern culture through anime and games. The creature known as Misdreavus in the popular Pokémon games is a nukekubi ... yes, children of all ages are playing with the vampiric head of a woman. She's not just a story to me, however.

I've seen one.

I was thirteen years old, living in Sweetwater, Tennessee with my Southern grandparents in a worn-out Victorian-style mansion long past its glory days. Faded red wallpaper with a raised pattern in black velvet, and lead crystal was everywhere. There were too many rooms to count, many of which served some outdated purpose like the sitting room, or the formal dining room. There was a main staircase, and then the hidden back staircase that connected the kitchen to the servant quarters. For a girl raised on too many ghost stories, it was a brilliant place to explore.

It was in one of these rooms, officially known as the formal parlor, that my grandparents kept a fully stocked bar. As owners of an actual licensed bar for many years, they always had plenty of everything booze. I'd decided to expand my education of alcoholic beverages every Friday at noon when my grandmother would walk across the street to visit Mrs. Jacobs, our elderly neighbor.

The trick was to act disinterested as she left. She'd ask if I wanted to "go visiting" with her. I'd decline, feigning extreme interest in whatever book I was reading until she was out the door. Then I'd stand out of sight in the hall to watch her through the diamond-shaped pane of glass around the door. As soon as I saw her enter Mrs. Jacob's house, I headed for the formal parlor, and the liquor.

The day I was introduced to my nukekubi was like any other until I was a few feet in the room. A loud, sharp noise stopped me in my tracks. Against one window was a big, wooden stereo console type player that included a (fancy for the time) 8-track cassette deck, AM and FM radio, huge wooden speaker cabinets, and a turntable on top covered in an amber plastic half box. It was from that amber plastic that I heard that first sharp rap.

It was curious, because there was nothing that could hit the plastic cover to make a noise, not from my angle of view. I moved closer to investigate when a second rap sounded, right in front of me, and I saw nothing. Nothing had shifted the light-weight box; the inevitable dust that clung to these contraptions was undisturbed. The noise had to be coming from something behind the stereo, out of my view. The third rap sounded as I stepped forward.

A noise to my left distracted me; all the pendants in the ornate chandelier were shaking. As they swung together, they sounded like a few dozen people frantically toasting each other with tiny glasses, but from beneath all the tinkling of crystal came another sound, welling up to drown out all others. It was a rising tempest.

I'm still not sure if the sound of rising wind was in the room or in my mind, but within seconds it filled my ears and I could hear nothing else. In the middle of the vibrating chandelier was a distortion in the air, like the heatwaves coming off a hot fire. I had a sense that it was sentient, perch-hovering, and fully aware of me. Then, it swooped.

I have stood in the winds of Hurricane Ivan (2004) as it laid waste to the gulf coast since then, and that hurricane tearing the roof off my neighbor's house was nothing compared to the noise filling my head in that parlor. It was loud enough to drown out my own thoughts. I was stunned and frozen until it swooped down at me.

I ran to the hallway and the sudden silence was as paralyzing as the noise. First deafened with storm, now with the utter absence of it, I turned around. The distortion hovered in the open doorway, rippling nothingness bobbing up and down. The only thing I was positive of was that it was looking at me. I was seen. Then it came at me again with all the accompanying cacophony of shrieking wind.

I'm not sure how I made it onto the front porch. I have fragments of memory—my hand slipping on the old, glass doorknob, the loose way it turned, and then the battered storm door slamming behind me. Again, the noise evaporated with such finality it shocked me to stillness.

I stood on the porch, back to the door, unable to move. I had a sense that if I kept running it would follow, and eventually catch me. Better to face it there, on familiar ground, than in the tobacco fields that surrounded us. Normal sounds filtered into my awareness just as a different type of awareness came over me.

A clear image formed in my mind, as clear as if I had eyes in the back of my head, and it was of the door behind me. I could also see straight ahead to Mrs. Jacob's house. In my vision of the door behind me, there was a head floating in midair behind the glass. A woman, her skin pale with a doughy, gelatinous texture. She was soaked. Liquid ran down her face and long black hair as if she had just risen from the water. Her hair was plastered to her bloated face like flat tentacles. Her mouth gaped open in a silent scream. Her neck was torn from her body. Shreds of waterlogged skin dangled, along with cords and flesh, dripping onto the carpet.

When my grandmother returned from across the street, I told her what had happened, and she believed me. Now I wonder if there was a trail of drip marks from the parlor to the front door, or if she connected it to a story of previous residents who had been beheaded in a car accident. This certainly wasn't the only supernatural experience in that house, but it was the last I know of. We moved almost immediately, possibly even that night.

Aside from a scary story I sometimes told, I hadn't thought of that experience again until I was researching for *Tortured Willows* (2021), the poetry collection I wrote along with Christina Sng, Lee Murray and Geneve Flynn. As I was researching my Shimanchu heritage, I came across the name in a chat. Someone else described what a nukekubi was, and I recognized my own experience in their words. This conversation inspired my poem, "The Nukekubi":

> *I thought she was there*
> *just for me—my own terror—*
> *a resident ghost.*

> *It made sense to me.*
> *The house was Victorian*
> *in the deep, deep South.*

> *Such places have ghosts.*
> *She hung behind me, mid-air*
> *her face contorted*

her hair streaming down
plastered to her shrieking face—
silent, hateful screams.

Like slick tentacles
her neck cords trailed to the ground
disembodied face

soaked wet from drowning
or perhaps from her own tears.
She couldn't tell me.

My nukekubi
out of place in Tennessee…
out of place like me.

As an adult, I see her not as a terrifying entity, but as another woman. Haven't I worn the same face, silently screaming in rage? Haven't I worn this hideous mask myself, and seen it in the faces of the women in my life? My children, adults now, have seen the nukekubi in my features. I'm sure, in my screams, they too heard the deafening tempest.

This is what happens when we swallow so much pain it begins to drown who we are. It's rude not to submit to others, it's selfish not to give of yourself. I saw my Shimanchu grandmother give herself away to the point of being a silent ghost in her own house, clinging to the words of radio evangelists for salvation. Salvation given in monthly donations. I saw my own mother, isolated by her own intellectual brilliance. I'm not sure she has ever had an adult friend.

It's the silent scream of being out of place in a world that takes and takes. I'm not sure what a Japanese ghost—a yokai— was doing in the deep and dark South, but I do know she didn't belong. Neither did I. We never have. Otherness transforms us into scapegoats, witches, dolls, and monsters. For many of us, monster is the label of choice.

The woman's face was already splitting wide. Her jaw thrust forward and down, unhinging like flesh made into a puzzle, revealing the dark, widening oval of her throat. Lining the throat were ridges, each ribbed with needle-sharp, inwardly curving teeth. A pearlescent bead oozed from each tooth.

MONSTER.

—Geneve Flynn, excerpt from "A Pet is for Life," *Black Cranes*

A nukekubi is a normal person by day. She does her best to blend in. Even if she doesn't read it, she carries the romance paperback with the over-muscled Caucasian man on the cover so others can see she is like, and therefore likeable. Later, when a flesh and blood man comes into her life, she submits to the things he wants, even if they hurt. Even if they feel wrong. By day, she is polite and accommodating. By night, she is a good girl doing bad things.

The nukekubi is released when her defenses are down. She can't control her dreams, fueled by rage. Her body is so heavy with pain the head must leave it behind. It floats, uninhibited, buoyed by rage to scream, to hurt, to wreak vengeance…to finally, finally feed herself.

They say if you hide the nukekubi's body while she roams, she will die. They say this like it's a bad thing, but why do you think she left it there to be found? Too often, women are given two roles. We are either saints, or succubi. We nurse and nourish with our breasts, or we inspire men to evil with them. Our hips can bear life or weave a spell that men are helpless to resist. That's what they tell us anyways, afterwards, when they are sated and human again. It was us, not them. We are just so beautiful-helpless-desirable. We should feel complimented. We smile. We forgive. We serve… secretly hoping the nukekubi will tear free from us.

Being an Asian woman, as I said in the beginning of this, is sacrifice. We slice pieces from ourselves to squeeze into the molds created for us. One of my favorite poems from *Tortured Willows* is Lee Murray's "cheongsam." Referring to a "a stunning cheongsam of pale silk decorated with dark piping" first worn by her grandmother, Wai Fong, Murray relates what we will do to fit in.

all it needs
is a minor alteration
to make space for me

I use the kitchen knife
slicing slivers from the hips
carving off the excess

and when at last I slip it on
my tainted blood blooms
red lotuses on sunrise silk

and I smile because it's fitting

In this banquet of pain, this feast of silenced voices and pieces of ourselves, I bring the roaming head of a nukekubi as my dish. This is what happens when we are no longer passive, when we let ourselves escape our bodies for a few moments and become us. My own nukekubi was silent, or maybe her scream was a pitch my adolescent ears couldn't yet register. Whoever she was—future me, my own mother trying to look in on a daughter left in a strange and unfriendly place, or my own grandmother finally getting a say—I no longer fear her.

I am the nukekubi, and I am no longer unquiet. I've become whole enough to keep my body with me as I travel. I am strong enough now to use my words in the light rather than reserving them for use only in shadow. I no longer have to act in rage and vengeance because I've learned to release the tempest in small gusts of *no*.

I offer this nukekubi to all my unquiet sisters whose bodies are still too heavy to fly. May this meal nourish you enough to be whole and amplify your spirits.

From my poem, "Four Willows Bound" from *Tortured Willows*.

Four willows stood bound
rooted to the shore, watching—
unquiet, waiting.

Individual—
different species, unique breeds—
but all were willows.

The storms came with wind
and lashing rain that stripped all—
every lovely leaf.

Silenced, their voices
no longer sang in the breeze...
and then came people.

They stripped away more
taking bundles of branches
leaving behind trunks

they couldn't budge, roots
too deep to pull. Left alone
and too bare to weep

the willows remained.
Around them, dropped twigs too small
to be of value.

Unnoticed, they grew
taking root beside mothers
with little to give...

but it was enough.
Four willows became a grove—
in numbers, came strength.

When the storms returned
the wind could only scatter
the smallest of twigs.

Four willows stood bound
in their sisterhood, in strength—
unquiet, waiting.

REFERENCES

Ninomiya, K. (2015). Science of umami taste: adaptation to gastronomic culture. *Flavour 4*(13). Retrieved from https://doi.org/10.1186/2044-7248-4-13

Cellania, M. (2012). 11 Legendary Monsters of Africa. *Mental Floss.* Retrieved from https://www.mentalfloss.com/article/12818/11-legendary-monsters-africa

Flynn, G. (2020). A Pet is for Life. In L. Murray & G. Flynn (Eds.). *Black cranes: Tales of unquiet women.* (pp. 61-77). Los Angeles, CA: Omnium Gatherum.

Forrester, S., Goscilo H. & Skoro M. (2013). *Baba Yaga: The Wild Witch of the East in Russian Fairy Tales.* Forrester, S (Trans). University Press of Mississippi. Retrieved from https://www.jstor.org/stable/j.ctt24hv8d

Meyer, M. (2015). The night parade of one hundred demons: A field guide to Japanese Yokai. Retrieved from https://www.academia.edu/41724642/The_Night_Parade_of_One_Hundred_Demons_A_field_Guide_To_Japanese_Yokai_Matthew_Meyer?pop_sutd=false

Murray, L. (2021). Willows. In A. Y. Smith & L. Murray (Eds.). *Tortured willows: bent, bowed, unbroken.* (pp. 2-3). Independence MO: Yuriko Publishing.

—cheongsam. In A. Y. Smith & L. Murray (Eds.). Tortured willows: bent, bowed, unbroken. (p. 32). Independence MO: Yuriko Publishing.

Smith, A. Y (2021). The Nukekubi. In A. Y. Smith & L. Murray (Eds.). *Tortured willows: bent, bowed, unbroken.* (p. 32). Independence MO: Yuriko Publishing.

—Four Willows Bound. In A. Y. Smith & L. Murray (Eds.). *Tortured willows: bent, bowed, unbroken.* (p. 32). Independence MO: Yuriko Publishing.

EDITORS

Lee Murray is an author, editor, screenwriter, and poet from Aotearoa, and a third-generation Chinese New Zealander. A USA Today Bestselling author, Shirley Jackson Award and four-time Bram Stoker Awards® winner, her work includes military thriller series, the Taine McKenna Adventures, supernatural crime-noir trilogy The Path of Ra (with Dan Rabarts), and short fiction collection, *Grotesque: Monster Stories*. Lee is the editor of nineteen volumes of dark fiction, among them *Black Cranes: Tales of Unquiet Women* (with Geneve Flynn) and *Asian Ghost Short Stories* (Flame Tree Press). Her short stories and poems have appeared in venues such as Weird Tales, Space & Time, and Grimdark Magazine. She is a former HWA Mentor of the Year, NZSA Honorary Literary Fellow, and a Grimshaw Sargeson Fellow. Read more at https://www.leemurray.info/

Angela Yuriko Smith is a third-generation Shimanchu-American and an award-winning poet, author, and publisher with 20+ years of experience as a professional writer in nonfiction. Publisher of Space & Time magazine (est. 1966), a two-time Bram Stoker Awards® Winner, HWA Mentor of the Year for 2020, she offers free resources for writers at angelaysmith.com.

FOREWORD

Lisa Kröger holds a PhD. in Gothic Literature and is the author of *Monster, She Wrote* and the forthcoming *Toil and Trouble*. She also co-hosts the *Know Fear* and *Monster, She Wrote* podcasts. Her work has won the Bram Stoker and Locus awards. Lisa's fiction and nonfiction work may be seen in *Lost Highways: Dark Fiction from the Road*, *EcoGothic*, and *Horror Literature through History*. Her edited essay collections include *Shirley Jackson: Influences and Confluences* and *The Ghostly and the Ghosted in Literature and Film*.

CONTRIBUTORS

Nadia Bulkin is the author of the short story collection *She Said Destroy* (Word Horde, 2017). She has been nominated for the Shirley Jackson Award five times. She grew up in Jakarta, Indonesia with her Javanese father and American mother, before relocating to Lincoln, Nebraska. She has two political science degrees and lives in Washington, D.C.

Eliza Chan is a second-generation British Chinese author. She writes about East Asian mythology, British folklore and madwomen in the attic, but preferably all three at once. Her work has been published in The Dark, Podcastle and Fantasy Magazine. You can find her on twitter @elizawchan or www.elizachan.co.uk

Grace Chan (www.gracechanwrites.com) was born in Kuala Lumpur, Malaysia, and migrated to Australia with her family before her first birthday. She grew up in quiet outer suburbia, with a bedroom view of bush-covered hills. She can't seem to stop writing about brains, minds, space, technology, ghosts, and identity. Her short fiction can be found in Clarkesworld, Lightspeed, Fireside, Aurealis, Andromeda Spaceways, and many other places. She has been nominated for the Aurealis and Norma K Hemming Awards. Her debut novel, *Every Version of You*, explores change, love, and loss through virtual reality and mind-uploading (Affirm Press, 2022).

Tori Eldridge is the IndieBound national bestselling author of *Dance Among the Flames* and the Lily Wong mystery thriller series— *The Ninja Daughter, The Ninja's Blade, The Ninja Betrayed*—two-time Anthony Award finalist, nominated for the Lefty and Macavity Awards, and awarded the 2021 Crimson Scribe for Best Book of the Year. Her shorter works appear in the inaugural reboot of Weird Tales and numerous anthologies, including "Missing on Kaua'i" in *Crime Hits Home*. Her screenplay *The Gift* was a semi-finalist for the Academy Nicholl Fellowship. Tori was born and raised

271

in Honolulu—of Hawaiian, Chinese, Norwegian descent—and currently resides in Los Angeles, where she earned a fifth-degree black belt in To-Shin Do ninja martial arts. Learn more about Tori at https://torieldridge.com.

Geneve Flynn is a Chinese Australian fiction editor, author, and poet; although she was born in Malaysia, she now calls Queensland home. She is the winner of two Bram Stoker Awards®, a Shirley Jackson Award, and an Aurealis Award. Her works include *Black Cranes: Tales of Unquiet Women* (co-edited with Lee Murray), *Tortured Willows: Bent, Bowed, Unbroken* (in collaboration with Lee Murray, Christina Sng, and Angela Yuriko Smith, and foreword by K.P. Kulski), and *Relics, Wrecks & Ruins* (edited by Aiki Flinthart, and as associate editor with Lauren Elise Daniels). She has been nominated for the British Fantasy, Australian Shadows, and Rhysling Awards, as well as the Pushcart Prize, and her work features on the Locus Recommended Reading Lists for 2020 and 2021. Her short horror fiction appears in various markets, including Flame Tree Publishing, Crystal Lake Publishing, Black Spot Books, and PseudoPod. Learn more at www.geneveflynn.com.au.

Vanessa Fogg is an American writer of Thai and Chinese descent, born and raised in the American Midwest. She received a bachelor's degree in Biological Sciences and a minor in Literature and Creative Writing from the University of Southern California. She received her doctorate in Molecular Cell Biology from Washington University in St. Louis. After years at the laboratory bench, she now works as a freelance technical medical/scientific writer and editor. Her short stories have appeared or are forthcoming in such places as Lightspeed, Podcastle, GigaNotoSaurus, The Future Fire, Translunar Travelers Lounge, and *The Best Science Fiction of the Year: Volume 4*. Her fantasy novelette, *The Lilies of Dawn*, is available in print and ebook from Annorlunda Books. For a complete bibliography and more, visit her website at www.vanessafogg.com

Kiyomi Appleton Gaines is a writer of fairy tales and other fantastical things. She was a 2018 Contributing Editor at Enchanted Conversation, and contributor to Mad Scientist Journal 2019 Spring Quarterly. Her work has also appeared in Nightmare Magazine, Quail Bell Magazine, and The Grimm Reaper. Find more of her writing at a work of heart and follow her on Twitter @ThatKiyomi. Kiyomi is a third-generation Asian-American of Japanese descent. She lives in New Orleans with her husband, two marmalade cats, and a snake.

doungjai gam is a Thai-Lao-Eastern European who ended up planting roots in New England. She is the author of *glass slipper dreams, shattered* and *watch the whole goddamned thing burn*. Her short fiction and poetry have appeared in LampLight, Wicked Haunted, Nox Pareidolia, and Cape Cod Poetry Review, among other places. Born in Thailand, she currently resides in southern Connecticut with author Ed Kurtz.

Frances Lu-Pai Ippolito is a Chinese American writer based in Portland, Oregon. When she's not spending time with her family outdoors, she's crafting short stories in horror, sci-fi, fantasy, or whatever genre-bending she can get away with. Her work can be found in Nailed Magazine, Red Penguin's Collections, Buckman Journal's Issue 006, Flame Tree Press's *Asian Ghost Short Stories*, Strangehouse's *Chromophobia*, and Moms Who Write's *Order of Us*. www.francesippolito.com.

Ai Jiang is a Chinese-Canadian writer and an immigrant from Fujian. She is a member of HWA, SFWA, and Codex. Her work has appeared or is forthcoming in F&SF, The Dark, Uncanny, Prairie Fire, The Masters Review, and her debut novella *Linghun* (April 2023) is forthcoming with Dark Matter INK. Find her on Twitter (@AiJiang_) and online (http://aijiang.ca).

K.P. Kulski was born in Honolulu, Hawaii to a Korean mother and American-military father. A wanderer by design and later by habit, she's lived in many places within the United States as well as Japan. A former history professor, her fiction is often inspired by history; most evident in her gothic horror novel, *Fairest Flesh*, from Strangehouse Books and novella, *House of Pungsu*, from Bizarro Pulp Press. She now resides in Northeast Ohio with her husband and children in a house in the woods. Find her at garnetonwinter.com and on Twitter @garnetonwinter.

Gabriela Lee teaches creative writing and children's literature at the Department of English & Comparative Literature at the University of the Philippines. Her fiction has been published in the Philippines and abroad, most recently in the Bram Stoker Award-winning anthology, *Black Cranes: Tales of Unquiet Women* (Omnium Gatherum, 2020). She received the 2019 PBBY-Salanga Grand Prize, which was published as the picture book *Cely's Crocodile: The Story and Art of Araceli Limcaco-Dans* (Tahanan Books, 2020). She recently contributed the chapter "Digital Liminality and Identities in Philippine Young Adult Speculative Fiction" to *Asian Children's Literature and Film in a Global Age: Local, National, and Transnational Trajectories*, edited by Sharmani Gabriel and Bernard Wilson (Palgrave Macmillan, 2020). She is currently pursuing her Ph.D. in English at the University of Pittsburgh. You can learn more about her work at www.sundialgirl.com

Rena Mason was born in Nakhon Sawan, Thailand. She is a first-generation American dark speculative fiction author of Thai-Chinese descent and a three-time winner of the Bram Stoker Award. Her co-written screenplay RIPPERS was a 2014 Stage 32 / The Blood List Presents®: The Search for New Blood Screenwriting Contest Quarter-Finalist. She is a member of the Horror Writers Association, Mystery Writers of America, International Thriller Writers, The International Screenwriters' Association, Science Fiction & Fantasy Writers of America, and the Public Safety

Writers Association. She currently resides on a lakefront in the Great Lakes State of Michigan.

J.A.W. McCarthy is the author of *Sometimes We're Cruel and Other Stories* (Cemetery Gates Media, 2021) and *Sleep Alone* (Off Limits Press, forthcoming 2023). Her short fiction has appeared in numerous publications, including Vastarien, LampLight, Apparition Lit, Tales to Terrify, and *The Best Horror of the Year Vol 13* (ed. Ellen Datlow). She is Thai-American and lives with her husband and assistant cats in the Pacific Northwest. You can call her Jen on Twitter @JAWMcCarthy, and find out more at www.jawmccarthy.com.

Celine Murray is a queer, disabled New Zealander with a multi-faceted cultural background, including Chinese, Māori, and Scottish ancestry. A short fiction writer from a young age, she published her first collection, *Seven to Seventeen*, at 17 years old. She is the winner of a Sir Julius Vogel Award for science fiction and fantasy for her novella, *Peach and Araxi*. At university, Celine pursued her interests in linguistics and communication and now holds a Masters of Speech and Language Pathology. Though just beginning to dip her toes into the world of horror, Celine has a longstanding enthusiasm for death, with work experience in the death industry. She also enjoys embroidery, drinking tea, and playing board games with her partner.

Christina Sng is the three-time Bram Stoker Award-winning author of *A Collection of Nightmares* (2017), *A Collection of Dreamscapes* (2020), and *Tortured Willows* (2021). Her poetry, fiction, essays, and art have appeared in numerous venues worldwide, including Fantastic Stories of the Imagination, Interstellar Flight Magazine, Penumbric, Southwest Review, and The Washington Post. Christina is a fourth-generation Singaporean whose grandmothers were Teochew and Cantonese. Visit her at christinasng.com and connect @christinasng.

Yvette Tan is one of the Philippines' most celebrated horror writers. Aside from short fiction collections in English and Tagalog, she's written a feature film that received nationwide release and co-written a libretto for a ballet that was performed by Ballet Philippines on the main stage of the Cultural Center of the Philippines. She was the official scribe of the Manila Biennale in 2018 and her story was the companion piece to the artwork that adorned the Philippine pavilion in the 2021 Frankfurt Book Fair. She co-hosted "Trese After Dark," the behind-the-scenes companion to the Netflix hit anime "Trese." Her 2009 collection *Waking the Dead* was re-released in 2021. Her works have been translated into Spanish, Czech, and Hungarian. Follow her on Twitter and Instagram at @yvette_tan and on Facebook at @yvettetanauthor.

Benebell Wen is the author of *The Tao of Craft: Fu Talismans and Casting Sigils in the Eastern Esoteric Tradition* (North Atlantic Books, 2016). She is a Taiwanese American occultist and currently at work on an annotated English translation of *The I Ching Book of Changes*.

Yi Izzy Yu left Northern China for the US in 2011. Since then, she has taught Chinese and English in high schools and colleges, given birth to the now eight-year-old visual artist Frankie Lu Branscum, and published work in magazines ranging from New England Review to Samovar and in the collections of translated Chinese weird fiction: *The Shadow Book of Ji Yun* and *Zhiguai*. Currently, she lives outside of Pittsburgh, where she teaches and translates Chinese and investigates shadows.